T0358521

STRUCTURAL ADJUSTMENT AND MASS POVERTY
IN GHANA

For my family.

The Making of Modern Africa
Series Editors: Abebe Zegeye and John Higginson

Ominous Transition
Joye Bowman

Contemporary Issues in Regional Development Policy
Edited by Wilbert Gooneratne and Robert Obudho

Oil and Fiscal Federalism in Nigeria
Augustine A. Ikein and Comfort Briggs-Anigboh

Religious Militancy and Self-Assertion
Islam in modern Nigeria
Toyin Falola and Matthew Hassan Kukah

An Aristocracy in Political Crisis
The end of indirect rule and the emergence of party
politics in the emirates of Northern Nigeria
Alhaji Mahmood Yakubu

The Golden Contradiction
A Marxist theory of Gold
Farouk Stemmet

Beyond the New Orthodoxy
Africa's debt and development crises in retrospect
Nikoi Kote-Nikoi

The State, Violence and Development
The political economy of war in Mozambique, 1975-1992
Mark Chingono

Incomplete Engagement
US foreign policy towards the Republic of South Africa, 1981-1988
Alex Thomson

Structural Adjustment and Mass Poverty in Ghana

KWABENA DONKOR

Routledge
Taylor & Francis Group

LONDON AND NEW YORK

First published 1997 by Ashgate Publishing

Reissued 2018 by Routledge
2 Park Square, Milton Park, Abingdon, Oxon, OX14 4RN
711 Third Avenue, New York, NY 10017, USA

Routledge is an imprint of the Taylor & Francis Group, an informa business

Publisher's Note
The publisher has gone to great lengths to ensure the quality of this reprint but points out that some imperfections in the original copies may be apparent.

Disclaimer
The publisher has made every effort to trace copyright holders and welcomes correspondence from those they have been unable to contact.

A Library of Congress record exists under LC control number: 97073380

ISBN 13: 978-1-138-34544-7 (hbk)
ISBN 13: 978-0-429-43786-1 (ebk)

Contents

Tables

Acknowledgements

I am especially grateful to Professor Peter Townsend of the School of Policy Studies, University of Bristol for getting me started on this challenging journey, and for his ever present support throughout the various stages of this book. Special thanks go to Dorothy and Dr Noel Tagoe for their support. I also thank the Administrative staff of the School of Policy Studies, University of Bristol for secretarial and other support. Finally, I also wish to thank the editorial staff at Ashgate.

Foreword

There has been widespread recognition of the need to reform the economies of African States. The bone of contention has been the form such reforms should take. Two well publicised views on this issue are the Lagos Plan of Action and the International Monetary Fund/World Bank Stabilisation and Structural Adjustment Policies.

This book looks at the rationale for, the implementation of, and the economic and social effect of the World Bank Structural Adjustment Policy (SAP) in Ghana from the early 1980s to the early 1990s. It shifts the focus from a primarily economic evaluation of these programmes and includes issues such as their impact on vulnerable groups within the Ghanaian society and on poverty in general. Thus it is not sufficient to ask whether or not wealth has been created as a result of these programmes. One must ask whether or not the 'ordinary Ghanaian' has gained any benefits from any wealth that has been created if at all.

The issues tackled in this book have both academic and practical policy merits and implications. From an academic view point, it speaks to the current debate in the development studies academy and offers some theoretical and empirical insights into some aspects of those debates. It allows the reader to evaluate the merits of various development theories using empirical material from Ghana. The practical and policy implications and merits of this book cannot be over emphasised when placed within the context of the number of 'Third World' countries already implementing or contemplating SAPs. The balance discussion on the relative merits and demerits of the World Bank's SAPs would be particularly relevant to policy makers in such countries.

Finally, this book uses ordinary language to communicate its central theme to readers. It does remove the discussion/debate of these important aspects of

'Third World' development from the arcane world of the academic literature and working papers of policy makers who often cloak 'and sometimes obfuscate' the issues in tedious and inaccessible technical jargon.

I recommend this book unreservedly.

Dr. Noel Tagoe
Department of Accounting & Finance
University of Manchester

1 Introduction

Although the antecedents of the contemporary economy and polity of Ghana are largely indigenous, any analysis must be in the specificity of an evolving world system of economic, political and social relations beginning in the sixteenth century. This leads to the gradual involvement of both Ghana and Black Africa in world-wide exchange relations. By the middle of the nineteenth century, this had turned into a more direct incorporation. Finally by the mid twentieth century, the inter relationship deteriorates into subordination to the economic and political needs and objectives of major western powers (see Adu-Boahen, 1975).

Before the arrival of the Portuguese circa 1500 AD, the Gold Coast had no dealings with Europeans. The people traded with neighbouring states and others from across the Sahara. The Portuguese arrival was to change the traditional forms of trade known to the various kingdoms, tribes and, or, states who inhabited the land. Until then, economic activities had centred on the production and exchange of goods and services basic to the survival of the community. The national economy was, therefore, self sufficient, with barter being the acceptable mode of exchange. This should, however, be seen as different from what occurred in continental Europe at about the same time of 'development'. The inability to differentiate between the two has often led to inaccurate analysis, especially by the Marxian school of the Ghanaian, or indeed, the African historical situation by transposing a schema of class relations characteristic of Western capitalism and its development from feudalism.

The interaction with Europe, beginning with the Portuguese, and before the incorporation of the Ghanaian economy into a world system, must be seen in its context. Both Ghana and her European colonisers were trading in each other's *external arena*. Each trading partner was relatively self sufficient of the other, none being a *periphery* or a *core* at this point in time. By this very

1

characterisation of trade, goods traded were classified as 'luxuries'. Luxury hereby being defined as goods for which the demand originates from the part of profit which is consumed. Each economy was self - sufficient in its essentials and was not at this stage [in the sixteenth and seventeenth centuries] dependent on the outside world for either consumables or raw materials.

The colonial penetration

The advance of Euro colonialism in Ghana had two dimensions; an earlier phase of economic encroachment and a later phase of total incorporation. In each case, the stimuli lay outside Ghana, and must be sought therefore in Europe. The carving up of Africa was the product of strong economic and political forces operating in Europe. By the second half of the nineteenth century, international trade had become very competitive in Europe as a result of the spread of the industrial revolution to continental Europe and America. Industrialisation brought production levels beyond the consumption ability of the home markets for manufactures. This was seen to be best resolved by the acquisition of overseas territories, whose markets could be exclusively quarantined. Additionally, the same revolution in production engineering generated the need for more raw materials to feed the increased production capacity of factories in Europe, especially British plants. New territories, therefore, provided a source of raw materials such as cotton, rubber, and palm oil, to name just a few. Where such materials were not in existence, the tropical climate of Africa provided basis for the development of materials such as cocoa, coffee and tea.

The upsurge of nationalism in Europe at about the same time as the spread of the industrial revolution led to a new desire for colonies. These were sought not only for their economic value, but also for their prestige value. France probably more than most, rushed into colony acquisition shortly after her defeat by Germany in 1871 partly to demonstrate and assure friend and foe alike that she was still a great power. This consideration was to some extent, true of both Germany and Italy. The foregoing was made possible, from an economic panorama, by the rise of industrial capital as a means and imperative of colonial structures. Thus colonialism was intensified as industrialisation spread and accelerated. The process was completed with the internationalisation of individual and finance capital in Europe during the last decades of the nineteenth and early twentieth centuries.

By 1900, a global imperial system was in place (MacKenzie, 1983). This significantly coincided with the British conquest of Ashanti, the major challenge to British hegemony in the Gold Coast in 1901. The consolidation of British rule in Ghana began as early as 1844, when the then British lieutenant

Governor of the 'colony'[1] got some coastal chiefs to sign a declaration with a view to regularising the *de facto* jurisdiction British merchants had appropriated to themselves over the estate of the said Chiefs. Thus, what later became known as the Bond of 1844 was signed on 6th March. Some historians, particularly of European persuasion, have regarded this as the *Magna Carter* of Ghana and basis of British Colonial Rule. This view is, however, erroneous. As the noted Ghanaian historian, Adu Boahen (1975, p.41) argues, the Bond was not even a Treaty, but a mere declaration and could, therefore, not have the force of law to subjugate a sovereign people.

The need for British control arose mainly from the burgeoning trade of the early eighteenth century. In 1840 for example, Ghanaian exports to Britain had reached £325,508 while imports rose to £422,170. This expanding market stood to be even more lucrative for the British establishment, as well as for the merchants who were administering the colony, if the larger Ashanti and the Northern Territories were brought into the fold. Worthy of note is the influence of mercantilism on the colonial penetration, mirrored by the attitude of the British government. Merchants operating in the colony appointed the president of the committee of merchants, who was the *de facto* Governor to run the colony with a grant from the Colonial Office. Here, as elsewhere in West Africa, the intent of '*a civilising mission*' did not arise until questions of the morality of colonial rule were raised decades later. At the center of the penetration was the economic. No wonder, when even in later years, around 1930, official opinion favoured the withdrawal of the British presence , the committee of merchants went to all lengths to counter the official thinking and indeed prevailed.

The strength of the merchants and other economic agents in colonial policy was deep seated and underpinned most major British policies affecting colonies in Africa. A case in point is the abolition of slavery. Contrary to popular belief, the abolition had more to do with economic trade - offs. Williams and Dyke[2] emphasised the role of British industrialists in ending the slave trade. Needing raw materials and markets, they advocated a policy of encouraging the African to produce more raw materials and consume manufactured goods at home, rather than enslaving and exporting the African. The future role of the colony was thus set in stone, that is, the Gold Coast best served the interest of the empire and later western powers by being *encouraged* to produce raw materials for Euro based factories while *learning* to consume the 'superior' goods and services produced in Britain. The later manifestation of this change in emphasis is the present situation where Africa produces what she does not consume, and consumes what she does not produce!

The collective lobbying of Parliament by industrialists, commercial interests and humanists that finally pushed for the passing of the Abolition Bill in Britain was, therefore, made possible because a new role had been found for the

African continent which was seen not just as more '*humane*' but equally, if not more so, of greater benefit to British interests than slavery.

Colonial penetration, from the foregoing, should be seen in its historic context. It indicates some form of 'direct' political and economic control by a metropolitan power.[3] In some cases, foreign occupation was accompanied by settlements of significant colonists population, such as Kenya, Zimbabwe and South Africa from the metropolitan power. The establishment of formal colonial structures are not necessarily synonymous to colonialism. In almost every case, especially so Ghana's, formal structures[4] came decades after the penetration and were short lived. Indeed as Chris Dixon put it, "*the establishment of formal colonial structures is therefore only one peculiar and comparatively short lived element of the imperial global system*" (Dixon & Heffernan 1991, p.2).

Production relations in the colonial economy

The structure of the present Ghanaian economy as established during the period of colonial domination has changed very little. By 1954, minerals brought in £21.5m out of the total export earnings of £113.25m. The changes in the character of mining was to be found not in the receipts or position of mining in the economy, but in the ownership structure of the industry during colonial rule. Prior to the formalisation of colonial administrative structures mining was not only undertaken, but was owned by Ghanaian merchants and investors. The development of 'formal' colonialism shifted the ownership base of the industry which had been indigenously owned until now. By 1945, Ghanaians had been completely eliminated from the ownership elite of the mining industry. This, coupled with the low rents paid for concessions, minimised the multiplier effect of the mining sector as a component of the local economy.

What was the nature of the dynamics of the Ghanaian economy? The economy was basically fashioned to maximise the gains of extraction and other forms of primary production to meet the needs of the metropolitan political arrangement. To this end, natural products which were growing wild such as products of the palm tree, attracted the attention of both missionaries and government officials. By 1840, palm oil had become a major exporter, beaten only by gold and ivory and by 1880, topped the list of export earners. It remained so, together with palm kernel until 1911 when cocoa took over. Until then, the two palm products accounted for 48% of the country's earnings from exports. Timber exports came in for equal encouragement from the colonial administration. By 1891, over a million cubic feet of timber valued at £22,000 was being exported per annum. This had hit six million cubic feet by 1901, fetching £55,000. Rubber, another tree product growing wild in the vast forests of Ghana, attracted the sponsorship of the colonial administration and by 1891, the country had become the largest rubber exporter in the world at a volume of 2.9m lb (Adu Boahen 1975, p.92). Gold and other mineral products equally caught the attention of the colonial state and by 1911, 280,000 ounces were exported at a value of one million pounds. Manganese was also being mined at Nsuta by 1910, with output consistently increasing until by 1951, Ghana had become the second largest producer of the commodity in the world [ibid.].

The increased production of primary products was the outcome of two major influences. Firstly, the deliberate policy of the colonial government to expand the productive base of the economy along colonial lines. Thus the peripherisation of production was geared towards reinforcing the metropolis' position in the global economy by transferring surplus and materials to the 'home economy' whilst assigning it a functional specificity. Thus a division of superior and inferior functions was introduced along lines akin to unequal division of labour. Secondly, the suppression and abolition of slavery created an economic vacuum[5] that needed to be filled. The development of legitimate trade was, therefore, seen by the colonial administration as both justifying the abolition and as a preferred void filling activity.

The abolition created favourable conditions for a fundamental re-structuring of the Ghanaian economy through what became known at that time as legitimate trade between Ghana and Europe mediated by Britain. This trade in primary products created the impetus for the construction of roads, railways and the introduction of currency and banking services.

The context of the preceding activities is very important. After a period of contraction in the world capitalist economy from 1873 - 1897 (Schumpeter 1939, pp.321-325), the subsequent period of expansion around 1900 - 1913 saw an alteration in the world terms of trade that favoured agricultural exports as a result of perceived shortages in supply of raw materials (Lewis, 1952). From this position, it was arguably profitable to initiate new or expand production of export crops in Africa.[6] Being under colonial rule however, the significant part of profits were diverted into European hands and economy either by direct ownership of the production infrastructure, monopsonistic control of transportation and, or, purchasing for exports or by direct taxation. For Britain, the colonial control enabled her to determine to a large extent, the choice of foods and raw materials developed and exported from any colonial territory. It goes without saying that, in the absence of Ghanaian and other new colonies, the gains from invisible trade and her security as an economic power and her position in the 'core' would have been compromised.

The favourable agricultural terms of trade mentioned earlier did not last forever. By 1911, the bubble had burst and the process of structural change had lost its momentum. Indeed as Szereszewski aptly puts it, "...the pattern between 1891 and 1911 almost froze for half a century" (Szereszewski 1965, p.112). The economic structure had undergone a fundamental change. The most noticeable characteristics were the neglect of industrialisation, over

5

dependence on the cocoa crop, and the total domination of mining, banking and foreign trade sectors by expatriate firms. The economy was a classical colonial economy marked by the exploitation of natural resources by the colonising power through officialdom and trading firms with little benefit or relevance to the Ghanaian economy. Development, although prevalent, was therefore, limited to sectors producing for export, in import trade and in structures and services required to collect raw materials and to distribute imports.

The Ghanaian economy was thus from the very colonial onset, consolidated into an imperial economic system, whose distinctive feature, according to Fieldhouse, lay in Britain's[7] ability to create the formal framework for economic activity and in some degree determine the character of development (Fieldhouse, 1971).

The state machinery in the colonial political economy

The role of the 'state' in shaping Ghana's political economy under imperial domination was very pro active. The seizure of state power and its utilisation to promote class, ideological and economic interest has its roots in the central position of the state in the shaping and nurturing of the Ghanaian political entity.

The Gold Coast was regarded by the British establishment as its model colony for Africa.[8] By this status, the entrenchment of British interests, both in the economic and political spheres was of utmost importance to the colonial administration. The chains linking the colony to the mother country were, therefore, tighter than would have been the case in a 'non model' situation. The inculcation of British values was very pronounced in the psychological domain, first through a British - type educational elitism and also by the nature of the economic system established. None of these could have been successful without the active participation and or co-operation of the 'state'. The state did not only become a facilitator, but also an active player together with such institutions as the Church,[9] the big trading houses such as Unilever [among others] in the metamorphosis of traditional, albeit, self sustaining society.

For the transformation to a dependent society to be effective, the colonial administration, as was true of colonial Europe as a whole, was wary of existing traditional rulers [and institutions at that] who were unable or unwilling to make the societal adjustment that the European presence demanded and commanded. Not even were the emerging merchant class [such as the leadership of the Fante Confederacy], who were to a large extent, the products of the European interaction, favourably received by the colonial system, since their interests were often divergent from those of the coloniser.

The needs of the metropolis, as represented by its economic actors, mediated through political pressures on governments[10] for an expanded cash crop production, coincided with the administrative needs of colonial officials. Export promotion was needed to provide a feasible tax base sufficient to cover the cost of the imposed administration. The State thus put its weight behind the production and export of selected commodities for a single market - Britain. Expanded production of these 'encouraged' crops as well as other extractive ventures also provided ideological and psychological satisfaction of *civilising the natives*, not ignoring the provision of a viable alternative to the banned trans Atlantic slave trade.

Cash production was also deemed by the colonisers of having a social function, that is, keeping the natives busy by providing them with opportunities to earn money and by so doing, make it unlikely for mischief and expensive threats to the new order to prevail as a result of idleness. This position, on looking at historical facts, is untenable. The idea of idleness did not arise in the Ghanaian environment. Society was so traditionally structured along work and social responsibility that very little, if any, room was left for idleness. The fear was, therefore, one of political opposition. The introduction of export related crops was in this context, more diversionary than social.

The pro active role of the State was at its intensive best in the timber and cocoa trade. In 1891, over a million cubic feet of timber was exported, worth £22,000. By 1901, this had jumped to six million cubic feet. The first cocoa export was made only in 1891, a mere 80 lbs of it, and yet in less than a generation, Ghana had become the world's largest exporter. During the same period, gold mining was also being encouraged with the first modern mine at Tarkwa accounting for about one - third of the national export of 25,000 oz in 1901. In determining which exports to encourage or introduce, the colonial administration was consciously charting the medium to long term development route for the country in a way that was to subsequently prove difficult to alter, notwithstanding the inadequacy of the chosen path. The choice also had serious implications on not only the desired direction of development, but also the composition of economic activity and its place in both the empire and the global economy.

The behaviour of the nation state after independence was directly traceable to the colonial experience. Imperial rule was bureaucratic, rather than political, it was authoritarian rather than participatory, it was centralist rather than devolved. Above all, there was no doubt where power resided - squarely with the imperial authority. There may have been a thin white line of administrators, but there was a line of steel to back them if, and when, it was necessary. Hodder-Williams argues that, "The readiness of imperial authorities to use their powers, whether legislative ones, permitting detentions and limiting political protests, or the physical one of troop movement, was rarely called into doubt" (1984, p.32).

Thus at independence, the inheritance of the new leadership was essentially, an authoritative one in which compromises and negotiations central to Anglo -

Saxon democracy were absent. The emphasis on central control, whether by party or the state, became a distinctive feature of the post colonial State. Not even the bureaucracy escaped the inheritance. The imperial bureaucracy's legacy was one of a schism between the emerging politicians and the Civil Service with the latter seeing the former as 'mere politicians' in the classical tradition of the colonial civil service.

The present political economy of Ghana is, therefore, in Wallersteinian terms, the outcome of various stages [and modes] of its involvement with Colonial Britain in particular, and Imperial Europe on the global stage. Any attempt to analyse, let alone plan and implement any macro programme to ensure a dynamic and self sustaining economy must therefore, start from its past.

Notes

1 The present day coastal Ghana.
2 Quoted by Adu Boahen 1975, pp. 90-91.
3 This includes the so called indirect rule favoured by Britain for economic reasons.
4 Formal structures here referring to organised structures of domination such as the Governor's office, Police, Judiciary, Civil Service etc.
5 Income from slavery was important as both a source of income and a means of acquiring important military hardware [guns].
6 Although it is even more powerfully arguable that processing such products in Africa would have been more profitable.
7 In her place as the metropolis of the empire.
8 See Governor Burn's address to the Parliamentary Association "Political and Other Changes in the Gold Coast" 24 October 1946.
9 As represented by 'Missionaries'.
10 Both at home and in the colony.

2 Self government to the second republic

The socio-political setting

The colonial state in Ghana was neo-mercantilist - in that, it monopolised surplus from peasant production of primary commodities and exported such in concert with foreign big business.[1] In the early years of cocoa production up and including the 1940-1950 period, little food production was lost through export activity. Cocoa was '*added*' on to food production or food crops were '*added*' on to cocoa farms where land had been acquired for cocoa cultivation. Yet from the 1940-1950 period, food constituted a high percentage of the total import bill of the country. This is explained more as a result of newly developed taste for European produced food than for any other reason. Although Rimmer (1992, p.34) sees this as "reflecting effective demand for diets superior to those local resources could produce," there is little to justify this assertion both scientifically and historically. Traditional Ghanaian food, cultivated without chemicals and often eaten fresh, is for every reason, more nutritious than milled rice, corned beef, butter, sardines etc. that constituted the bulk of food imports. What is both credible and certain is the conscious promotion of European food sales by European controlled commercial concerns and the colonial State.

It is useful to point out at this stage that the colonial state had a vested interest in promoting a culture of consumerism. The consumerism was one directed at British products as against locally produced products. This probably should not come as a surprise, since as argued in chapter one, the whole basis of British colonialism was the promotion of British commercial and industrial interest.

The above, in concert with the neo-mercantilist nature of the Ghanaian state, reinforced the centrality of the state[2] and the political elite as source of accumulation and patronage politics. At the root of the country's rapid evolution was the process of political elitism and state formation. The

9

interaction between state and civil society,[3] as cited by Poggi (1978, pp. 77-78) laid the foundation of the country's political economy, especially in the 1950s. The institutional and associational forms of civil society mediated [and still do], between the state and the individual *qua* economic actors, giving such, a significance as well. As Crook so brilliantly put it, the "realm of the State begins at the point where the State enforces, upholds or represses particular relationships within civil society" (1990, p.25). A traditionally strong civil society had thus been put in the shadow of a more powerful state. The state became the pre-eminent actor, although the fractured civil society had tried in vain to prevent a dominance by the state.

Nothing expresses the antipathy of the state to the strong civil society better than the relationship between the Convention People's Party [CPP] and the economically powerful cocoa farmers. The CPP, having won the first general election under universal adult suffrage in 1951, and invited to form an '*internal self-government*' that covered areas the colonial state felt could be competently handled by the 'locals', broke up with the cocoa farmers over the government's decision to continue with the inherited system of state marketing of cocoa. The conflict set the seal on the 'new' state's attitude to the cocoa sector. The surplus accumulated from cocoa exports were to be used for state financed development and bureaucratic expansion. The sector was viewed by the CPP state as a '*cash cow*' whose fate was to be historically transcended by a state led - industrialisation [and not encouraged to expand further].

This policy, dubbed socialist by Kwame Nkrumah's CPP, not only fitted the interests and statist aspirations of the CPP, but also accorded with the Party's view of cocoa farmers as 'opposition'. The most dynamic geographical growth area of cocoa during this period was Ashanti, whose cocoa farmers were regarded by the CPP with the same venom as Mrs Thatcher had for the NUM coal miners in 1980s Britain!

It needs be said that the CPP state was strongly contested from the very beginning, [and thus] it matters that the character and representativeness of the Ghanaian state was not agreed, and that one of the most fundamental interests of both the regime and the state (the peasant economy) was alienated and excluded from all national consensus.

Economic setting 1951 - 1957

Other than the 1891 - 1911 epoch, the period under examination can be said to be the most significant in Ghana's economic history in terms of the stratification of the macro economy. The firm anchoring of the country's political economy in its assigned global periphery role, tethered in the earlier afore-mentioned period, was concretised during the period 1951 - 1957.

Equally significant was the programme of metamorphosis of the colonial state to a neo-colonial 'independent' state. Economic structures had to be solidified to withstand the possible 'shocks' of independence, considering the CPP's theoretical flirtation with socialism. In discussing the economic underpinning of the period therefore, it is important to look at specific sectors and or activities.

Cocoa

Cocoa was the predominant sector of the economy during this period and accounted for two-thirds of the country's export earnings. Annual output averaged officially at about 233,000 tons. This figure was obviously an under-estimation. Cocoa was being smuggled to the Ivory Coast and the then French Togoland, where producer prices were higher. At least, an equivalent of another ten percent of whatever the CMB purchased was lost to the production calculation through smuggling. Geographical reality, considering the role of three border regions -Western, Brong Ahafo and Volta in cocoa production makes the ten percent a conservative estimate. Other than Ashanti and Eastern Regions, the border regions accounted for total cocoa production. The specificity of colonial state creation is also a contributory factor to the high incidence of smuggling. Some farmers either lived in Ghana and had their farms in the Ivory Coast or had their farms in Ghana and their houses in Ivory Coast. This phenomenon was also applicable to Togo. In some cases, houses straddled the borders, with the same house technically in two countries.

Export prices of cocoa were very unstable, fluctuating wildly from year to year as table 2.1 indicates.

Table 2.1
Cocoa production 1949 - 1958

Year Oct/Sept	CMB Purchases 000' tons	Av.realised per ton (£)	Av. Producer per ton (£)	Public receipt from cocoa (£M)	Agg. payments to farmers (£)
1949/50	247.8	178.4	84	21.5	20.8
1950/51	262.2	268.5	130.7	33.5	34.3
1951/52	210.7	245.1	149.3	1.82	31.5
1952/53	247	231.4	130.5	22.4	32.2
1953/54	210.7	358.7	134.4	45.1	28.3
1954/55	219.8	355.1	135	46.5	29.7
1955/56	228.8	221.8	148.5	15.4	34
1956/57	263.7	189.5	149.2	6.8	39.4
1957/58	206.4	304.3	134.2	32.8	27.7

Note: Government receipts were made up of cocoa export duty plus CMB trading surplus.

Source: Cocoa Marketing Board Annual Reports.

Aggregate payments to farmers were unstable as the table 2.1 indicates, notwithstanding the intentions behind the Marketing Board Ordinance. The producer price per headload [60 lb.] was raised from forty five shillings to seventy shillings in 1950, and for the rest of the period until 1958, was fixed variously between seventy and eighty shillings. Although these prices were about three times higher than what farmers received in the last pre-war farming season and even the immediate aftermath of the war (Killick 1966, Table 15.3), there is no doubt prices were extremely low in comparison to export prices and producer prices being paid in either the Ivory Coast or Togo. And yet, so long as the difference in producer and realised export prices accrued to the Marketing Board as surplus, it had been rationalised by some, (e.g., Rimmer, 1992) that the statutory export monopoly served the interests of farmers, as had been the objective of the White Papers of 1944 and 1946.[4] This argument is porous. With the surplus growing, and proceeds used in supporting Britain's post war reconstruction, the hidden agenda could not be ignored. Why were such surpluses not invested in the colony or on high interest yielding bonds on the London Stock Exchange rather than the low interest government bonds on which such surpluses were 'wasted'?

Although grants were made by the marketing board from the surplus to the West Africa Cocoa Research Institute and the University College on the grounds of being in the producers' interests, it was still indefensible, from the farmers' perspective, that the large differential between producer prices and realised prices from 1951 was attributed to taxation.[5] The marketing system had effectively become a tax collection mechanism. Before 1948, the basis of duty was *ad valorem*, enabling government revenue as well as CMB surplus to benefit from rise in world prices. Thus a rise of about 50% in realised export prices in 1950/51 crop year led to a three fold increase in duty payments, which then absorbed one-fifth of total proceeds (Rimmer 1992, p.55). This, in addition to the 1951 change that allowed duty to be graduated so that 50% of realised export prices above £100 became payable as tax, affected the distribution of proceeds as the first three years following the change showed. CMB surplus fell sharply, whilst export duty on cocoa approached half of realised earnings in 1953/54. In short, farmers were over - taxed.

Table 2.2
Cocoa board purchases 1949/50 - 1957/58

Year Oct/Sept	Purchases 000' tons	Sales £m	Payment to farmers (% of sales)	Export duty	Other Trading expenses	Surplus
1949/50	247.8	45.1	46	8	7	39
1950/51	262.2	70.3	49	19	5	27
1951/52	210.7	51.6	61	28	7	4

1952/53	247	57.1	56	28	8	8
1953/54	210.7	74.7	38	46	5	12
1954/55	219.8	77.5	38	50	5	7
1955/56	228.8	52.3	65	28	9	-2
1956/57	263.7	50.7	78	24	10	-12
1957/58	206.4	62.9	44	42	7	8

Source: Cocoa Marketing Board Annual Reports.

The Cocoa Marketing Board had lost every semblance of being a sectoral resource by 1956. Appropriations were wantonly used to build up overseas reserves [mainly British Government Bonds], but by 1956, even this was discontinued. Assets were drawn on by the state to finance public expenditure and increased money supply.

For the cocoa farmers, who were wrongly viewed by the state and its apparatus as the 'upper tenth' of the taxable population and thus equivalent to the 'super tax' group, (Niculescu 1954), the rewards of their sweat had been appropriated by the sate without their consent and under a false premise. At best, only middle size farm owners, who were a tiny minority, could be near the 'well - off' classification. The majority of farmers were peasant producers with less than five acres of cocoa under cultivation.

Gross National Product/Gross Domestic Product

The calculation of Ghana's GDP as can be expected in an economy with a large non-formal component contained a significant estimate of subsistence production and consumption. Even the more advanced household expenditure survey of 1961 - 1962 found two-fifths of all consumption of locally produced foodstuffs and one-fifth of all private consumption to be non-marketed output (Szereszewski 1966, p.108). Subsistence production was estimated by the study to account for about 15% of the GDP.

These difficulties notwithstanding, in 1950, estimates of gross national expenditure showed a breakdown of 74.1% consisting private consumption and 4.2% of government consumption. Gross capital formation took 8.6%, increases in stocks 2.9% with resource balance [exports less imports] or net investment abroad accounting for 10.3%, that is, the equivalent of £20.1m. The ratio of exports to gross national expenditure was 39.5:100, indicating a very export oriented production structure. This ratio was more likely to have been influenced by the comparative ease of assembling data on exports as against the quality of data from the larger but often less formalised non - export sector that for all probability was highly under-estimated. Of the estimate of private consumption, food accounted for 57.1%, food, beverages and tobacco together increased to 64.2% of all private consumption (Ghana 1957. Approximation of Tables 2&4).

Estimating private consumption was not problem - free either. It held major difficulties, as was miscellaneous incomes. Prominent in the figures were the low level of government consumption, signifying a non-active state in development, and the large resource balance accumulated. The latter, added to domestic investment, gave a domestic savings rate of 22%, generated entirely from income harnessed by the local population.

While recognising that data from the 1950 household survey and subsequent years may be more incomplete than in 'advanced' economies, the Ghanaian economy was still very commercial. No household had been left untouched by commercial activities or totally detached from the money economy.

Fixed capital formation entered the national accounting calculations during the early 1950s. It took in the formal sectors of the economy much more completely than the rural sector. Many aspects of capital accumulation in the rural sectors were omitted altogether. For example, production of canoes and traditional tools and equipment - a main occupation along the coastal fishing belt - and increases in livestock were excluded. Others such as land clearing, cocoa planting, and food crops were only partly covered. Thus capital accumulation during the period tended to be on the low side. Even with the omission of large sub-sectors in the calculation of capital accumulation,[6] by the end of the period under consideration, real per capita GDP had doubled from the 1911 rate, despite rising population (Omaboe 1966, p.18). Accounting for this rapid growth of real GDP per capita was essentially, cocoa and mining.

Labour market

The labour market statistics of Ghana around 1950 indicated a 200,000 waged population out of a working population of 2.4 million. This figure, classically interpreted, was misleading. Historically, and particularly around the period under consideration, Ghanaian labour has been very fluid - taking on wage related jobs after the farming season and reverting to self employed status during the farming season. The 200,000 could only, therefore, refer the bottom line of the wage market within the year rather than the average waged labour. The Watson Report in 1948 for example, cited an estimated 210,000 employees on cocoa farms alone.[7]

The labour market, hence, contained an enumerated core of regular jobs in formal organisations and an amorphous, but larger periphery of unrecorded, informalised and often intermittent sale of labour to small scale employers.

Notwithstanding the above, there was a discernible trend in the gradual shift to wage earning labour, although the degree was not dramatic. Between 1950 -

1958 for example, recorded employment increased by about 50% from 200,000 to 300,000, with the Public sector largely accountable for this increase. The increase was concentrated in Southern Ghana - about 40% the increase in Eastern Region, 30% in Western and Central Regions combined and Ashanti and Brong Ahafo collectively accounting for 20%. The geographical spread is important, reflecting to a large extend, the concentration of public resources on resource rich Southern Ghana. Seventy percent of recorded labour was daily rated, reflecting the unskilled qualification, with nearly 50% of employees earning less than seven shillings a day at a time when Government recommended daily minimum wage for unskilled labourers in Accra was 5s/6d [£85 per annum]. There was little difference in this regard between public and private sectors. Although pay differentials were high, only 15% of recorded employees were earning more than £186 per annum in 1958 and only 8% more than £234 per annum (Ghana 1962, Tables 86&94).

In the context of war and post war wages, one is tempted to conclude that money wages during the 1950s rose significantly compared to the preceding period. Before 1950, the minimum daily wage for the unskilled labourer was 3s/3d [three shillings and three pence]. Real wages also rose by 25% between 1950 - 1958. The rise in real wages was, however, not absolute, having only made good the erosion of wages by inflation during the war and immediate post war period. Indeed, Birmingham argues that the index of the lowest paid real wages in 1958 was only marginally higher than in 1939 (Birmingham, 1966).

The low level of recorded employment and the difficulty of collecting data on work practices in Ghana is also accounted for by the predominance of buying and selling in the economy. In urban Ghana, it was the single largest source of employment (Busia 1950, pp.15-16). Buying and Selling also happens to be a predominant female enclave. In a survey conducted in Accra in 1955,[8] Accra markets recorded 5,890 traders, of whom only 379 were males. Of the recorded 18,672 women employed in Accra in 1948, 16,526 or 89% were traders.[9]

On the industrial front, the labour scene was marked by an absence of heavy industries and a small number of secondary establishments. The largest of these employed 341 workers in Accra - incidentally the industrial as well as the administrative capital (Acquah 1958, p.63).

Under the condition of absence on any significant scale of industrial establishments, worker organisations were weak and confined to the formal sector. Such organisations were further disadvantaged by being very new in a powerful colonial state. Legal recognition was only attained in 1941 and an umbrella Trades Union Congress did not come into existence until 1945 with very negligible effect on labour relations.

Development strategy

Internal Self Government, evolved in a relatively favourable economic environment. The country's post war export boom continued in the 1950s, although export prices and value had started falling by 1954 as Table 2.3 shows.

Table 2.3
Commodity trade: Imports and exports 1950-1957

	Export value (£m)	Import value (£m)	Export price index	Export volume index	Import price index	Commodity terms of trade	Income terms of trade
			1954 =100				
1950	77.4	48.1	59	93	114	63	72
1951	92	63.8	77	111	103	69	71
1952	86.4	66.6	74	117	100	63	63
1953	89.9	73.8	71	106	109	67	73
1954	114.6	71.1	100	100	100	100	100
1955	95.7	87.9	85	98	98	87	85
1956	86.6	88.9	68	101	111	67	74
1957	91.6	96.7	65	102	123	64	79

Source: (Adapted from) Ghana 1962 Statistical Year Book 1961Tables 109 & 119 Accra. Central Bureau of Statistics.

The context of strategic choices was therefore, relatively hawkish, in that it was an aggressively expanding economy largely reliant on export of raw materials and it is only fair that any examination of the strategic choices ought to be undertaken with the historical environment in mind.

The various instruments of development adopted were informed by the dominant development theory of the day in the Western sphere of influence - Modernisation. Modernisation theory had many facets, but suffice it to say that the mainstream interpretation put economic growth, quantified by rising per capita income as the defining characteristic of economic development. In other words, economic development entailed the transformation of the traditional subsistence oriented and often stagnant economy into a dynamic capitalist economy based on wage labour, capable of sustained growth and of providing, in the long term, rising wages (Lewis 1954, Rostow 1952). The institutional and organisational structures making for modernisation included the building of western style financial infrastructure to support export, the integration of the domestic economy into the global, increasing growth of the formal sector at the expense of the informal, the monetisation of transaction among others. It was argued under modernisation that, once economic growth took place, the benefits of development would trickle down to the whole population.

Economic direction, especially from 1955, was very growth oriented, reflecting the influence of modernisation. Yet up until 1958, fixed capital formation was only about 15% of total expenditure, which in itself, contradicted the priorities implicit in modernisation theory, recognising the premium on capital formation that modernisation entails. In a situation where the State, through the activities of the marketing boards, could impose savings on earnings, not much was done to redirect GDP to capital formation through increasing investment in education, health, roads, enterprise development, research and development.

Two specific developments, more than any other set of factors, set the tone for the period *vis a vis* socio-economic development strategy. First was the 1951 Ten Year Development Plan, and secondly, the "Report on Industrialisation of the Gold Coast" by Arthur Lewis on the invitation of the colonial government.

The Ten Year Development Plan, 1951

The Ten Year Plan for the Economic and Social Development of the Gold Coast was launched in 1951. The Plan per its preamble "... provides an outline of what is hoped will be achieved in all fields of development during the ten year period....", with the ten year period being seen as "merely one phase in the development of the country which has been going on steadily for many years and would continue beyond the decade with which this plan is concerned."

The colonial planners recognised the basic aim of planning in the 1951 framework document, but could not hope to achieve over all balance and development that socialist planning aimed for. The 'shopping list' approach, spitefully called 'colonial planning' because of its comparative ease of design and the love of colonial officials for such simple plans, was adopted as was expected in the model colony. This Plan simply assembled information from all government departments relating to all projects they would like to see implemented during the plan period. This was matched against available resources, [10] with projects dropped or modified not for their necessity, but for reasons of resources. This technique lacked the coherence needed to take account of close inter - sectoral relations of the macro economy and often ended up with a series of uncoordinated projects. Of course, the Plan itself was not coherent, in the class of subsequent comprehensive plans such as the Seven Year Plan of 1963. While the Plan was an advance over previous plans, it was too much to have expected it to achieve all its goals because of its lack of inter-sectoral sophistication.

The obligation of the government in this Plan was not, according to Rimmer, so much to create capacity but to deliver welfare (1992, p.61). Rimmer and others of this view seem ignorant of the correlation between such 'welfare' issues as education, health and increased productive capacity in both the medium and long terms. Indeed, both are now recognised as productive investment in human capacity resource development.

Development expenditure was largely on economic and social infrastructure and social overheads, and in line with the *laissez faire* economic philosophy of the colonising power, little attempt was made to directly alter the structure of existing production. The Plan had four major components:

- Economic and Productive Services. £G12,444,000, or 16.9% of total planned investment was allocated to this component.
- Communications. An allocation of £G26,110,000 or 35.3% of TPI and the largest was assigned to this sector.
- Social Services had the second largest allocation - £G24,542,000. This was 33.1% of total allocation.
- General Administration was allocated £G10,896,000. This was 14.8% of the total over the plan period.

The Plan was to be financed largely from internal earnings, with a loan and grant component of £G26m. The Colonial Development and Welfare Fund was expected to meet £G3m of this, while £G23m was raised by way of loans. The large internal mobilisation through the use of existing assets, including loans made to the UK Government during the Second World War and increased taxation mainly on Cocoa, underscored the relative strength and buoyancy of the Gold Coast economy at this stage.

The Plan contained a number of industries the colonial government had targeted for promotion. Included were, textiles, shoes, breweries, tobacco and canning, building materials, cement, bricks, tiles and timber.

The development of these industries had been the subject of debates for a considerable time, but the Plan represented the first attempt at formally integrating them into an Industrial Sector Programme. The Plan sought to 'take the bull by the horns' by allocating £G2m as *seed* money for the cement component of the sectoral programme. The amount was, however, never, utilised during the plan period.

The most ambitious scheme under the plan was the development and enhancement of communications. Recognising the vital importance of communications in development, the sector came in for attention. Extensions to existing railway lines were effected, new feeder and trunk roads constructed,

Takoradi Harbour, the only modern harbour was extended and improvements to post, telegraphic and telephone services were sought. The allocation of 35.3% of planned investment to this sector emphasised the commitment. Services considered 'social' such as education, health, nutrition, social welfare and community development witnessed massive improvements during the Plan period. New schools and colleges were built, extensions made to physical facilities of the University College, a medical school was proposed and provided for and a number of health centres and hospitals were to be constructed during the Plan period. The increased expenditure on social provision was a natural consequence of the increased influence of post war agitation by Ghanaians as well as a logical outcome of the strides made by the economy.

The Plan, however, was not bereft of problems. The new internal administration[11] duly changed the Plan from a ten year to a five year Plan without altering to any significant extent its direction and or choice of strategy. The repackaged five year Plan recognised, at least on paper, the importance of agriculture to the Gold Coast economy. The Gold Coast, according to the Plan, was predominantly an agricultural economy. Concrete action however did not live up to the rhetoric, as signified by the paltry £G3,650,000 voted for the agricultural sector. This amounted to only 5% of planned capital expenditure.

Report on the industrialisation of the Gold Coast: Arthur Lewis, 1953

Arthur Lewis, invited by the colonial government to advise on the desirability and sustainability of industrialisation in the Gold Coast, issued a Report in 1953 that became the blueprint for economic policy during the period. The report zeroed onto essentially two sectors of the Gold Coast economy:

Agriculture

A fundamental error made by Lewis on the Gold Coast economy was the Report's position that:

> the secret of industrialisation is a rapidly progressing agriculture, and more particularly, since food production is the major part of agriculture, the number one priority in a programme of economic development is measures which increase food production per head (p.604).

This may be valid of some countries, but in 1950s Gold Coast, the problem with food production in particular was not one of production per head, although that was important, but that of inadequate markets for agricultural products. Increased food production meant less revenue and above all, wastage through post harvest losses.

Arthur Lewis' diagnosis ought to have been one of inadequate marketing infrastructure for agricultural produce. The magnitude of this is appreciated upon the recognition of increasing food imports from Europe during this period. Increased imports were not to alleviate any shortage or scarcity of food [since there was none], but to meet changing taste for 'European food' encouraged, promoted and nurtured by the state and state favoured transnational companies. The failure of Lewis to read the situation correctly[12] had its reverberation in poorly devised strategies.

Industry

Lewis approach to industrialisation in the Gold Coast was very conventional and lacked the radical direction which a relatively well endowed colonial state at the throes of independence needed. He reasoned:

> the main difficulty in the way of capturing the processing of raw materials, and thus of getting the consuming countries to import finished products instead of its raw materials, lies in the superiority of consuming countries as centres for manufacturing ..... Today, the gap between industrialised and underdeveloped countries is even wider......and therefore, the obstacles to successful competition are even wider (Lewis 1971, p.597).

Lewis here ignores the ability of a country's industry[13] to produce initially for the local and regional markets where cheaper products locally produced stand a good chance of being successful whilst gearing resources and expertise for an onslaught on the global market.

The Report introduces another premise for the Gold Coast's non industrialisation by contending that "the decisive factor locating the processing of raw materials is, thus to summarise, usually not low wage cost, but loss of weight in the process of manufacture" By this argument, except in cases such as timber and the removal of precious stones from the 'useless ores in which they are buried', industrialisation could not be pursued because such would be uneconomical.

The Report also argued that existing conditions did not favour industrialisation. The first need, argued Lewis, was to raise productivity in food farming, as a means of providing markets and freeing labour and capital for manufacturing, the second being to improve the public services and so lower manufacturing cost. 'Very many years' would elapse before it becomes economical to switch resources to manufacturing from these very 'urgent priorities.' In the interim, the Report recommended that government supports such industrialisation as could have been undertaken 'without large or continuing subsidies' and where training was provided for the citizens in senior positions.

A small set of industries were identified - beer, bricks and tiles, cement and wood products - for whose production, conditions were favourable. A second group - biscuits, soaps, cigarettes - for which conditions were 'marginal' could also be tackled. The Government should encourage foreign businesses to set up, particularly, those willing to go into partnership with the citizens. The Report also saw the need to give assurances to foreign investment and possible grant of special assistance for a limited period to help such investors. The colonial government under Nkrumah promised such assistance recommended in a Statement to the National Assembly in 1953, hoping to see new industries established that would in due course, become fully self supporting under normal competitive conditions (Kay 1972, pp.82-92).

Lewis concludes his Report by stating *inter alia:*

> measures to increase the manufacture of commodities for the home market deserve support BUT (sic) are not of number one priority. A small programme is justified, but a major one in this sphere should wait until the country is better prepared to carry it. The main obstacle is the fact that agricultural productivity per head is stagnant .. (Lewis 1971, p.612).

My main criticism of Arthur Lewis is his globalist view of the Gold Coast economy. Whereas his training had equipped him for the mainstream academic based development economics, it did at the same time inhibit any radical thinking devoid of an immediate globalist perspective. The history of development in our time points to the realisation, that countries that have been bold to undertake very radical programmes and efficiently carry them out have chalked very major successes. None of the radical programmes pursued by South Korea or Taiwan or even Hungary's variant of economic planning made sense by the standards of the various orthodoxies current at the time and yet, these countries have short - circuited Rostow's stages of growth.

What the Gold Coast needed, with its physical resource endowment and a relatively high technical skill component - it had the most skilled labour force in Sub Sahara Africa at independence (Killick 1978, p.4) - was a radical plan that recognised the deficiency of agriculture as not necessarily one of low productivity per head, but most importantly as one of the absence of a market for most traditional Ghanaian food crops, leading to a low incentive for increased productivity.

A shift of labour to industry would therefore, have created the market for increased agricultural productivity as well as increase money earnings to stimulate productivity. By not doing this, valuable years were wasted and a favourable economic climate allowed to glide by unutilised.

Other than the influences of the Ten Year Plan and the Lewis Report, the *laissez faire* economics of the colonial state had a most noticeable effect in the strategic direction of national development. The economy, according to Seers and Ross (1952) imposed no checks on an inflationary wave of spending, either through increased savings or capital formation. Virtually, the only consumption goods being produced in the economy were foodstuffs. All other goods had to be imported, usually with delays running into months as a result of inadequate handling facilities. Low stocks guaranteed inflexible supply in a period of increasing money incomes. Yet, there was very little taxation or other outlets for remunerative savings to stem the tide of consumption. What was called for was a systematic programme to expand the local manufacturing base by re - channelling excess liquidity into investment in plant, machinery and training. Regrettably, the GDP was put to use more in meeting the foreign derived consumption needs of the economy rather than on capital formation (see table 2.4).

Table 2.4
Uses of GDP [%]

	1950	1951	1952	1953	1954	1955	1956	1957
Private consumption	74.1	78.2	77.7	81.4	69.3	75.4	75.9	80.2
Gov't consumption	4.2	4.4	6.2	6.1	5.8	7.8	8.7	9.1
Gross capital formation	8.6	8.7	11.4	11.5	10.8	15.6	16.2	15.4
Changes in stocks	2.9	0.7		-0.1	0.4		1.4	-1.7
Resource balance	10.3	8.1	4.8	2	13.8	1.2	-2.3	-3.1
GDP at current market price (£m)	195.8	239.5	239.1	259.2	259.3	334	345	363

Source: Ghana, Economic Survey 1957, app. Table 2; Economic survey 1962, Table 3.

Balance of payments/international trade

The Gold Coast was a very active player on the international trade scene. The share of exports of goods and non-factor services for 1955 - 1957 for example, averaged 27.66% for exports and 29.06% for imports as a component of GDP [expenditure] (Walter 1963, p.20). The trend of a trade dependency and deficit was one that was to continue into the post independence period.[14] For 1955, the foreign trade dependency ratio was 46% (ibid. p.43)showing a high dependency on international trade. The only period of significant international trade surplus was, as was the case in Latin America, the inter - war period. Strong reserves were built up in the UK, part of which was drawn on by the metropolitan government as war loans.

The nominal value of the country's overseas balance at the end of 1950 was £118m, reflecting the high surpluses generated during the inter war period as mentioned earlier. The colonial government alone held £19.1m as revenue surplus, £63.1m held by other public bodies and enterprises, including £56.2m held by the Cocoa Marketing Board (Central Bureau of Statistics, 1962 Table 145).

It must be emphasised that the Gold Coast balance of payment, as well as its international trade as a whole, was very influenced by the macro policy of the colonial administration, and particularly, as it affected cocoa. The metropolis, notwithstanding the immense commercial gains derived from the colony, contributed very little even before 1939 [when the highest contribution of 5% was made by the imperial treasury to the financing of development].[15] Indeed, the policy of imperial Britain was that colonies should be self - financing, and that they should contribute to, and not take away from the imperial treasury (Howard 1978, pp.156-157). Under such strictures, the stabilisation agenda of the Cocoa Marketing Board in particular, and marketing boards in general, had become in reality, and particularly so after the loss of German markets in 1939, instruments of supporting both the colonial and metropolitan economies. 'Surpluses' appropriated from farmers were invested in government securities, tantamount to enforced lending by farmers producing for exports without any guarantee of being repaid In 1950/51 alone, export duties on cocoa brought into the treasury £5.6m while CMB 'earned' £19m as operational surplus. Thus the statutory collectivisation of savings had produced low return on savings and used exclusively for the acquisition of UK financial assets.

Government revenues were dependent on the value of cocoa exports, rather than internal taxation, so that they increased by almost 85% in 1951/52. In 1954/55, there was again a 60% rise on the back of favourable cocoa market conditions. This was followed by a fall of about 40% and again a recovery in 1957/58. The share of export duties in total revenue averaged two-fifths, but fluctuated between one quarter and three-fifths, providing a very unstable base for development. (see Table 2.5).

Table 2.5
Central government revenue and expenditure, 1950/51-1957/58 (£m)

	50/51	51/52	52/53	53/54	54/55	55/56	56/57	57/58
REVENUE								
of which %								
Import duty	34.6	25	22.2	24.8	16.1	28.5	33.1	25
Export duty	23.7	50.3	39.2	38.3	61.1	38.5	25.4	37.9
Income tax	20.3	12.2	15.8	11.7	7.4	9.6	10.5	9.1
Other taxes	1.5	1.4	3.9	6.2	1.7	2.6	5.7	7.2
Non tax	19.8	11.1	18.9	19	13.7	20.8	25.3	20.8
Consolidated Fund								
expenditure	17.8	18.4	24.8	34.3	32.7	45.9	43	47.2
Development Fund	-	6.7	13.9	15.6	15	25.3	17.5	16.6
Expenditure surplus	3	13.9	4.2	0.6	33.1	-6.7	-11	-3.5

Note: Fiscal Periods are April to March from 1950/51 to 1954/55; April - June i.e, *15 months in 1955/56; July to June 1956/57.*

Source: Ghana 1962, Table 140; Kay 1972, Stats. Abstracts, Table 24a.

The colony's overseas balance, and for overseas substitute Britain, continued to accrue and by 1955, a peak of £211m had been attained, far higher than two year's combined exports.

The first post independence era 1957-66

Ghana's independence on 6 March 1957 dawned at a time of high political expectations. Independence signalled a new era for the anti-colonial movement not only in Africa but in the wide global movement both East and West. Optimism was also generated because the self-government experiment begun in 1951 had been deemed a success. Massive infrastructural as well as other forms of development had taken place under self-rule and the economy had been fairly competently managed.

Independence was, therefore, seen not just as a logical conclusion to the decolonisation process but for most Ghanaians and their sympathisers elsewhere, the beginning of the great march to 'nirvana'. Not least was the charismatic leadership of Kwame Nkrumah. As the founder-leader of the governing Convention Peoples' Party and the sitting prime minister, his leadership had galvanised the expectant population to believe that the massive development of the country was being held up by colonialism and once independence had been won, the country would in no time be rubbing shoulders with the developed countries of the world.

In examining the period between 1957 and 1966 therefore, it is appropriate to look in more detail at the themes anticipated in this introduction: leadership; the institutionalisation of development planning; the evolution and management of the wide political [CPP] programme. The first post independence period was probably the most significant era to study, in understanding the subsequent developments of the Ghanaian economy and polity in later years. This period also happens, to have coincided with the peak of the cold war on the international scene. The politics and economics of the country could not, therefore, escape from the ramifications of the cold war. Ghana, like other African and Third World nations, unwillingly became an arena for the titanic struggle between the divided worlds of East and West, Socialism *vs.* Capitalism and international solidarity against free for all capitalism.

Leadership and ideology of the country

The character of the leadership of the country and the ideology which it reflected during the period under consideration can be divided into two epochs; 1957 -1960 and post 1960. At Independence, the CPP did not alter to any significant extent, its style of leadership. The party continued with its private sector led growth policies accompanied by massive infrastructural outlay by the state. The political posturing of anti imperialism was adopted as an extension of nationalism and the specific African liberation struggle. Thus, in terms of the ideological direction of the national economy, and its area of interest, nothing had changed from the self-government era during the first years after independence.

However, the face of the administration changed from 1960. By 1958, Nkrumah had begun to put the challenges of development in the right perspective. The period of the struggle for independence and the miraculous gains in the 'good life' were over. Nkrumah himself puts this succinctly:

> One may sometimes wonder if the western powers fully understand the dilemma facing political leaders of emergent lands. They have gained independence for their peoples. The hazards and excitements of the struggle lie behind. Ahead lies the workaday world in which people must live in hope and prosper. Independence of itself does not change this world. It simply creates the right political atmosphere for a real effort of national regeneration. But it does not supply all economic and social tools. The leaders are now expected, simply as a result of having acquired independence to work miracles (Nkrumah, 1958).

Another influencing factor for change was the need for the government to demonstrate quick economic progress coupled with job creation despite the threats to the economy of falling cocoa prices. Ashanti, Volta and to a lesser extend, the two northern Regions had been threatening secession even before independence and this threat had not been shaken off. The government had thus to prove through real improvements in peoples lives that their best interest lay in a united Ghana (see Killick 1978, p.36).

The CPP government had become disillusioned with the efforts of the private sector in bringing about rapid national development. This was contrary to an earlier period of concern about the creation and development of a Ghanaian private sector. The earlier concern was reflected in measures such as the setting up of the Industrial Development Corporation which was encouraged to set up a number of publicly owned enterprises with the aim of selling them to Ghanaian businesses when they became viable (Killick 1972, p. 19). Furthermore, a Committee was set up to investigate 'the best means of assisting Ghanaian businesses to overcome their difficulties' (Esseks 1971, p. 13). Out of this disillusionment, the government sought another model for achieving its objectives.

The purely ideological break cannot also be discounted. Nkrumah, after his state visits to USSR and China in 1960, saw the task of throwing off the distorting effects of the colonial system, escaping from dependence upon primary product export, breaking out of the circle of poverty and dependency as a whole as the main goals of the development process of the 1960s. The strategy was revolutionary. This revolution, in the words of the Party, could only be carried out via the ideology of socialism (CPP 1962, para. 7). It is worthy of note that Nkrumah believed in the primacy of politics over economics and once the political decision [even if informed by the economic] had been taken, it was all systems go! With this mentality, the goal of socialism itself, and not the objective factors leading to the choice became the raison d'être. "...we could be hampering our advance to socialism if we were to encourage the growth of Ghanaian private capitalism in our midst."[16] There is not, however, a universal acceptance of the socialist credentials of the CPP government and its ideological leadership of the country. Genoud (1969, p.78) argues that, notwithstanding official state policy and terminology branding this phase of the country's political practise as socialism, what actually prevailed could most appropriately be termed modernism or nationalism. Land ownership was not affected by the changes, although the state could acquire land for public interest purposes and for which compensation was payable. Foreign capital was courted as the 'accelerator' while domestic small enterprises were tolerated.

In a post mortem of the Nkrumah government in 1966, Fitch and Oppenheimer concluded that the two approaches - pre and post 1960 were motivated less by ideology than by objective conditions. The neo-colonial period was dominated by the Lewis model of development. The failure of the model was caused by deterioration in balance of payments, loss of huge reserves and most significantly, failure to attract foreign capital which Lewis counted on to assure Ghana's industrial development and future. This also explains the abandonment of the Second Five Year Plan. They argue that the second period was not so much a flirtation with socialism as the search for alternative strategy. The second period too failed because of the rather late attempt to break from the vestiges of the colonial past coupled with the unwillingness [or inability] of Nkrumah's leadership to make the break decisive even when they attempted (Fitch & Oppenheimer, 1966 pp.82-84).

The greatest indictment of the CPP on ideological grounds is provided once again by Fitch and Oppenheimer. They are not surprised by the failure of the government in both the political and development arena. The strong influence of the Sixth Pan African Congress on Nkrumah in particular is seen as the major culprit. Themes of the Congress embraced by Nkrumah, they argue included:

a series of contradictory positions: anti - communism and anti - imperialism; non - alignment and economic development through foreign investment ..... it was the clash between these contradictory principles that produced and led finally to his undoing ([ibid. p.19).

But Nkrumah also displayed significant naiveté politically in believing that small nations could relate favourably to both superpowers whilst avoiding becoming a client state of either in the tensed cold war period of the 1960s. This posture caused apprehension in both Moscow and Washington and throughout the First Republic, Ghana was never trusted by either camp. On Tito's visit to Ghana in March 1961, Nkrumah further alarmed both camps, but more so the West, when he said at the state banquet in his guest's honour:

I am determined to build a socialist society in Ghana, entirely Ghanaian in character and African in outlook and based on a Marxist philosophy .... I see before my eyes, a great monolithic party growing up out of this process, united and strong and spreading its protective wings over the whole of Africa .... All people are equal, born equal and have an equal right to self-determination, and have an equal right to manage or mismanage their own affairs in their God given land and country.[17]

Rooney's summing indictment of Nkrumah's socialist credentials is appropriate here: "A clear and coherent outline of Nkrumah's socialist policies is difficult to achieve because, although his overall aim remained fairly constant, his views and attitudes often appear contradictory, paradoxical and almost schizophrenic" (1988, p.169).

Development planning

The government opted for a comprehensive development programme for rapid economic growth at independence. This was more ambitious than the existing 1951 Ten Year Plan provided, hence the existing plan was jettisoned. In any case, most of the planned targets, especially that of social overhead capital, had been attained. In place of the Ten Year Plan, a holding Consolidated Plan covering 1958-1959 was put in place. This was to 'tidy' the planning process and to give attention to planned targets that had not received adequate attention. The tidying up period was also needed to facilitate the drawing up of a new Five Year Development Plan. This interim plan was no different from previous plans in the techniques of design adopted.

The second Five Year Development Plan, 1959 - 1964

Although this was to be the first specifically named Five Year Development Plan, it was called the Second Five Year Plan because the preceding Ten Year Plan had been abridged and referred retrospectively as the First Five Year Plan. (Omaboe 1966, p.446).

The Plan in Nkrumah's words, '...*would give us a solid foundation to build the welfare state.*'[18] The Plan was to:

show what we have to do - by our own hard work, by the use of our natural resources and by encouraging investment in Ghana - to give us a standard of living which will abolish disease, poverty, and illiteracy, give our people ample food and good housing, and let us advance considerably as a nation (ibid.).

If the above was not expecting too much of a medium term plan, then one cannot but envy the vast resources available to the country at this point in time. Notwithstanding the relatively large resource base at the disposal of the Nkrumah government, the Plan was still too ambitious, at least in the rhetoric.

It was, however, surprising that the very ambitious Plan did not depart from the 'shopping list' approach to planning so favoured by the colonial bureaucracy. Targets were mostly set in expenditure terms, probably arising out of the constraints of the poor state of statistical data in the country. But even at this stage, a more scientific linkage enhancing model could still have been used with a bit of creativity.

The total amount of capital investment proposed by the Government over the Plan period came to about £G350 million. This included £G100 million earmarked for developing the country's hydro - electric potential via the Volta River Project. The possibility of obtaining the necessary finances to fund such an ambitious development undertaking was contested by the techno-bureaucracy. To circumvent this challenge, a creative compromise was struck between the politicians pressing for the plan [with an eye on the propaganda value] and the bureaucrats [who would provide a convenient scapegoat for politicians if targets are not achieved].

A number of projects were selected for 'immediate implementation' totalling £G132m. The other amount, £G118m, that is, excluding the £G100m for hydro - power, was maintained as part of the total planned expenditure over the five year period. Thus, whereas the total £G350m could be bandied around for public consumption [and satisfying the politicians], the more cautious and realistic £132m was slotted for immediate implementation to satisfy the non politicians who were more concerned with their professional reputations! The two sums thus became the 'small coat' and the 'large coat' in the corridors of power (Omaboe 1966, pp.446 - 447).

Table 2.6
Capital allocation under the second Five Year Plan

Sector	(£Gm) Immediate implementation	Total allocation
Agric. & Natural resources	10,425	24,668
Industry & Trade	15,418	25,331
Electricity	7,000	8,765
Communications	28,679	53,010
Local & Reg. Gov't	9,220	18,852
Education	14,150	27,852
Information	1,693	2,677
Housing	7,093	17,000
Health, Sanitation & Water	19,675	43,650
Police & Prisons	4,786	7,677
Miscellaneous	7,718	13,684
Contingencies	6,143	6,834
TOTAL	132,000	250,000

Source: Office of the Planning Commission, Ghana.

The Plan is said to have recognised the importance of agriculture (Omaboe 1966, p. 448). The ratio of the working population employed by the sector could not have decided otherwise. The Sector, in the words of the document, was to be developed into a 'highly efficient and productive occupation.' To this end, the plan provided for six priority activities:

- Raising the yields of the cocoa industry.
- Establishing large acreage of rubber and banana in the Western Region.
- Establish the foundations of a cattle industry.
- Raise the yields of cereals in the Northern Regions.
- Bring the Volta flood plains under irrigation.
- Study and promote the use of fertilisers.

In addition to the above, proposals for research, education and extension services were included in the sectoral input. It is, however, difficult to accept this overarching concern for agriculture on the basis of actual monetary commitments. Of the £G132m earmarked for 'immediate implementation' projects, only 7.89% was for agriculture, whereas the 'large coat' was only marginally better at 9.86%. Against these figures, Communications were allocated 21.72% for the 'small coat' 11.68% for industry and trade, 14.9% for health and 10.71% for Education.

Industry was, in consonance with Nkrumah's perceptions and attitudes, the lead sector of the Development Plan. The Plan was planned to establish six hundred factories of varying sizes producing a range of over a hundred different products during the Plan period. These industries were expected to bring substantial benefits both in terms of national wealth creation and job opportunities for the increasing army of school leavers. Not least was the belief that industrialisation would give the macro economy the balance it so dearly needed.

To achieve the goals projected, foreign direct investment [FDI] was to be encouraged through the use of incentives. However, not all sectors of the economy were to be opened up to foreign capital. Three distinctions were made in this connection:

1. Sectors reserved exclusively for the State; railways, electricity generation and sales, waterworks and sales, export of cocoa, telecommunications, arms manufacture, atomic energy etc.
2. Sectors where State participation was obligatory, e.g.. manufacture of alcohol, narcotics and alcoholic beverages.
3. Sectors opened freely to private enterprise.

In the case of (3), certain rules had to be followed. These included the recognition of trade unions, training Ghanaians for senior posts and the use of local raw materials wherever possible.

The industrial map chartered by the Plan was a mixed economy with the state actively participating in the wholly State Owned Enterprises, in partnership and as a provider of social overhead capital to stimulate and encourage the private sector. To this end, £G10m was provided by the Plan through the Industrial Development Corporation for direct State investment in industry. A comparatively meagre facility of £G500,000 was provided for under the Plan to enhance Ghanaian businesses pending the recommendation of a Special Committee appointed to consider ways in which Ghanaian owned industrial units could be strengthened (ibid. p.450).

Finance of the plan

The Plan was expected to be financed largely from internal sources. The country's free reserves were to provide £G50m with the Cocoa Marketing Board providing another £G50m from its reserves. Resulting from the convertibility of the Ghanaian pound [at par with Stirling], the country could gear up £G75m for planned expenditure even before the detailed work and politicking associated with the Plan had been concluded. This amount, representing over 50% of the hard-core Plan expenditure, underscored the relative strength of the economy. So strong and convertible was the currency that no distinction was made between local currency and foreign currency requirements in plan expenditure projections. Hence foreign capital was used in areas where greater reliance on local currency would have been optimal. Reserves were thus unnecessarily run down. Of course, with the satisfactory terms of trade prevalent at that time, the country did not foresee the difficult days ahead.

The Second Five Year plan was, however, abandoned in 1961 with no official reason(s) assigned. One can therefore, only speculate [even if informed] that the Plan's demise after the return of the Presidential entourage from a trip to the then USSR, China and other parts of the former East European bloc and the subsequent formal adoption of Socialism as the way forward were not unconnected.

Needless to say, the differences between the 'techno - bureaucracy' and the CPP politicians and the ensuing outrageous compromise did not leave the Plan a strong one, once its propaganda value had been milked by the politicians. It therefore, becomes an exercise in futility to assess the impact of the Plan. Historically, the first year of medium term plans, not only in Ghana, have often been expended on gearing or what engineers prefer to call 'mobilisation' and thus the short lifespan of the plan makes any attempt at analysis or indeed review, very slippery.

It is also important to note that by 1960, the Lewis - Gbedemah conservative approach to finance and financial management had been jettisoned and Gbedemah demoted from Finance to Health minister.[19] Nicholas Kaldor and Joszef Bognar had replaced their approach and in 1961 influenced by them, compulsory savings were introduced without much debate or discussion in the nation. This naturally led to strong resistance from the population at large.

The CPP Programme for Work and Happiness

The discontinuation of the Second Five Year Plan in 1961 left a strategic void on the development horizon that needed urgent filling if the developmental momentum was to be maintained. The effective use of propaganda as a mobilising tool has been one of the strengths of the CPP administration. This was called into play to forestall any slide by the party into oblivion by the introduction of the Programme for Work and Happiness in 1962.

The 181 paragraphed Programme's basic significance lay in two areas; reiterating Nkrumah and the Party's belief in the primacy of politics over economics and as a threshold of a new era of socialism as formal state policy as opposed to just party policy. The Programme, ostensibly a party programme in a multi party state[20] was promoted as State Policy, over which Parliament had very little control. It was never put to the electorate as a party manifesto commitment, and yet imposed on the State machinery.

Most importantly, a political choice of ideology was made by a governing party for the State without thoroughly debating the implications of such a choice outside the party. Kwame Nkrumah's well known 'seek yea first the political kingdom ...' approach was most pronounced in the Programme.

Whereas socialism had been intimated in the past, it had never been declared the formal state ideology or option. The previous Five Tear Plan was officially meant only to turn the country into a 'welfare state.' As Omaboe postulates, the first attempt at translating the previous hazy references of socialism to praxis in the form of technical programme in anything resembling an economic blue print was this Programme (Omaboe 1966, p.452). The Programme thus was a watershed in the government's commitment to Socialism.

Provisions of the Programme

A central thrust of the programme can be picked from paragraph 54. "... socialism implies central planning in order to ensure that the entire resources of the state, both human and material are employed in the best interest of all the people." Here, socialism is seen as a panacea. This prognosis became a fatal flaw throughout the Nkrumah regime. Socialism, like any other system of production and production relations, needs efficient, capable, creative and knowledgeable managerial mechanisms as much as it needs the directional beacon of an 'ism' The inadequate, if any, emphasis on collective and individual creativity in the production process left the regime bereft of any credible counter balance to the promotion of distributional justice in the economic realm that worked so well during the struggle for independence.

The strategic objectives of the Programme for Work and Happiness were industrialisation and socialism. An attempt was made to parry the undue political concentration of the Programme by justifying it as more or less that of political necessity. Removed from the forefront was the very strong social justice and or ideological considerations:

> The Party has always had a consistent theory for enlarging the country's prosperity. ...this ...has been tried out in practice during the difficult circumstances of the last years. The progress that has been made is indispensable proof of the practical correctness of the party's line. ..This theory has its basis in the principles upon which the party is pivoted. What are these principles? They are:
> 1] Socialism, because of the heritage of imperialism and colonialism, is the system by which Ghanaians can progress.
> 2] Socialism can be achieved only by a rapid change in the socio - economic structure of the country. To effect this, it is absolutely essential to have a strong, stable, firm and highly centralised government. This means that power must be concentrated in the country's leadership.
> Imperialism - colonialism left Ghanaian without the accumulation of capital in private hands which assisted the western world to make the industrial revolution. Only the government therefore can find the means to promote those basic services and industries which are essential pre requisites to intensive, diversified agriculture, speedy industrialisation and increased economic productivity (CPP 1962, para. 6-8).

The Programme's self justification lay strongly in its identification of criticisms against the colonial economic system (para. 28 -31). These included the division of labour, the colonial pact, low wages, inadequate educational system and infrastructure, inadequate health facilities etc. These criticisms were correct and well known, even if unoriginal. Recognising the foregoing, the Party and Government saw the need to "grapple quickly with the problem of re-organising the whole of the life of the nation based on improvements - in all sectors" (para. 32). The thorough re-organisation of the nation was deemed necessary because:

33

the basic aim of our economic development is to free our economy from alien control for the State to participate in the wholesale and retail sectors of trade throughout the country. This is the only means of protecting the people from unbridled exploitation by alien monopoly interests. The Party is firmly of the view that planning of the national economy can only be really effective when the major means of production, distribution and exchange have been brought under the control and ownership of the State (para. 55).

The Programme goes on to take the position that, development would not be possible without real liberation, which it deemed necessary because "Ghana's trade and industry remains largely under the domination of alien monopoly interests. This is a relic of colonialism which the Party is determined to eradicate ..."(ibid. 35).

The Programme and agriculture

The Programme for Work and Happiness envisaged the progress of agriculture through four basic steps. The first was to increase the production of export crops; second to introduce new cash crops which could find a market abroad; third to use at home for food and industry, the cash crops now produced or which could be produced but for which processing facilities do not presently exist, e.g.. cocoa, and lastly, producing at home foodstuffs that are presently imported (para. 77).

Critics such as Genoud point out the absence of clarity in the Programme as to who was to bring about the changes enumerated for agriculture. This critique is justified by the silence of the Programme on the mode of production and forms of ownership in agriculture. However, one has to look at the Party's broad attitude to industrial and other forms of production to find an answer. Notwithstanding CPP's displeasure with particularly peasant cocoa producers, just as in its industrial policy, the Party did not envisage nationalisation or basic land reforms to achieve a hold over agriculture. The perceived wisdom was for the State to set up rival production units to compete and outperform existing modes of production.

By investing heavily in newly created state owned agricultural units, particularly the Russian influenced Workers Brigade, the State hoped to beat the private sector through higher productivity and plantation based complexes under competent scientific management. Mechanisation was thus a major element in the armoury of the State in this direction.

The Programme and industrialisation

The creation of an industrial economy under the direction of central government was the ultimate aim of the Programme. Industrialisation was to result from the creation of three main industry types:

1. "The Party proposes that the Seven Year Plan[21] contain proposals for establishing those types of heavy industry which are large consumers of power and for which raw materials are locally available" and also "immediate study should be made of the possibility of starting a heavy chemical industry (fertiliser, artificial yarns and plastics)". The Programme further dilates that, "the use of our iron ore resources might form the basis of an iron and steel industry" (para.88 - 89).
2. " A second type of industrial development consist of industries which utilise new cash crops and thus provide considerable agricultural employment. The sugar industry is a case in point. For every man employed in the factory, ten agricultural workers are needed..." (para. 90).
3. The third type of industrial development envisaged comprised light industry such as textiles, making of shoes, clothing, furniture, diamond polishing and fittings for the building industry etc. (para.91).

To underpin all the above, the complete electrification of the country was regarded as imperative, if the envisaged was to come to fruition (see para.33). The drive for electrification was particularly urgent and was pushed to the top of both the political and economic agenda.

The preponderance of ideology over all other considerations in the determination of national development policy under the Nkrumah regime seemed to have been temporarily put on the backburner with regards to the ownership of the means of production. This is most reflected in the attitude to capital. Five sectors were designated for different treatment vis a vis capital injection and investment. Sector one referred to industrial units reserved solely for State enterprises; Sector two referred to wholly foreign private owned; Sector three joint State and Foreign ownership; Sector four was solely co-operative ownership and sector five 'small scale' Ghanaian private enterprises. The Programme tasked State enterprises to:

> ensure an ever-growing and steady employment for the people; to increase national income and the revenues of the State; ... to have at the command of the State, significant and growing stocks of commodities in order to influence the market; the influenced being aimed at the stabilisation of price levels and that of currency; to supply those services which the private sector does not wish or is not allowed to supply.

The Government defended the acceptance of large scale foreign enterprises in the country along the lines of needing accelerated growth of Ghana's capital stock and the need to conserve foreign exchange arising from its commitment to 'maintain the national reserves at safe levels'. What was most significant about ownership in the Programme's industrial trajectory was the almost disdain the government had for Ghanaian owner enterprises. Paragraph 103 - 109 made no attempt to disguise this. "..... in order to encourage and utilise personal initiative and skill, Ghanaians can undertake small scale enterprises, provided that they are not nominees or sleeping partners for foreign interests".

Although the intention was to build a socialist economy and society, the economy was to remain for an unspecified transition period, a mixed economy [with as little Ghanaian private large scale component as possible]. External capital was courted and assigned to act as accelerator. Why was the CPP and Nkrumah welcoming to foreign capital but not the national bourgeoisie?

The Volta River Project

In line with the aspirations of the CPP government [and indeed most Ghanaians] to transform Ghana from a primary production based economy to a modern industrial one, the Volta River Project, which had been gathering dust in the cobwebs of time, was put on the fast track. The history of the Volta River Project [VRP] is one of a long gestation. In 1925, under the colonial administration of Governor Gordon Guggisberg,[22] an aluminium industry, based on the country's bauxite deposits and hydro - electric power from the Volta river was seen as a priority for national development. Commercial investigations, however, did not commence until 1938, only to be interrupted by the Second World War. The investigations were, however, restarted in 1945 by a private group -West Africa Aluminium Ltd., later to be joined by Aluminium Ltd., another British controlled company in 1949.

The Gold Coast Government appointed Sir William Hakrow & Partners as consultants and who submitted a favourable Report on the Project in 1951, arising out of which serious negotiations between the Government,[23] the UK and interested British Aluminium Companies. Agreement was reached and a White Paper[24] published setting out the outlines of the project.

The estimated cost of the project at this time was £144m, divided into two phases costing £100m and £44m respectively. The UK government's condition for participation [in its model colony!] was an option at the ruling market prices for 75% of the total aluminium output arising from the project be given to British buyers for a thirty year period.

Based on the favourable technical report from the government's consultants, a Preparatory Commission was set up utilising once again the expertise of the same consultants, but with an expanded membership and remit. The Commission reported in 1956 that " the Volta Project can be regarded as technically sound and could be carried out successfully" (Sir William Hakrow & Partners 1956, p.3). The Commission costed the project at £231m [the first phase taking up £162m]. The release of the Report however, coincided with an increased supply of aluminium on the world market by about 60%; leading to a depression in the previously engineered high world market price arising from supply inadequacies. This contradicted a World Bank forecast of a fourfold increase in demand for aluminium in the twenty years after 1950 (Rooney 1988, p.154). The British government's interest, true to form, waned once supra-profits became no longer feasible and British business interest was no longer served by the project.

With the withdrawal of the British interest, the Nkrumah government turned to the USA. This culminated in the State Visit of Nkrumah to the USA in the furtherance of this objective. The Kaiser Corporation, with the encouragement of the Kennedy White House, responded favourably and put forward a variant of the British designed scheme under which a larger dam would be built at a lower cost. An aluminium smelter was also to be built but would run on imported alumina instead of developing Ghana's own bauxite deposits for the purpose. This possibility was relegated to a later stage.

With the backing of the USA administration and that of Kaiser Corporation secured, the World Bank was approached. The Bank's own team investigated the project and was enthused about it. The Bank therefore provided a £17m loan to Ghana for the project, the largest such loan it had ever made for any single project in Africa. The World Bank's lead was followed by the USA and a lacklustre Britain, both providing additional funding in the form of loans. The funding arrangements thus were:

Table 2.7
Funding of the Volta dam hydro-electric project

Lending Agency	£G1,000's
IBRD, 53/4%, 25yrs	16,785
USAID, 31/2%, 25yrs	9,643
EXIMP Bank(US), 53/4%, 25yrs	3,572
UK-ECGD, 6%, 25yrs	5,000
Total International Finance	35,000
Ghana Government	35,000
Total financing (core)	70,000

Source: Seidman, 1978 p 138.

In addition to the core project, the Ghanaian State was to underwrite the cost of building about 500 miles of transmission lines and the construction of both a new township - Tema, to house 70,000 people and a brand new harbour, said to be the largest and most modern in Africa at the time as part of the peripheral support for the core project.

The Ghana government, with financing arrangements secured, entered into a contract with the newly created Volta Aluminium company [Valco]. Valco is usually described as a consortium, but it is most appropriately described as a partnership. Kaiser Aluminium and Chemical Corporation holds 90% of the equity shares with Reynolds Metals Corporation owning the remaining 10%. The two companies were to supply alumina to the new smelter from their various global operations and dispose of ingots produced by the smelter in proportion to their holdings (Killick 1966, p.402). Valco was and is in reality, only a tolling smelter. It does not buy alumina and smelt it into aluminium product. What it does is to process the alumina for its customers and in its special case, its two shareholders for a fee. It would not accept custom from elsewhere. What effectively goes into the Ghanaian economy is the cost of power, labour and the purchase of materials necessary for its operations as well as contributions to the Valco Fund administered solely for the use of Ghana and any taxation and the transfer of foreign currency through the Bank of Ghana to meet its local operational expenses.

The contract obligated Valco to build a smelter at Tema and provided *inter alia*:

1. The price at which electricity was to be sold to the smelter was fixed for the first 30 years at 2.625 mills i.e. 0.225 cents per kilowatt hour! The price was virtually at cost and was comparable to the lowest existing market price for electricity anywhere in the world at that time (ibid. p 397).
2. Valco was to consume or pay for a maximum of 370,000 kilowatt per year out of the expected total capacity of 919,000kw when the project is fully on stream.
3. Imports by Valco for construction and running of the smelter to be duty free for the first thirty years (Articles 15&20).
4. No restriction, control or taxation of aluminium exports (Article 19).
5. Imported alumina to be duty free for thirty years (Article 20).
6. Valco to be guaranteed pioneer company relief, which exempts it from all taxation of its income for at least five years, extending beyond that to a maximum of ten years if profits have not totalled a specified minimum (Schedule B).
7. From the years when income tax does become payable until 1997, the rate at which tax shall be levied is that applicable to companies on January 2, 1961 i.e. 40% of retained profits plus a further 2.5% of profits transferred out of

Ghana. With certain exceptions, no other taxes can be levied on Valco's business within this period (Schedule c).

Ghana made two important concessions to Valco that had far reaching consequences:

- The agreement not to insist on a firm commitment on the part of Valco to install in due course an alumina plant in Ghana.
- Agreement to sell power at a fixed price rather than prevailing world prices.

In trying to understand why Ghana under Nkrumah, the radical leader of African politics signed such an unfair agreement, one has to look back at the influence of the modernisation paradigm reinforced in the Ghanaian case by the Soviet influence of power industries, e.g.. steel, iron etc. The need to move away from agriculture, particularly strengthened by the CPP distaste for cocoa producers, was worth any price. "The government is conscious of the great - and perhaps decisive - contribution which the Volta project could make to the diversification of economy, and to reducing our dependence on the basic cash crop, cocoa" (Nkrumah, 1961, p.105).

The optimism of the project also rested on providing water for irrigating the Accra plains for large scale capital intensive crop production,[25] providing cheap water transport of raw materials and equipment across its three hundred mile long artificial lake connecting the south of the country with the north. The discovery of large deposits of iron at Sheini in the North was an added tonic.

The project was significant in another sphere. It was seen as the battleground between East and West. The then US ambassador to Ghana, Russel, was so outraged by the attack of the Ghanaian press on US foreign policy, particularly on the Congo whose Prime Minister - Patrice Lumumba was a close friend of Nkrumah, that he argued funding the Volta project would reward Ghana for her virulent anti-Americanism but conceded that refusal to finance it would play into the hands of USSR (JFK Lib. NSF Jan 1961).

The cold war hysteria surrounding the project was not helped when Nkrumah in a National Assembly debate on the Volta River Project in January 1961, announced that the USSR had offered to build another dam on the Black Volta at Bui. Neither did Nkrumah's oratory when Brezhnev visited Accra in the February of the same year smoothen matters.

It needs be pointed out however, that throughout Ghana's subsequent economic problems, which included a major rescheduling of debt, the Volta River Authority [VRA] had been able to meet interest and loan commitments on the project as a result of the agreement by all parties involved to pay all of Valco's power bills into an offshore account out of which interests and loan repayments were first made before any residue was paid to Ghana.

The Seven Year Development Plan, 1963-1970

The Seven Year Development Plan was introduced in 1963 following the abandonment of the Second Five Year Plan by the CPP government as a planning manifestation of the new direction of the country's political economy and sign posted by the Programme for Work and Happiness.

The foundation of the Seven Year Plan can be perceived as arising from of the need to utilise the massive social overhead capital [SOC] created during the fifties and early sixties. Hirschman generally proposed the stepping up of investment in SOC creation as a precondition for development for countries just emerging from colonialism. In the specific Ghanaian context, Seers and Ross argued for increased investment to open up the country and its potential for development. Thus Ghana, as indicated in the preceding chapters, decisively increased its stock of social overhead capital only to discover in the early Sixties that, the economy was not responding sufficiently to this stimulus and that the SOC thus provided was under utilised. Omaboe, the then Government Statistician who chaired most of the Planning Committee meetings in the absence of the President, remarked that Ghana was in possession of an infrastructure that was capable of supporting a higher level of productive services (Omaboe 1966, p.454). JH Mensah, the Executive Secretary of the Planning Commission noted that:

> a general presumption of planning for the next seven years has been that existing level of social services is under utilised in terms of the volume of economic activity which it could support, and that a good deal of which expansion could take place without any need for corresponding increases in social and administrative services (Mensah [ca Sept. 1962] p. 20).

The Plan, in tandem with the Programme of Work and Happiness, started from the point that Ghana was to become a socialist state and that this long term objective was to be achieved through the successful accomplishment of a series of development Plans in the general framework of a mixed economy. The Government was to progressively acquire a dominant position in the economy through its investments in the productive sector. Genoud (1969 p 75) estimates that this could have taken place over a twenty year period.

The underlying spur for the Plan could be viewed from either a politico-social perspective or from an economic perspective. This is not to say that it is always easy distinguishing between the two.

Politico - social

The Plan had the decisive advantage of being drawn up not in a political vacuum as other Plans have suffered. Its authors derived fairly explicit guidance from the CPP Programme of Work and Happiness. The Plan therefore, was in its main trajectory at least, consistent with the political outlook and aspirations of the power cells of the country. It also had, according to Killick (1978, p.53), the tacit approval of some of the radical left's leading economic doyens of the day. These experts, including Joszef Bognar, HC Ross, AO Hirschman, Nicholas Kaldor, WA Lewis, KN Raj, Dudley Seers, Killick et al, at a conference called to debate and discuss the draft plan in April 1963, with few reservations, 'passed' the plan as technically sophisticated and competent and also as a step in the right direction.

The Seven Year Plan aimed at the rapid economic growth, the socialist 'transformation' of the economy and the complete eradication of its colonial structure (Seven Year Plan p.ix). Thus for the first time, development planning in Ghana was to be the instrument of not just economic transformation, but also the transformation of production relations and society as a whole. Whereas the previous plan aimed at the creation of a welfare state (see page 28) the current plan goes further to establish its socialist credentials. The transformation was to be achieved through the rapid development of the state and co-operative sectors.[26]

Economic

Nkrumah [and the CPP] believed massive industrialisation to be the only way out of the poverty of the nation. The Seven Year Plan was seen as a vehicle for achieving the above and also transforming the colonial production structure of the economy and increasing economic independence by processing materials for export and by producing local substitutes for imported manufactures. Page 3 of the Plan nominated the production of manufactured consumer goods as the type of industrialisation on which "it is intended to lay the main emphasis .... under this plan". The drive for massive industrialisation can be understood in its simplicity by linking it to the need to create jobs for the increasing numbers of middle school leavers. Myrdal notes a similar (Myrdal 1968, p.150) nationalist identification of industrialisation with development in South Asia.

General provisions of the plan

The Seven Year Plan aimed at achieving a shift in the end use of capital formation from the provision of social overhead infrastructure to directly productive activities [PDA]. It emphasised modernisation of agriculture and an accelerated process of industrialisation (Seven Year Plan pp.7-12). The post-war period and particularly the 1950s had come up with the inadequacy of social overhead capital [SOC] as a major drawback to industrialisation. In accordance with Hirschman's general treatise of development, and in the specific Ghanaian case the work of Dudley Seers and HC Ross on the potential for industrialisation, the building up of infrastructural capacity had become the pre-occupation of previous efforts. New roads, hospitals, schools, power stations etc. were built.

This Plan however, veered towards rapid economic growth. This was to be accomplished by "maximising the rate of productive investment." It provided for the maximum utilisation of existing plant capacity, followed by an expansion whenever possible of the productive capacity of existing enterprises in preference to the setting up of entirely new factories, the completion of projects under construction and lastly the erection of new buildings and installation of new machinery to commencing entirely new industries (p.105).

Socialism, formally adopted by the Plan, required absolute and relative growth of the Public sector "until by the end of the transitional period, the State will be controlling on behalf of the community, the dominant share of the economy." The colonial mould was to be severed by the production of manufactures on the basis of markets to be provided by the inevitable forthcoming Union of African States (7 Yr.P chapt. 1). The Planners were adamant that the dominant position of the state sector in the economy was to be achieved:

> without ...ever having to resort to much expedients as nationalisation which, if carried out without full compensation, would only change the ownership of the means of production without adding to the capacity or employment opportunities, and if carried out without such compensation, would inevitably incur such a large measure of hostility as to make our development plans very much more difficult to achieve (ibid. p.3).

Sectoral divisions and relationships

The Plan as argued earlier, represented a major departure from previous plans, in that, emphasis of investment was directly on productive undertakings as against infrastructure and services.

Table 2.8
Proportionate distribution of government investment under various plans

Plan	Productive investment (agric & industry)	Infrastructure & social services
First 1951 - 56	11.2%	88.8%
Second* 1959 - 64	20.3%	79.7%
Seven Year	37.3%	62.7%

* Discontinued after two years.

Source: Birmingham et al. 1966 pp 455 Table 18.3.

It is useful to note that the use of percentages conceals the real allocation in absolute terms. Notwithstanding the percentile decreases, the total allocation to infrastructure and social services under the Seven Year Plan exceeded the total for the same under the two previous plans put together. Between 1951 -1959, the average allocation to social services was £G6.2, compared to the Seven Year Plan's provision of £G21.5m per annum. Infrastructure was also allowed £G6.6m per annum during 1951 -59 as against the Seven Year Plan provision of £G12.8m for each fiscal year (Omaboe 1966, p.455).

Under this Plan, the bulk of the £G476m Public Investment still went to indirect sectors of infrastructure and social services, although the relative downgrading in favour of directly productive investment is a highpoint. Omaboe, one of the architects of the Plan, asserts that it had concentrated on directly productive services (ibid.). This was an obvious exaggeration. Significant however, is the nature of individual projects chosen for promotion and investment by the State. Such projects had to have the capacity for high rates of return on investment and short pay-off periods. The Planners believed that only when this is effected can they "ensure that investible resources in the hands of the State will grow rapidly, thereby enabling the State to extend further participation ..." (Seven Year Plan p.3).

The Plan hoped to achieve both in its present manifestation and subsequent instalments, four cardinal results:

• It was planned to reduce what was often referred to as the colonial structure of the economy, that is, an economy based mainly on the export of primary commodities.
• The achievement of full employment or the eradication of unemployment.

- Ensuring that Ghana will be able to play her full role in a Pan-African Economic Community.
- That the socialist goals set would be accomplished mainly through the participation of government in the economy to ensure the full implementation of this ideological orientation.

In achieving the foregoing, the Plan aimed at a total break with 'primitive' agricultural methods; and the rapid development of large scale agricultural schemes which would safeguard the supply of food to the planned large industrial settlements. The governing party had very little confidence in the ability of hundreds of thousand peasant farmers to carry out the task of the envisaged agricultural revolution.

Planned investment

Planned total investment for the period was estimated at £G1,016m. This covered both government and private sector investment. The private sector investment target of £G540m was to be obtained as follows.

Table 2.9
Breakdown of private sector investment

	£Gm
'Direct labour' investment	100
'Residents' net private savings	340
Net Foreign capital: Valco	60
Others	40
Total	*540*

The detailed investment portfolio for the period was therefore as follows:

Table 2.10
Investment breakdown

(a) By Investor	£Gm
1 Planned investment [State sector]	333.3
Housing	20.0
Infrastructure [excluding transport]	75.7
Volta River Project	33.7
Social Services	127.9
Mining	10.2

Agriculture	65.8
2 Projected Investment [Private sector]	273.7
Mining: bauxite and alumina	16.4
gold	10.3
other	4.8
Agriculture, direct & recorded	110.8
Housing: Urban	24.5
Rural	31.7
Other	75.2
3 Industrial investment	
(State and private)	269.3
Aluminium smelter	43.6
Basic industrial enterprises	79.3
Other industry	43.6
Industry for post 1970 period	30.0
Transport	62.9
Depreciation	140.2
Total Investment	1016.5

(b) By economic sector

Agriculture	176.6
Industry	206.4
Mining	41.7
Transport	62.9
Housing	76.2
Infrastructure	109.4
Social services	127.9
Other	75.2
Depreciation	140.2
Total	*1016.5*

Note: Social Services refer to education, health etc.
Source: Seven Year Development Plan p271.

Table 2.11
Financing of Ghana's investment bill

	£Gm
Recurrent budget surplus	100
Profits of State corporations	23
Small savings	12
Foreign loans & grants	240
Long term domestic borrowing	14
Short term borrowing	87
Total	*476*

Source: Omaboe 1966, p.457.

The strengths of the Plan

The Seven Year Plan was distinctive from previous plans, for amongst other reasons, it differed from the 'shopping list' approach in technique. It employed a more sophisticated generic approach, closely mirroring the increased spasm of expertise available to the country. The planners also had the advantage of operating from a relatively strong data base built up from previous exercises. Not to be omitted is the qualitative and quantitative improvements in the state of development economics in general and development planning in particular globally. Thus closer attention was paid to inter sectoral relationships in the working of the economy than had previously been the case.

The Plan recognised the need to take a long term view of the economy and attempted to build this perspective into the planning process. The planners argued it is only in the long view that it is rational to project any really radical transformation of an economic system. The Seven Year Plan was, therefore, only the first instalment in a co-ordinated series.

A most remarkable feature of this particular Plan was that for the first time, growth targets were set for the economy. This was pegged at five and half percentage growth points per annum. However, providing for population growth of two and half percent during the period, the targets did not seem ambitious enough.

A major strength of the Seven Year Plan was the willingness of planners to deviate from Nkrumah's perceived wisdom. Although the planners took inspiration and guidance from the CPP's Work and Happiness programme, they recognised a facet of Ghanaian reality that did not tally with the expressed views of the political leadership. The planners argued that 'the most readily available way of raising national income is by concentrating our efforts in the coming seven years on modernising agriculture' (pp.54-61). They went on to state that however much progress was made in the non-agricultural sectors, the general level of prosperity in Ghana could not increase significantly unless agriculture, the employing sector of nearly two thirds of the labour force underwent a revolutionary change in output per acre and or per unit of labour. The rate of growth in agriculture would thus condition the rate of growth of the whole economy (ibid. p.61).

On the industrialisation component of the plan, the architects again showed considerable understanding of the Ghanaian economy in a way that diverged from Nkrumah. The long term perspective was to begin with manufacture of consumer goods,[27] building materials and the processing of Ghana's traditional exports. The second stage would then be to move basic industries such as metals and chemicals and only then to proceed to the creation of heavy industries and the manufacture of sophisticated electronic equipment (ibid. pp. 11 -12). Nkrumah's view however, was that:

> secondary industries, important as they are to making us economically independent, will still leave us reliant on outside sources and skills unless we build up those industries which alone provide the fundamental basis of industrialisation.[28]

The diagnoses and prescription offered by the planners were the most realistic and consistent at that period of the country's development history.

Weaknesses of the Plan

The Plan, notwithstanding its strengths, had a number of weaknesses that marginalised its positive impact on the development horizon. These could be classified under structural or technical weaknesses and those of implementation or human/political factors.

Structural deficiencies Transformation of a structural kind required an extensive use of imported inputs and foreign factors, notwithstanding the aspiration of economic autonomy being preached. This happens to be in direct contrast to the plan periods preceding the Seven Year Plan when growth was primary product led and more local factors were therefore utilised. Large scale manufacturing, modern service industry [including air and sea transport], mechanised agriculture and power generation were capital intensive activities and given the resource availability at the time, also import intensive. To this extent inappropriate choices, or at the very least, inadequate assessment, attention and recognition of the degree of the structural problem led to the selection of inappropriate activities for diversification and this contributed to the malaise of the national economy.

Additional biases towards capital intensive and import substitution industrialisation heavily burdened the economy, particularly with the country's obsession with the latest available technology. Equally, the over-valuation of the currency occasioned primarily by inflation and monetary policy rigidity had cheapened foreign exchange by about 25% between 1960-65 (Killick 1978, p.118). Borrowing, under this condition was indirectly subsidised whereas savings was discouraged leading even to more inflationary pressures. The net effect on the investment climate was to encourage foreign exchange based speculative activities such as imports of easily tradable goods rather than putting the country's resources geared from savings into directly productive non service activities.

It is estimated that as applied to Ghana's structural transformation, Domestic Resource Cost [DRC] of saving [or for exports, earning] a unit of foreign exchange was largely negative. Out of forty firms surveyed by Steel (1972) in broadbased manufacturing, using the official foreign exchange rate and the shadow rate of the currency which assumed the currency [cedi] to be over valued by a third, only six firms were seen to be efficient in the sense that they were transforming domestic resources into foreign exchange at a rate equal to or less than the value officially put on foreign exchange. A further four firms became efficient at the shadow exchange rate. The other thirty were inefficient in that it cost them more to save foreign exchange than foreign exchange was worth even at the shadow price. The inadequate costing of individual projects, particularly those in the directly productive category only burdened the plan with unsustainable demand for foreign exchange which in the long run, made the economic viability of the plan questionable.

Implementational/political weaknesses The undue politicisation of economic decision taking led to a decline in the quality of investment decisions. A number of such decisions had very weak economic rationale and others could not even be said to have any. A mango canning factory, for whose products a market did not locally exist and whose capacity is said to exceed the then global trade is only one of the most bizarre ones taken (ibid. p.229). Investment decisions, in short left much to be desired and under such circumstances, no plan, irrespective of its sophistication, has any chance of being successful.

The decisive shift of investment in favour of directly productive services provided for by the Plan did not materialise. The only official review of the plan observed that "the pattern of governmental expenditure had not shifted decisively as envisaged" (Rep. of Ghana, 1965).

It is not surprising that a fundamental shift in the government's pattern of investment could not be achieved. The annual budgets of 1963 to 1966 bore very little relevance to either the whole Seven Year Plan or to even the annual plan instalments prepared by the Planning Commission to effect the implementation of the former. For example, the Budget Speech for 1963-64 financial year made only a single passing reference to the Plan and even then in direct opposite to the plan strategy proposing increased government consumption relative to capital expenditure. The 1965 budget speech[29] did not even make any mention or reference to the Plan.

The 1966 budget retreated even further from economic services towards spending on general administration and services (Uphoff 1970, p.709).

The Planners were equally unsuccessful in exerting influence on balance of payments policy. The Seven year Plan stated that the country's external reserves should remain around the end of 1963 level and should not be further reduced (p.220). This was simply ignored by both the Finance Ministry and the

Central Bank. The Planning Commission could also not enforce the important and desirable proposal of screening all governmental investment projects with the finance ministry before submission to Cabinet as provided for by the Plan (pp.288-290 & 295 -299). Ministries and ministers found it convenient to ignore plan discipline and procedures.

Last but not least, the Planning Commission was unable to enforce spending discipline on projects, particularly new ones. The Plan had given preference to full use of investments already made at the expense of new projects but this was again totally ignored by the politicians. They simply set up new factories without exhausting the capacity of existing ones as stipulated by the Plan (p.105). No wonder the Executive Secretary of the Planning Commission, JH Mensah, resigned in 1965 frustrated.

Assessment

In analysing the Seven year Plan, it is important to note that Ghana is ultimately not a *plannable* economy. The export sector is unusually sensitive to one of the world's most volatile commodity markets - cocoa. In a study of export markets, Michaeli (1962, Tables 8 & 10) found Ghana had the fourth highest index of export price instability and the second largest fluctuation in national income derived from changes in terms of trade. This extreme variability of world cocoa prices disfunctions not only the country's import capacity, but equally critical, the tax revenue of the State. Exacerbating this is the natural dependence of a largely agricultural economy on the vagaries of the weather. This dependence imposes on key variables, considerable year to year instability.

The volatility of national economy in turn induces a pre - occupation with the short term, and yet more often than not, the short term is at discord with the medium to long term aspirations of sustainable development of a country.

The foregoing notwithstanding, the Seven Year Plan suffered particularly from a lack of will by the political elite to submit themselves and their ambitions, both personal and national, to Plan discipline. It was true that some of the economic projections of the Plan were flawed, particularly assumptions of an average cocoa price of 400 cedis per ton (Plan p.233) since actual prices fell to 356 cedis in 1964 and 276 cedis in 1965 respectively. Even then, arising from the bumper harvest of 1965 [and Ghana's expansion was a significant contribution to the over - supply on the world market], total projected proceeds did not suffer unduly because of the increased volumes. The shortfall for the two years combined came to only twenty-five million cedis. Thus one cannot justify the naked disregard for plan implementation. The absence of political will was the major debilitating factor that hindered the effective implementation of the Plan. Infact the Plan remained basically a paper tiger.

Killick in assessing the Plan, wrote "the Seven Year Plan was a piece of paper, with an operational impact close to zero" (1978, p.140).

Sectoral performance during the First Republic

Agriculture

The most important drawback of the country's developmental effort during the period as amplified especially by the Seven Year Plan was the relegation of agriculture to the background, notwithstanding the country being basically agricultural:

> Industry, rather than agriculture is the means by which rapid improvement in Africa's living standards is possible. There are however, imperial specialists and apologists who urge less than developed countries to concentrate on agriculture and leave industrialisation for some later time when their populations shall be well fed. The world's economic development, however, shows that it is only with advanced industrialisation that it has been possible to raise the nutritional level of the people by raising their levels of income (Nkrumah 1966, p.7).

This position of Nkrumah summarises the official line on agriculture during the First Republic better than any policy document. Nkrumah's attitude [or that of the Party for that matter], showed a Lenin-like disdain for peasant farmers and what they represent. From Nkrumah's perspective, rural development meant mechanisation and state farms and in concert with this position, withdrew assistance from small scale farmers who made and still make the bulk of the population (Killick 1978, p.41).

To Nkrumah, a break from 'primitive' agriculture was called for. Agriculture, the largest component of GDP [41% in 1965] was thus starved of resources consistent with its proven mode of production and output. State Farms into which whatever resources allocated to agriculture went, hardly made any impact largely for wrong choice of technique and massive mismanagement.

Growth and productivity

The 1957 - 1960 period recorded satisfactory annual average GDP growth rates of 6%. This was reasonably encouraging performance of and within the capability of a country that was in 1960, far ahead of most developing countries. For instance, Ghana's per capita income of £70 compared favourably

50

with Egypt [£56], Nigeria [£29] or India [£25] (Huq 1989, p.2). This growth rate was not sustained and from 1960, and throughout the 1960s, averaged 2.8%. With a population growth rate of 2.6%, 2.8% GDP growth rate left only a 0.2% gain in real GDP per capita.

The most outstanding feature of the Ghanaian Economy therefore in the 1960s was its failure to grow. Per Capita GDP therefore declined [at constant prices] from ₵140 [cedis] in 1960 to ₵125 by 1969. The decline raises questions even about the recorded growth rates of the early 1960s since there were generated almost exclusively by the expansion of public sector consumption. Kuznets (1966, p.224) questions the nature and desirability such 'artificial' growth that has no roots in increased production.

Industrialisation

If there was one major area that symbolised the development approach of the First Republic, it was industrialisation. State participation and involvement was at its maximum in the drive to industrialise. It is still useful to note that direct state participation was achieved by creating new enterprises rather than nationalisation. In a few cases, the state purchased at going rates from the private sector such as in the case of the State Gold Mining Corporation which was created from a number of failing private mines or in the state buying control of AG Leventis and turning the trading concern into the Ghana National Trading Corporation. The state's industrial strategy of outperforming the private sector rather than absorbing and taking control in its 'scientific socialist' approach drew a lot of flack some left wingers both inside and outside the country for 'supping' with the devil (see Fitch, & Oppeinheimer, 1966). The industrial strategy of the period was import-substitution led but the policy witnessed the regular symptoms of 'structural inflation'. On this Killick writes:

> with the domestic structure of industrial production proving too inflexible to accommodate major new demands being made on it as a result of import restrictions. it was not merely that Industry could not catch up quickly with demand: the industrialisation was highly inefficient, fostering the emergence of high cost producers charging prices well in excess of the imports they were replacing. (1978, p.159).

An important element of the period was mismanagement of the development process, especially as this affected industry and commerce. Dowse puts it as: "... signs of obvious industrial and commercial mismanagement were everywhere ... (By 1965) some £40m had been invested in 32 state enterprises, only two of which showed profits.." (Dowse 1969, p. 96).

Capital formation

At constant prices, domestic capital formation increased from 14.1% GDP in 1957 to 22.6% in 1960 (Huq 1989, p.2) but started sliding down in 1961 when it amounted to 20.2% in addition to a decrease of -2.0 of stocks (ibid. p.50 table 2.4). The ratio of gross fixed capital formation to GDP at current market prices increased from 15% in 1957 to 20% in 1960 and went above 20% in 1961, but varied between 17% and 18% during 1962 to 1965 (ibid. p.48). On exports, the value of exports was as high as one-quarter of GDP during the late 1950s but started declining from 1960 when it amounted to 25.73%, 1961 23.87%, 1962 21.93%, 1963 19.37%, 1967 18.20%, 1965 17.12% and 1966 14.62%.[30]

Investment policy

Whereas the government from the 1960s did not encourage Ghanaian business, there was a conscious attempt to attract foreign direct investment [FDI], pointing out that this brought in much needed managerial and technical skills which could be passed on to Ghanaians. A Capital Investment Act was thus passed in 1963 offering a wide range of fiscal and other concessions to would be investors. However, the Act stipulated that large scale enterprises by foreign interests should give the government first option to buy their shares whenever they wished to dispose part or all of their equity holdings. Foreign private enterprises and enterprises jointly owned by the State and foreign private investors were required to re-invest 60% of their net profits in Ghana.

It is significant to recognise that, notwithstanding the very massive development outlay during the 1960 - 1966 period, the economy did not respond to the stimulus. Investment ratio had been raised from the fairly high 16% in 1958/59 to 23% in 1964/65. Net investment had also increased from 12% to 16% of net national product (Killick 1978, p.67). This was Ghana's 'big push' and was seen by many economists as a gigantic investment effort. The ratio was higher than the Rostowian ten percent minimum prescribed as necessary for take-off. The big push was further supplemented by a huge increase in national capital stock that dwarfed the high 50% increase talked about in the 1950s. Net capital accumulation in 1960 - 1965 was put at 80%+ of the 1960 stock capital (see Brown Economic Bulletin No. 1&2 table D1).

Notwithstanding the substantial investment during this period as elucidated earlier, the Nkrumah regime failed to attain any appreciable growth rate commensurate with investment outlay. This draws attention to an economic fact: there is no strict connection between investment and growth. Although one is a facilitator of the other, reaction is not automatic. Unfortunately, this seemed to have been taken for granted in the Ghanaian case. The inability to translate investment into growth in the Ghanaian specificity arose more from the low productivity of investment from the late 1950s to 1960s. The most lasting character of investment in this period was its remarkable failure. This failure becomes more stunning when juxtaposed with the relative success of earlier periods.

Public finance

It has been argued that low income countries experience a vicious circle of low income leading to low savings, investment and back to low income! (Nurkse 1953, Lewis 1953, Myint 1980). Any development pattern, whether capitalist or socialist, must aim at via various instrumentalities, exerting major influence on improving the savings ratio of the national economy.

The savings ratio had witnessed a very fluctuating trend, 14% in 1957 [relatively high] reaching 22% in 1964. Decline set after this landmark and by 1984, only 5% of GDP was saved. In another manifestation, Gross Domestic Savings declined from 18% of Gross National Savings in 1958-1959 to 15% by 1964. The decline was more noticeable in Net National Savings which fell from 14% of GNP to 5% within the same period. Disturbingly, this was happening at a time when investment ratios were going up. The gap between gross savings ratio and gross investment changed from a saving surplus of 2% of GNP in 1958/59 to a deficit of 8% in 1964/65 (Killick 1978, p.69). In other words, the country added to its external reserves in the first part of the period, but by 1964/65 one third of gross investment had to be financed by drawing on these reserves as inflows from abroad. Large balance of payment deficits were the inevitable results culminating in the major foreign exchange crisis of 1965 - 1966. The year 1960 marked what Ahmad saw as "the beginning of an uninterrupted series of sizeable budget deficits as well as the use of money creation as an instrument of financing the deficits" (1970, p.24) The Budget deficit was 7% of GDP in 1961, increasing to 9.4% in 1962 and 9.9% in 1963. This fell on the wave of high cocoa incomes in 1964 but rose again to 10.9% in 1965. Government revenues increased by 42% from 1961-1965, with expenditure increasing by 66% in the same period. Even recurrent expenditure increased faster than government revenues, having increased by 53% and development expenditure by 79% in the period under consideration (Huq 1989, p.13). Money supply was increasing at an annual rate of 12%[31] from 1961 - 1965. The average GDP growth rate was 3.2% during this period, and yet government consumption at constant prices averaged an annual 15% between 1960 -1965 with gross domestic investment at 3.45 (ibid.).

Internal Public Debt increased from ȼ76.5m to ȼ407.1m - that is a five-fold expansion - while external debt rocketed from a negligible ȼ12.7m to ȼ378.4m by the end of 1965. More disturbing was the Suppliers' Credit component in the external debt. In 1964 for example, out of a total external debt of £187m, Suppliers' Credit alone accounted for £157m. By the very nature of such credits, they attract higher interest rates than medium to long term development loans. Most of these Suppliers' Credits originated from imports from UK [30%] and Germany [24%], the two leading sources of Ghanaian imports. Not to be sidelined was the more fundamental issue of these suppliers credit violating the very principle of cost effectiveness of imports as enshrined in the Seven Year Plan. The Plan advocated for long term loans that were preferably not tied to specific projects.

Following this trend, the country's debt servicing ratio, negligible in the 1950's had reached 18.5% on Suppliers Credit alone by 1965 (Rimmer 1992, p.282). Payments due in 1966 and 1967 totalled £G33.5m and £G40.5m respectively, equivalent to over 25% of export receipts for each year. By the end of 1966, long term loans owed to western countries and the World Bank totalled £G37m. Another £G29m, other than the Suppliers' Credit aforementioned, was owed to suppliers from the USSR and other Eastern bloc countries.

Trade

The most unique feature of the Ghanaian trade regime during the period was the over-dependence on the West, principally UK, Germany and the USA for both imports and exports. Notwithstanding governmental attempts to diversify the country's internal trade, very little was achieved in real terms as shown by table 2.12.

Table 2.12
Trade with socialist countries [£m sterling]

	1960	1964
Imports from Socialist countries, Israel* etc.		6.5 22
Total Ghana Imports	129.6	121.6
Exports to Socialist countries, Israel etc.	5.8	15
Total Ghana Exports	115.9	114.6

Source: Ghana, Central Bureau of Statistics Economic Survey 1964.
* Israel, UAR, Mali, Guinea. i.e. all had bilateral trading agreements with Ghana.

The absence of diversification was not for want of trying. Ghana commenced cocoa exports to USSR [a non-traditional market] in 1955 and yet by 1964, this market together with the expanded Eastern market accounted for an almost insignificant percentage of Ghana's cocoa exports, with cocoa accounting for over 60% of her Ghanaian export trade.

Table 2.13
Export of cocoa to USSR 1955-1964 [thousands of tons]

	1955	1956	1957	1958	1959	1960	1961	1962	1963	1964
Total Export	204	233	259	195	252	297	406	423	404	382
Export USSR	13	9	36	1	8	34	19	25	43	33

Source: ibid.

Social

The need for expansion and increased supply of skilled labour as a basic requirement for industrialisation pushed the country into an ambitious educational expansion. Basic school education was made free and compulsory [1961] and tuition fees for secondary level education abolished in 1965. Under the Seven Year Plan, provision was made for the doubling of secondary school enrolment with University intake increasing sixfold.[32] The supply of skilled labour via other technical colleges and avenues was boosted by over a hundred percent during this period.

A worthy social indicator of the development direction was the distribution of income in the country. Income distribution in Ghana has historically been less unequal than other African countries. This was aptly captured by Derek (1972, table 5) in his examination of evidence from 18 developing countries. He found Ghana's distribution to be more equitable than the average for countries in a similar state of development. His multinational finding was that 50% of the population [in the combined 18] accounted for 19% of income, the highest 20% earners accounting for 55% on income and the topmost 10%, 41% of income. The Ghanaian figures below compared favourably to the above.

Table 2.14
Distribution of income in Ghana

Year	lowest 50%	highest 20%	highest10%
1956	33%	37%	22%
1962	29%	43%	30%
1968	26%	50%	27%

Source: K. Ewusi: Distribution of Monetary Incomes in Ghana. Institute of Statistical, Social and Economic Research. 1971 graph 6 & appendixes 1 - 5.

Ghana experienced a relative decline in living standards in the 1960s as measured by consumption per capita. Total consumption, measured at 1960 prices, increased only marginally from ¢790m in 1960 to ¢836m by 1966. This against an average population growth rate of 2.6% translated into a decline per capita from ¢117.4 in 1960 to ¢106.5 by 1966. The decline was even steeper for private consumption per capita, which fell from ¢103.2 to ¢88.3 for the same period. The higher private consumption decline rate *per se*, need not be viewed negatively as this was partly triggered off by increased socialisation of consumption during the First Republic. What was worrying here was the concealment of impoverishment that resulted from the ability and willingness of the political and bureaucratic elite to appropriate a large share of the increased social consumption at the expense of the average Ghanaian. The allocation of publicly built houses at Kanda and Kaneshie was an embarrassing example of the middle - senior level bureaucrats and the political masters using their positions to acquire multiples of houses when they already owned private houses as well as occupied duty post accommodation.

The National Liberation Council period 1966 - 1969

The overthrow of the CPP regime in February 1966 brought into power, a military *cum* police junta that rejected what Nkrumah's CPP had sought and progressively set out to reverse the policies of the previous regime. Doing away with central planning and control, monetary and fiscal stability was the foremost item on the Regime's development agenda. This, for example, pushed growth to the back burner, opened up the economy and returned to a private sector market led and an economically decentralised system. The state was increasingly disengaged from direct participation and control of the production process and instead, sought to regulate the economy through the instrumentality of the market devices.

The coup occurred against a background of drawn out negotiations between Nkrumah's government and the Bretton Woods institutions. No agreements had been reached by the coup date. In both May and September of 1965, the Fund and Bank respectively were invited by Nkrumah to advise on the Ghanaian economy. Both the Bank and the Fund rightly observed the need for a pause in the speed of investment to allow for consolidation and desirability of putting a lid on public sector expenditure, particularly, the dependence of the exchequer on the central bank facilities to finance these deficits. The operation of state industries, state farms and other aspects of macro-management, were also rightly questioned by the twin institutions.

However, on the direction of the economy, the Bank/Fund's expressed reservations were contestable. A major bone of contention was the CPP's emphasis on equity as opposed to the Bretton Woods accent on growth. And indeed, there are theories of economic development, including those using Keynesian prepositions, which suggests that sustainable or swifter growth is dependent on more equitable or less extremely unequal social structures.

Public finance

If any area of national politics could be described as NLC's battleground during its period in power, that was Public Finance. Ideological posturing aside, the major bottleneck of development in most developing countries has been the management of the national economy. Arising from low savings, the state has constantly been called in to lead the funding of prime development projects and programmes. The ability of the state to effectively prime the process is in turn limited by its inadequate resource base. Too often therefore, the state has had to resort to borrowing to make up its deficits. Whereas such borrowings in the first world are derived almost exclusively from bonds and other forms of borrowing from within the country, developing countries have had to fall on central bank financing and equally, if not more damagingly, on external loans. The decisive difference between public sector borrowing in advanced economies and the developing world is one of the nature their currency. In the former, such borrowing is accomplished in local currency [sterling, dollar, yen etc.]. But in the case of the latter, other than domestic bank borrowing, the bulk of the borrowing is defined in a foreign unit of account. Debt servicing, therefore, becomes not only one of the state meeting its debt obligations, but doing so in a foreign currency. This must be done with the built-in disadvantage of differential exchange rates and interest rates.

57

The National Liberation Council's approach to public finance had a number of strands: debt payments and debt arrears, curtailing imports, review of government tax and spending programmes, bringing the balance of payments into equilibrium, building up the country's reserves and reaching an arrangement with both the World Bank and the International Monetary Fund.

Debt and payments The country's net increase in external principal debt was from ₡687m on February 1966 to ₡768m at May 1969. Rescheduling of past debts had however, increased total interest payments to ₡197m, an increase of ₡80m. Annual debt payments on the external account therefore constituted about 10% of exports in the medium term. As if this drain was not cataclysmic enough, a number of loan moratoria were scheduled to run out in the next five years, aggravating the export to debt servicing ratio.

The debt position was exacerbated by the run down of the nation's external reserves. At the end of 1960, foreign exchange reserves stood at ₡357m [$416m] but by the end of 1965, this had all but disappeared and instead, an external debt of $1bn had been established, including nearly $600m [60%] worth of suppliers' credits, with 75% maturing within five years. By the beginning of 1966, payments due on both the principal national debt and suppliers' credit amounted to 28% of export earnings.[33] By march 1969, however, net external reserves had risen from the all time low ₡10m at the onset of the NLC to ₡39.6m as against a worsened external debt position as indicated by table 2.15.

Table 2.15
Summary of external debt, May 31 1969
(₡m post devaluation)

A. Principal debt at 23/2/66	-₡687.3
Less cancellations or suspensions	-₡55.5
Plus effects of rescheduling	₡53.8
Total rescheduled debt: Pre Feb. 23, 1966	₡685.6
New debt incurred from 24/2/66	₡240.6
Less payments since Feb. 24, 1966	-₡158.1
Total Principal outstanding	₡768.1
B Interest [estimate]	
Interest at 23/2/66	₡201.6
A:Before rescheduling	₡118.0
B:Effects of rescheduling	₡83.6
Less Cancellation or suspension of debt	-₡11.2
Less Actual payments since 24/2/66	-₡34.6
Plus interest on new debt incurred since 24/2/66	-₡40.9
	₡196.7
Total Debt (P+I)	₡964.8

Source: Omaboe 1969.

Recurrent expenditure If the NLC was to bring public expenditure under control, then it was imperative that public spending was closely kept under wrap. In an attempt to curtail recurrent expenditure, modest school fees were introduced [breaking the holy writ of compulsory free basic education for all]. A freeze on public sector recruitment was also imposed. Job losses arising from natural wastage and limited redundancy measures were pursued. It was the National Liberation Council's position that the marginal productivity of excess labour was zero and that the state was paying such labour for no work done (Budget Statement, 20 July 1966).

The first year of NLC saw the recurrent budget forced down by £8m from the 1965 level of £110m. Notwithstanding the success that year in not only holding down current expenditure, but actually achieving the above saving, the subsequent years proved more difficult to handle. In this year [1966], recurrent expenditure reached the 1965 level and shot up to £148m by 1968. This was largely accounted for by a 5% increase in public sector wage bill in July 1967. The dilemma faced by the government was how to halt the decline of real public sector reward that had been manifesting itself since 1962 without increasing public sector expenditure, particularly in the wake of Mills-Odoi Commission's recommendation against increases in public sector wages for sometime (1967, p.30).

The NLC was apt to propose reducing government expenditure rather than increasing taxes. Taxation was deemed to be already too high and did not therefore provide a viable option in bringing the current account into equilibrium. Public expenditure discipline, therefore, went beyond the recurrent. Overall reduction in budgetary expenditure was on the cards. Against the actual expenditure of ¢467.6m in the preceding year, expenditure for 1966/67 was pegged at ¢401.2m. A chunk of the reduction was borne by the capital budget.

The drive to bring down recurrent expenditure had mixed results. Between 1966 and 1969, recurrent expenditure actually increased by about 9%. The increase compared unfavourably to a 3% increase in current revenue. The claim was made (Omaboe 1969, pp.3-4) that the increase was inevitable and arose from augmented expenditure on social services notably education and health resulting from expansionist policies of the past; increased security spending, and the effects of past development activities on recurrent expenditure. It is, however, useful to speculate on what the levels of recurrent expenditure would have been if the CPP plan had continued.

Deficit financing Financing of budgetary deficits was an improvement over the Nkrumah approach which depended largely on foreign borrowing in addition to central bank borrowing, with the latter being inflationary in character. The deficit during NLC's period in power was largely covered and from 1967-68, entirely from non-inflationary domestic borrowing, revolving IMF medium term credits and inflows of long term low interest or interest free foreign aid.

Fiscal policy was also utilised in reducing government reliance on banking finance of budgetary deficits. Spending was compressed from ₡401m in 1965 to ₡358m in 1967/8, notwithstanding increases induced by the devaluation of the cedi. In 1968/9,[34] state spending was still around ₡400m. The reduction in government expenditure being borne by the shrinking of the development budget from ₡147m in 1965 to ₡78m in 1968/9 (Omaboe 1969, p.3).

The economic thrust of the NLC

The management and thrust of economic policy was decisively pro market under the National Liberation Council. This differed considerably from the Nkrumah approach, although a fair amount of keynesian doctrine was prevalent all through the 1960s and 1970s. To buy time for the regime while deciding its options, the NLC was quick to declare its commitment to meeting all of Ghana's debts, even though some of its radical supporters had advised against this line of action. This gave the NLC time to prepare remedial measures and to negotiate a standby credit with the IMF. NLC, thus unlike the Nkrumah government accepted and indeed signed up to the 'soundness' of IMF's advice (see Omaboe, 1969).

The International Monetary Fund's advice centred initially on a stabilisation programme that aimed at reducing central bank finance of budgetary deficit, eliminating such finance as a second step, cutting back on deficits on the current account to levels that could be balanced by inflows of long term capital.

Ghana's IMF inspired stabilisation of 1966-1968 did not depart from the classic stabilisations associated with the IMF's right stabilisations the world over. The government's budgetary deficit was to be drastically pruned down. Budgetary expenditure as well as extra-budgetary ones were to be matched to revenue receipts, and whatever deficits existed were to be financed from non-inflationary sources.

The IMF package of proposals included the following; Bank of Ghana lending [other than cocoa pre-finance] was to be limited to a ceiling of ₡159m. Loans and other advances to the private sector and commercial banks were not to exceed ₡15.3m. The lending rate [rediscount] of the central bank was to be increased from four and half to seven percent. To further control money supply, commercial bank lending was to be pegged to ₡200m, while advances to non-priority sectors from the same banks were to be reduced from thirty three and a quarter percent to twenty five percent of their lending portfolio. Thus a squeeze on liquidity was to be the golden nugget in stabilisation.[35] The Stabilisation Programme consisted of four important facets:

- A squeeze on public spending;
- A 'shake out' of excess labour from public sector;
- Tariff, duty and import licence changes and
- Devaluation.

Public spending

To deflate the economy, stringent economies in public employment and a temporal halt on public investment was called for. The government was also to keep public expenditure within budget as stated earlier, a feat that had for a long while, become unattainable for the CPP government. This was achieved by the NLC (see Krassowski 1974, p.111). Moreover, a saving of 2.5% was actually made.

Public Sector shrinkage

A favoured tool of 'stabilisation' the world over has been[36] public sector cuts and Ghana was no exception. It was perceived that at the bottom of Ghana's inflationary pit was the unwieldy and largely inefficient public sector. Any realistic attempt at stabilising the economy, it was believed, could not ignore the imperative of shedding excess labour in the public sector as well as other cost excesses.

The government therefore, aimed at reversing the trend of increased growth in the public sector[37] through increased emphasis on private sector and joint venture projects.

> It is obvious that only a partnership between the government and private individuals and businesses in the country can create the resources with which a welfare state can be built.(Foreword Budget Statement,1966/67).

The distinction in both usage and rhetoric between the NLC's 'welfare state' and the mid sixties 'socialism' of the Nkrumah government is worthy of note. Paradoxically, the influence of the socialist experiment [even if naive] is clear and strong. Here was an obviously right wing military junta eager to establish its welfare credentials.

A ban on employment was instituted as a component in holding down public sector growth. Natural wastage was also allowed to be instrumental in this direction. Pruning down the numbers in public employment, particularly the civil service and subvented organisations was essential to the task.

Devaluation

A most powerful weapon in the stabilisation armoury was devaluation. The World Bank and the International Monetary Fund had earlier in their discussions with the Nkrumah government noted the over- valuation of the cedi as detrimental to sound macro economic management. Devaluation, however, was unacceptable to the Ghanaian left, most, if not all of whom were by definition, structuralists. And among structuralists, devaluation has hardly ever held any credibility. It is the structuralist argument [particularly those from the developing world] that the very nature of developing economies make currency and balance of payment disequilibruim inevitable. Elasticity of demand and supply can hardly be used to justify devaluation. Elasticity, according to the structuralist perspective, works well in economies with the capacity to react fairly quickly to external and market conditions, but very rigid structures [and third world economies fall under this classification] are not gifted with this ability.

It is worth mentioning that the Ghanaian devaluation experience was regarded, even by its Ghanaian supporters as mainly one of preventing further deterioration of exchange rate disequilibruim, at least in the short to medium term. Devaluation should therefore be seen as part of a package, and not a panacea on its own (see Leith 1974, p.140). The cedi was thus devalued from ¢0.71 to the US dollar to ¢1.02 to the same in July 1967, a 30% devaluation.

The 30% devaluation could not be said to have been successful, at least not during the NLC's period in office. By the very nature of the Ghanaian economy, and particularly its traditional exports, the time lag between policy initiation [and or incentive] and the manifestation of results is about five years. The leading export commodity, cocoa, has a gestation period of at least five years. It takes about this period of time for a new crop yield to come on stream. Arising from the shortage of venture capital and the capital intensive nature of the other major earner [mining], there would always be a time differential between export incentives and realisation of increased exports.

What probably conspired most against the success of Ghana's devaluation was the convergence of devaluation, import liberalisation and reduction in levels of international trade related taxation.[38] It was necessary, if not critical for the NLC to raise taxes, particularly import tariffs to counteract the effect of liberalisation of licensing. With an over-valued currency attracting very high patronage rent, a thirty percent devaluation was incapable of forcing down the level of imports on its own, particularly recognising the very high marginal propensity to import. Yet the NLC, even without an electoral base, shied away from taking the harsh but necessary step of raising tariffs to stem the flow of imports for fear of being unpopular with the masses.

It has to be said that the major beneficiary of the stabilisation policy was the manufacturing sector. The ease of importing raw materials and spare parts helped the sector to increase both capacity and profitability. Between 1966-1969, gross output and manufacturing value added grew by 85% and 61% respectively. The sector's employment record, in contrast to other sectors, grew by 43%. The number of small manufacturing units rose from 230 in 1966 to 346 in 1968, with textiles, clothing, footwear, food, beverages and tobacco recording substantial increases. In 1968 for example, textiles, clothing and footwear accounted for 21% of the increase in gross manufacturing output and 47% of value added. Food, beverages and tobacco also accounted for another 13% and 52% respectively. These rises were faster than in the previous three years (Hutchful 1987, p.36).

Budgetary and fiscal policy

Economic policy was centred around budget balancing, rather than economic transformation. The total state budget was for this purpose cut by ₵60m in 1966/67 over the 1965 figure with ₵58m coming from the development budget. When inflation is accounted for, the magnitude of the cut becomes more sobering.

The 1966/67 budget marked the beginning of the stabilisation programme pursued by the regime which aimed at 'the rehabilitation of the economy and the preparation of the ground for sound economic policy leading to a resumption of a satisfactory rate of growth'. (Budget Statement 1966/67, July 20 1966 p.3). It assigned specific sectors to the private sector. Agriculture, commerce and housing fell under the domain of the private sector. The state was to move out of these. The containment of inflationary pressures, fuelled primarily by the public sector was central to this move.

In the light of the above, it is ironic that the devaluation of 1967 and the concomitant increase in cedi debt servicing charges [both internal and external] sparked the rise of recurrent expenditure. For here was a tool designed to sap out excess liquidity by charging consumers a realistic value for imports rather aggravating domestic spending. This is the dilemma most low income developing countries face. The government, being often the largest employer in the formal sector as well as the most important player in the economy, is often under conditions of devaluation, saddled with having to spend more in local currency buying the necessary foreign denominated currency to service its external debt.

Fiscal policies were adopted to induce a 5% increase in the volume of economic activities particularly in 1968 when the stabilisation induced recession threatened to derail the economy. The volume increase was made up of about a

3% increase in private consumption and a 20% upturn in government expenditure on public services. More worryingly, investment recorded only a 2% increase. Private sector investment did make up for the massive drying up of state investment. The Gross National Product therefore increased by only 1.7% out of a Gross Domestic Product increase of 2.5% (Budget Statement 1969/70, p.2.).

Foreign trade

Whereas the Nkrumah government stressed the internalisation of economic activity, placing emphasis on import substitution reinforced by import and exchange controls, the NLC era was with minor exceptions, characterised by an open market approach. The exception was the cancellation of bilateral agreements with China, Albania and Guinea and the suspension of such agreements with other COMECON countries. What was unquestionable was the preference of a western *laissez faire* approach to the keynesian macro-economic management with only the minimal controls and regulations that the peculiarities of the national economy demanded.

Attempts were made to secure inflows of long term public and private capital. This was buttressed by the experiment in import liberalisation where the main elements were decontrol of imports and devaluation. In ridding the economy of import controls, the commissioner for finance stated "... of the NLC to free our foreign trade and payments from artificial restrictions and controls" (NLC 1967,p.4). The government, however, soon found out that the 1967 devaluation did not go far enough in establishing exchange rate equilibrium to warrant the total removal of import controls. The controls, at least most of them, were therefore left in place. The 1967 devaluation was therefore seen in a new light as 'cutting down' rather than eliminating [as it was first touted] the difference between the official rate and the parallel market (ibid. p.10). The emphasis thus shifted to the decontrolling of imports of mass consumption, spare parts for industry as well as raw materials for the manufacturing sector. By 1968, when the Two Year Development Plan was launched, the idea of liberalisation had virtually been dropped and on the agenda came improvement in the licensing system. (ibid. p.4).

The use of import licence did not favour capital expenditure. This was in harmony with the NLC's desire for greater utilisation of installed capacity as against the creation of new productive units. Despite the soundness of the foregoing, the inability of the regime to regulate or cap the importation of consumables wrecked the attempt at creating a stronger balance of payments position. Imports of consumer goods exceeded by a very large margin, planned levels. Thus the overall fall in imports during the years of NLC was attributable to the steep cuts in imports of capital items. Against the 1965 figure of £188m, imports totalled £140m in 1966/67 and £128m in 1967/68 before rising to £142m in 1968/69. Another source of decline was imports from former Eastern Europe, which had previously accounted for a significant percentage of capital machinery imports from 1960.

The NLC's philosophy of private sector led development naturally drew the country into the IMF sphere of influence. The Fund, and indeed the Bank as well, had previously come up against Nkrumah's altercation in 1965 and found reaching agreement with Ghana extremely difficult. The NLC, for reasons stated above, did not have any serious problem striking an agreement with the two institutions. It is arguable that the NLC's *repose* with the Bretton Wood's institutions and the West in general was the only logical move since the bulk of Ghana's outstanding external loans were due to these sources and their banks. The country's external trade was also dominated by trade with these countries.

The external environment favoured the NLC government. Although the volume of exports did not increase, especially in 1968,[39] total export revenue increased by about ₡100m above the 1967 level on the back of improved world market price for cocoa. The increase volume of imports, twelve and a half percent, could therefore be accommodated while enjoying improved balance of payment. Total deficit on the current account, which stood at ₡ 129m in 1966 had fallen to ₡87m in 1967 and a further decrease to ₡57m in 1968, notwithstanding the devaluation effect. (Budget Statement 1969/70,p.2.)

The biggest folly of the NLC in its management of the external trade relations was the use of the cocoa windfall to finance consumer imports of non critical national significance such as milk, alcoholic beverages etc. This might have been allowed to court popularity, but it made the work of the next administration extremely difficult by denying it of the resources for real development.

The Two Year Plan

The Two Year Development Plan, effective from mid 1968 to mid 1970, was conceived as a forerunner to a more comprehensive Plan. Its general purpose, as stated by the foreword to the Plan by the Chairman of the ruling junta [Gen. Ankrah], was to 'stimulate economic, social and cultural progress which would provide a higher standard of living to Ghanaians in a manner compatible with human dignity' The Plan signalled the end of the stabilisation phase of the government's programme, although it still encompassed elements of stabilisation. The Plan was more directional than pro-active, reflecting the 'less government' approach favoured by the IMF, the World Bank and the government's external advisors. It was prepared with the assistance of the

Harvard Advisory Group. In reality, the Plan was more of a '*progress*' report than a 'plan' as previously known. It is, therefore, not surprising that this is the least known of all plans in the country's developmental history. It made for a modest expansion in the national economy by encouraging the maximum use of existing productive and infrastructural capacity supplemented by selective additions and fundamental reforms aimed at attracting and encouraging private capital.

The use of the Harvard Group was the first time since independence when a single outside group had been associated with a Ghanaian Plan, although individual foreign academics and practitioners had been used in the past. The use of the Group could also be linked with the growing influence of the International Monetary Fund and the World Bank during this period.

Investment

The investment scene was characterised by a desire[40] of the state to withdraw from all productive investment other than infrastructural and social services such as education, health and welfare. This was in consonance with the NLC's 'small government' approach to macro- economic activism. This strategy, for a developing country with low per capita income and a least developed financial market, has consistently been attacked as heresy by nationalists of the Nkrumah mould, political economists and Keynesian economists.

Public investment, not suprisingly, fell from one hundred and forty two million pounds sterling in 1965 to one hundred and fifteen million in 1966/67 financial year and one hundred and twenty seven million in 1967/68. Although a general downward move in economic activities triggered off by the stabilisation programme is often credited with this steep fall in public investment, this approach begs the answer. A political decision had been taken to cut public sector investment in order to consolidate on previous investment. This in itself, was laudable. But consolidation ought to involve reinforcement, and not inaction. If an appropriate programme had been drawn up, setting the parameters for consolidation, then the argument would have been more tenable. But in the absence of any such programme, one is tempted to see consolidation as a weak justification.

Under the NLC, the domestic savings-investment gap was reduced with fixed capital formation declining by 23% of GDP in 1965 to 13% in 1968/69 (Killick 1978, p.304). Import licence was as stated earlier, not geared towards increased capacity but more towards consumption, raw materials and spare parts. At best, one can argue that such allocation of import licence, critical in a third world economy, was too much tilted in favour of capacity utilisation, but at worst to promote blatant consumption.

The regime's position on public investment was that the 'overall levels of government expenditure has run too far ahead of the growth of the economy. There must be a pause for consolidation' (Budget statement 1966/67,p.4). The consolidation period was to see the completion of projects already started. The exception was meant to be those which would supplement the profitability of those in the earlier classification. Of particular attention was the importation of additional tractors in agriculture. No extra tractors were to be imported into the public sector until the capacity utilisation of existing machinery was appreciably raised from the existing 10%.

The position of the junta on investment was probably fashioned by the World Bank's thinking on the Ghanaian economy. In a preliminary report on the economy, the Bank (22 Sept 1965) concluded that:

> the primary cause of this relatively low effective return to effort has been the result of understandable desire to attain a very rapid rate of development. ...Although top management is competent, its capacity has been overstrained by the rate of introduction of new projects. This has run ahead of the rate at which middle and junior levels of management and technical personnel could be developed. ...Financial resources have been similarly overstrained. Despite the rapid increase in taxation, recurrent development expenditures have grown at an even faster rate, resulting in very high levels of budgets deficits.

Thus the bank was calling for a halt to further investment. One is not disputing the need for reappraisal, but the seemingly blanket clamp down was not necessarily, the most appropriate and cost effective. Notwithstanding NLC's criticism of the Nkrumah regime's investment programme, particularly its composition, its own record did not break new grounds.

Table 2.16
A sectoral distribution of public investment

	seven year[1964-65]	post Nkrumah [1966-69]
%age shares in total		
Agriculture	10	12
Manufacturing & mining	26	13
Infrastructure/public works	41	38
Education	5	9
Health, social & housing	7	12
General government	12	16
Total	100	100
Total investment [annual]	108	60

Notes:
1. Annual investment in pounds sterling.
2. Includes two months covered by 7yr plan.
3. First two years of 7yr plan.

Source: Andrzej Krassowski 1974, p.160.

The relative increase in allocation to agriculture has been consistent with the increasing trends even under Nkrumah. Of significance however, was the decrease in allocation to manufacturing and mining. This was in accord with the government's stock taking and consolidation of investment line.

The capacity utilisation approach of the NLC paid dividends in at least one area. The manufacturing sector recorded increased output arising from the liberalisation of parts and raw materials imports. New capacity, relatively small but new, was also added to the private sector. This was especially true of the textile industry. The new additions were capital intensive, import sapping and lacked appropriate linkages, both backwards and forwards. The textile and footwear industry was particularly import dependent, as the Table 2.17 below illustrates:

Table 2.17
Textiles, weaving apparel and footwear industries: imported inputs as a percentage of total materials in 1968

	SITC Classification	% of imports
Textile	2311	100
	2312	NA
	2319	90
	2320	100
	2391	94
Footwear	2411	94
	2430	98
	2442	95
	2443	69
	2444	100
	2449	100
	2451	46

Source: Bank of Ghana [quoted in Hutchful 1987, p.37].

Social and political

At the heart of the NLC regime were policies with very deep social implications. Although most of these policies were primarily economic, the distinction between the economic and social, if not political, is often hazy, more so in the developing world where as a result of the pivotal role of the state, the fusion becomes even more prevalent. In considering the social dimensions of the NLC period in power, the researcher is often confronted with seemingly political or economic decisions which impact severely on the whole of society in ways other than narrowly economic or narrowly political.

The first of such decisions is the employment effect of stabilisation. Inbuilt into the programme was worker retrenchment in the public sector. The NLC argued that workers (whose marginal productivity in the public sector it had calculated to be negligible) would, upon retrenchment, find themselves in agriculture and other private sector activities. This was over-optimistic and anecdotal at least in the short term in the context of an economy where the public sector was the biggest employer. The Ghanaian private sector's capacity was small and thus it was naive to expect increased absorptive capacity almost by fiat to take in tens of thousands of retrenched workers.

The IMF influenced policies brought in its wake, unprecedented levels of unemployment in the urban zones of the country. Between February 1966 and August 1968, over 66,000 workers, nearly 10% of the formal waged labour force, had been retrenched. Thirty six percent of this number was in Accra-Tema metropolitan area (Hutchful 1987, p.22). The construction sector alone lost 26,000 jobs during this period. As if the foregoing was not enough, the private commercial sector also shed 50% of its labour force in the same period (ibid.).

The share of labour in total value added in large scale manufacturing units fell from 30.4% in 1962 to 20.6% in 1970. The NLC period recorded the highest fall in labour input as the profit motive became virtually the only yardstick of success with very little regard to social cohesion and responsibility. Capital had increased its share of earnings from the manufacturing process at the expense of labour. A study by the World Bank (1974, p.4) covering this period concluded that industrial workers did not gain from the growth of productivity [and] recipients of non-wage income, that is capital, gained most from the industrial expansion that occurred. This was partly brought about by the extensive concessions given to foreign capital by the National Liberation Council. The Valco agreement, signed by the previous regime, had also come into operation with all its built in incentives.

The relatively good macro-economic stability did not remedy the worsening unemployment situation and by 1969, the Minister of Finance had to moan that "... the problem of unemployment has proved to be one of the most intractable problems that the National Liberation Council has had to cope with" (Budget Statement 1969/70,p.3). For those still in employment, real wages hardly rose from the depressed 1965/66 levels. When compared to the early 1960s, however, real wages actually took a tumble.

Table 2.18
Income distribution

Year	minimum wage (₵)	index of nominal wage	index of real min.wage
1960	0.65	100	100
1964	0.65	100	74
1965	1.00	100	59
1966	0.65	100	56
1967	0.70	108	64
1968	0.75	115	65

Source: Ewusi: 1974 p. 34.

The above figures indicate only a slight improvement in the living standards of Ghanaian workers relation to 1965, that is if we for this purpose, equate income levels alone with standard of living.

The steep recession witnessed under the NLC, lasting longer than any since independence, was therefore unavoidable, considering the reduced state expenditure accompanied, in synchronised harmony, by stagnation in private sector investment [contrary to government predictions]. Of critical importance to poverty considerations was the stabilisation effect of exasperating income differential in the waged economy. For the lowly paid, survival, according to the Ghana Trades Union Congress, became a miracle (TUC, 8 May 1968).

The NLC's most lasting legacy was incidentally in the field of social programmes. The introduction of a Population Policy Document for the first time recognised the correlation between unbridled population growth and national development. The Ghana Family Planning Programme was, therefore, set up to provide free advice, training and ancillary services as well as raising the general consciousness of the population on the subject.

Political

The reliance of the NLC on its western advisors was probably the most striking feature of the NLC regime. The fact that all members of the Council trained at one time or the other in some of Britain's most elite military and police institutions had a bearing on the regime's western outlook. The role of the

Harvard Group has been aired in the preceding pages. What is often downplayed is the secondment of a senior official of the IMF to Ghana as resident representative with offices in the Bank of Ghana [central bank] from mid 1966 up to early 1970 (see Killick 1978,p.55). The sovereignty of policy making was thus subjected to the Fund at the very heart of the nation. No new external loans with less than 12 years maturity [except normal trade credits of up to 360 days maturity] were to be contracted without prior consultation[41] of the Fund. The Fund thus was granted wide supervisory powers over the Ghanaian economy. The country was obliged to "remain in close consultation with the Fund, and to keep the Fund informed of developments in exchange, trade, monetary, credit and fiscal situation" (Hutchful 1987, p.63).

Even as a military government, the NLC was often confronted with the hostility of the population, particularly on economic issues. The state's divestiture programme for example, run into serious political boulders. There was strong intellectual hostility to details, if not the thrust of the whole issue of divestiture. Divestiture programmes have historically had the tendency of off-loading the most profitable enterprises in the first instance. A typical example of this in Ghana was the botched attempt to sell the state pharmaceutical corporation to Abbot Laboratories [of USA]. The terms were seen as too favourable to the buyer and this set off a general protest against the whole idea of denationalisation of industry. The NLC was forced to back away from this particular sale. Here was the NLC having to walk a tight rope between its creditors who were criticising the uneconomic state ownership and control of public corporations and a Ghanaian intellectual class, which although conceding the problems of some state enterprises, was nevertheless, against denationalisation.

It is tempting to generalise all of NLC's denationalisation attempts on the purely economic. However, apologists for the regime find it difficult applying the economic criteria to the abandonment of the Russian built Reinforced Concrete Factory, completed at a cost of ₵2.3m and awaiting only working capital to commence operations. With a housing shortage raging, the factory's products had a waiting local market and yet the government chose to abandon this factory. Neither could the Tarkwa Gold Refinery, also Russian built and 90% completed by early 1966, have its abandonment justified by the national interest. The general unprofitability of some state enterprises might have poisoned the concept of state industrialisation, but for some projects, it was cheaper to complete than to abandon, and yet the NLC chose the latter. Reasons would therefore, have to be located in the ideological. The National Liberation Council closed its political chapter by supervising a smooth change over to constitutional rule in August 1969.

By the end of NLC's stay in power, the economy was fairly more stable than it was in 1966. However, the drive towards industrialisation had been halted in stock taking. Politically, the economy was more relaxed, westernised and less self radical than when the NLC first shot its way into power.

The Busia Regime

The Second Republic, installed in 1969, saw the coming into power of the Progress Party under Prof. K.A Busia, an Oxford don and former leader of the Opposition prior to the institution of 'one party' by the Convention People's Party in 1964. The constitution of the Second Republic, fashioned after the Westminster model, brought into government, technocrats most of whom had previously worked for the NLC in various capacities.

Basic elements of the economic programme started under the NLC were, therefore, with minor exemptions, carried over by the Progress Party government of Busia. These were mainly improvements in management of balance of payment, especially imports, by devaluation and related measures, liberalisation of imports and parallel improvements in allocation to priority needs, rationalisation of the structure of import duties, and the introduction of incentives for exports, including an increased producer price for cocoa.

The Second Republic witnessed the collapse of its macro-management policies under the weight of massive pressure from imports. Its policies were torn apart at the seams by the confluence of massive pressure from imports arising from its ambitious liberalisation programme and the cyclical fall in cocoa prices on the world scene.

The liberalisation programme had initially been sustained both under the NLC and the Progress Party government largely by improved revenues from cocoa exports. For the period between mid 1966 to 1969, the introduction of price instruments in place of the previous quantitative restrictions imposed a curb and did not permit imports to get out of hand. However, when cocoa prices tumbled at the end of this period, it became imperative to institute severe cuts in imports if the economy was not to return to previous near disaster levels of the mid 1960s. The major instrument selected for this re-adjustment was a massive devaluation in December 1971. The Cedi was devalued from a previous ₵ 1.02 to the US dollar to ₵1.82 to the same. Unfortunately, this measure was not allowed time to work through the economy. The Second Republic was aborted by the military in January 1972, the very month in which the devaluation became effective.

The Busia government's time in office was too short to be able to draw major conclusions from spending patterns as to developmental direction, but suffice it to say that rural development attracted marked attention. A ministry of rural development with cabinet status was created and rural development in all its facets was put at the top of the country's developmental agenda. One of the most unfortunate consequences of the abortion of the Second Republic was the denial to the nation of a concerted rural development approach.

The disregard of cocoa farmers by the Nkrumah government in the 1960s caught up with the country during the Second Republic in the form of lower production figures. Output declined by some 20% over the 1962-1965 average tonnage of 425,000 and although revenue, on temporal price rise on the commodity market did not fall [in current price terms] in 1969/70 financial year,[42] the decline in prices from the second part of 1970 and increased output from traditional competitors as well as the new producers of South East Asia and Brazil, brought forcibly home, the consequences of earlier decisions.

The Progress Party administration did not find much success in the reallocation of public spending, especially to more productive purposes in the short-term, although a pattern favourable to rural development was emerging. Neither did the rehabilitation and re-structuring of state enterprises go far enough by the beginning of 1972 nor the attention given to food production go beyond gestation.

The continuos dislocation of Ghanaian economy, and especially industry at the level of its imports dependency was acknowledged by both the administration and other bodies as a major bottleneck. By early 1972, Ghana, an agriculturally endowed nation with excellent facilities for cotton, for example, was only producing 3% of its cotton requirements. This disjointed nature of the economy favoured foreign capital since it reduced the risk of nationalisation of an internally consistent industry. Such foreign operators, whether MNCs or individuals, could continue to import from their plants and or private sources, raw materials [and thus increasing profit margins through sharp businesses practises associated with such imports].

Even the World Bank, an ideological concubine of MNCs, had to write this about Ghana:

> flour mills are devoted entirely to grinding foreign wheat. Flour, bread and biscuits are almost exclusively derived from imported grain, yeast, milk powder and added nutrients. The GIHOC meat slaughtering, butchering and packaging factory relies upon imported cattle for 98% of its output. All the hops, malts, concentrates and yeast, and most of the sugar used by large scale breweries, distilleries and soft-drink manufacturers come from abroad. This is true of milk powder used for tinned milk and much of the oil which goes into margarine (World Bank 1974, Annex 1 p.3).

The Busia administration was more critical of the international community's lukewarm attitude to Ghana debt problem than the NLC was. In its very first budget statement, the administration asked for long term re-financing aid to cover debts due in the short term. And the willingness of the same western creditor nations and institutions to take a very sympathetic position on Indonesia's debt while refusing to extend the same to Ghana was hammered upon by the administration. Britain, to whose interests Ghana owed about 40% of its total commercial debt, came in for particular strong criticism for its lackadaisical attitude to the call by Ghana for a conference on its debt. Ironically, Britain, by virtue of being the largest single creditor, was by convention, to be in the chair for such a conference. The conference finally took place in May 1970, agreeing to re-open negotiations on debt reduction measures in July of the same year.

Ghana's debt servicing commitments were estimated at £43m for 1970 and £35m for 1971. At the July conference, Ghana forcibly drove the point home that the debt servicing position was untenable and needed urgent and sympathetic attention. The major creditors then offered a 50% relief on supplier's credit debt due but left each creditor nation to choose the mode of such relief. Three variants were offered by the conference, viz.

- A re-financing loan with a minimum grant element of 61%;
- A straight forward ten year moratorium without extra interest payment;
- Additional aid with a minimum of 6% grant element and the rest on concessionary terms.

Ghana accepted this outcome on the understanding that another conference would be convened to look at further ways of reducing the indebtedness in mid 1972, and that a neutral arbitrator would be appointed out of Ghana's dissatisfaction with Britain's performance in the chair (Krassowsk1 1974, p.132).

The next chapter would examine how some of the threads woven through these years, particularly the fiscal indiscipline of central government and the statist domination of the Ghanaian economy made for the worsening macro environment in subsequent years, albeit with the help of some very inept leadership.

Notes

1 Usually British owned.
2 This was probably more pronounced in Ghana because of the model state status conferred on the country and run largely by civil servants from the colonial office.
3 Civil society being seen in its broader perspective [rather than the narrower confines of Marx.
4 see HMSO, 1944 & 1946 on the two reports on cocoa control and cocoa marketing in West Africa.
5 As different from setting aside a percentage of realised earnings for a rainy season.

6 A trend not uncommon even in 1990s Ghana as a result of the large contribution of the informal, largely rural and unrecorded sector.

7 Gt. Britain, Colonial No. 231 1948, para. 353.

8 A trend not uncommon even in 1990s Ghana as a result of the large contribution of the informal, largely rural and unrecorded sector.

9 Office of Government Statistician: Notes and Tables on Africans in Accra, 1948 Census Report.

10 More often than not financial. Thus human capital was hardly ever taken into the equation.

11 The CPP, led by Kwame Nkrumah, having won the 1951 elections, was allowed to form a limited government with control over the country except in areas of finance, defence, and foreign affairs which were the preserve of the colonial civil service. The governor could also veto any legislation or Executive Instrument.

12 Probably arising from his fixation with a conservational economic perspective at the expense of the socio - political.

13 And indeed history, as the Latin America economic examples point out.

14 The index of dependence of foreign trade - the Foreign Trade Ratio, is computed by dividing the sum of GDP and imports, this later sum being the total of available resources.

15 Based on raw figures from Kay 1972, Table 24a, p 348 - 55.

16 See National Assembly Debates, 11 March 1964 vol. 25.

17 see JF Kennedy Library NSF Jan 1961.

18 Nkrumah, 4 March 1959 at the launching of the Plan.

19 He subsequently fled the country for fear of his life.

20 Although the operational opposition parties in the National Assembly were in the process of being conscribed to the dustbin of history through repression and intimidation.

21 Preparations were already underway for the Seven Year Plan to be drawn up to replace the existing Five Year Plan. The reference to the Seven Year Plan here was therefore, to prepare the minds of the general public and the party faithful to the abandonment of the then current Second Five Year Plan and the adoption of a more 'Socialist' Seven Year Plan.

22 He who more than any other colonial governor made capacity building his priority.

23 With Nkrumah as first, the Leader of Government Business and later Prime Minister, the CPP having won the 1951 elections.

24 see White Paper on Volta River Project, 1952 cmd 8702, London. HMSO.

25 And most likely state controlled.

26 see National Assembly Debates, 11 March 1964 col. 21

27 Which was seen as simpler and would provide a base for managerial and industrial aculturalisation.

28 Nkrumah K, quoted in Friedland and Rosberg [eds.].,1964 p 260

29 The country having changed to calendar year budgets.

30 Central Bureau of Statistics, Economic Surveys (various).

31 including "quasi-money" consisting of time and savings deposits of commercial banks.

32 Chapter 7 of Plan.

33 See Proposed Letter of Intent, 26 April 1966.

34 When payments had resumed.

35 see Gov't of Ghana, 1966 Proposed Letter of Intent op.cit.

36 Indeed, the 1980s and 190s seem to have reinvented this tool.

37 And which was hardly ever accompanied by increased productivity.

38 Once the volume of international trade had fallen, the state's revenue base is automatically affected as duties on imports and exports, special duties on imports etc. fall. Additionally, resulting from the country's excessive dependence on imported raw materials, any reduction in raw material imports brings about a further fall in excise duty paid by manufacturers.

39 Decreased slightly as a result of shipping bottlenecks encountered by cocoa industry.

40 This desire could have been influenced by a lack of resources to continue with the previous direction as well conditionalities for western and particularly IMF/World Bank assistance.

41 And for consultation, substitute approval.

42 Earnings were about £1m higher than the reference base of £72m per annum.

3 Accelerated decline 1972 - 1983

During the 1970s and early 1980s, Ghana became the supreme example in Sub-Sahara Africa of economic mismanagement. This contrasted sharply with the country's image as the development and political pace setter less than a quarter of a century previously. During the earlier period, Ghana was the richest country in the sub-region and had the most developed educational and health infrastructure.

The Progress Party government under the premiership of Dr. K.A Busia was overthrown on 13 January 1972 in yet another coup d'état after less than two and a half years in office. The leader of the putsch, Colonel [later General] I.K Acheampong offered as their principal justification, the reduction in real incomes of the military and public servants as a result of the severity of the two Busia budgets aimed at deficit reduction. These measures were in a large part, a compliant response to international financial pressure. The coup makers also complained of the devaluation of the cedi and the redistribution of resources in favour of the export sector implied by the devaluation of the currency.

But the National Redemption Council[1] government then attracted the reputation of having the worst macro-management competency in the history of the country. The World Bank wrote about the period of their stewardship:

> (The) economy has been steadily deteriorating throughout the past decade but the situation has recently become critical. Past years have been characterised, in varying intensity, by persistent high inflation, declining production and exports, flourishing illegal activities and political instability. A gradual decline in per capita income has increased the incidence of absolute poverty and has been accompanied by a worsening of income distribution, growing unemployment and the emigration of skilled professionals (World Bank 1984, p.xv).

The peculiar nature of most West African states, indeed almost all developing countries, in which the fusion of the state and the economy is almost cast in concrete further intensified the national malaise resulting from the incompetence of the Acheampong regime. The appearance of a separation of state and economy, as Hart noted, is not even plausible and thus impacting very heavily on the very fibre of society when an incompetent regime gets into power whether by constitutional or unconstitutional means (Hart 1982, p.14).

The political and state bureaucracy

The new leaders' [NRC] policy objectives were to restore allowances and benefits to the Public Services[2] and to partially reverse the devaluation of the cedi announced by the Busia government only a month previously. Of equal, if not more far reaching consequence, was the repudiation of the country's medium to long term debt.

A constant criticism of the Ghanaian state has historically been the extent of its influence outside the non-formal sector. Civil society seems to be limited only to the informal sector, both in the economics and politics of the state. The dominant position of the state is reflected in the extensive nature of the state machinery. The National Redemption Council, rather than curbing the bloated state machinery as initiated by the Busia regime, co-opted the machinery into power and even expanded it. This temporarily placated those in charge of state institutions, leading to even greater consumption by the state bureaucracies at the expense of the creators of national wealth, particularly, the rural farmer. And as long as benefits accrued, the state bureaucracies were content.

The benefits could not, however, accrue forever. As basic economic laws on the relationship between consumption, savings and investment caught up with the country, the government could no longer ensure the continuation of a parasitic state, absorbing the benefits to which it had become accustomed. With an enlarged state, increased demands were foisted on an economy starved of investment. Something had to give. What happened to the defence budget probably provides the best example.

The Busia government, on assuming office in 1969, prioritised the bringing down of the country's defence expenditure to a more manageable level, departing from the increases associated with the NLC. That government also abolished vehicle maintenance allowances for all public sector workers, including the armed forces. For the first time in the nation's colonial and post colonial evolution, the military were to pay tax in the form of a national development levy of one percent on all salaried workers.[3] The military, forever a powerful cog of the parasitic state in the developing world, reacted by staging the coup that gave birth to the NRC. The new government in accordance with the wish of its military constituency, abolished the special tax.

Again as part of the extension of the state, the NRC in 1974, established fifty eight District Councils [later increased to sixty-two]. These councils were headed by civilian chief executives in what the regime saw as marking a phase of administrative reforms. The councils had limited powers, with all the appointed District Chief Executives being career civil servants [as opposed to politicians]. The members of the councils were all appointed, rather than elected, and by so doing stifling a potential source of dissent by local elite. These councils were commissioned to implement government policies and were given limited administrative powers. But they lacked democratic credibility at the grassroots.

The revaluation of the cedi effected by the NRC on coming to power left them with no alternative but to return to comprehensive import controls which were mal-administered even more thoroughly than under Nkrumah. In addition, the attempted justification of the overthrow of Busia on the grounds of unacceptability of devaluation placed a political imperative on the NRC not to devalue even as the foreign exchange crisis deepened. Despite nominal control of imports, an excess demand fuelled by increased money supply in the economy[4] led to record high price levels in the economy, especially for consumer goods.

Notwithstanding the implications of policy directives issued by the NRC in its first few months in office, as well as its initial ethos, the Ghanaian economy at first reacted positively and recorded fair growth rates. The explanation for this 'abnormal' occurrence is provided by JH Frimpong-Ansah, a former Governor of the Bank of Ghana. As part of the negotiations between the Bank and the new regime, the Central Bank got the government's agreement for sound fiscal and financial management. The Bank under this agreement initially tightly controlled the management of the external sector to avoid trade deficits as a counter to the repudiation of the country's debt obligations[5] (Frimpong-Ansah 1991, pp.108-110). This, coupled with the reintroduction of restrictive trade policy and an emphasis on domestic food production - championed by a nation wide impressive campaign captioned 'Operation Feed Yourself'- and a general campaign of self-reliance made the economy in the short term, fairly efficient in the use of reserves, foreign exchange and installed capacity.

The above scenario did not last, as subsequent analysis would point out. Within two years, political pressures and mismanagement had wrecked the discipline imposed by the Central Bank.[6] One of the reasons for the breakdown was the creation of a large mass of intermediaries between formal state resources and actual users of such resources through political and social patronage thus exerting even more pressure on resources.[7] Import licence and foreign exchange allocation became by-products of patronage. Inflation and

79

over-valuation of the cedi made it more attractive financially to be a beneficiary of state patronage than to produce. More worrying was the involvement of state officials and representatives[8] at the highest levels in these pervasive practises of corruption (Frimpong-Ansah 1991, p.110-111, Chazam 1983, pp.194-197).

The political bureaucratic management of the country was painfully aggravated by the almost criminal relationship between the ruling cabal and multinational corporations operating in the country. The Ghanaian intellectual and to a large extent the youth, have historically been wary, if not antagonistic to MNCs. The fiasco over the sale of GIHOC Pharmaceuticals to Abbot corporation of the US by the NLC is a pointer in this direction. Disappointment was therefore major, and rightly so, over the agreement signed with Agripetco of Canada for oil prospecting. Under this agreement, the country was entitled to and actually only received 12% of output when Agripetco brought the Saltpond oil fields into production and the rest of the crude destined for foreign refineries. At a time when fuel shortages were severe, this increased the anti-multinational hostility of the conscious Ghanaian. The de-linking of Firestone International from its Ghanaian operations, notwithstanding the myriad of excessive concessions provided by Ghana did not help to ameliorate this mood.

Domestic policy and planning

The obstacles that confronted the NRC were not new and were essentially the same at the macro level that previous regimes had faced. These included external debt, decreasing foreign exchange earnings per capita, deteriorating terms of trade, low agricultural productivity, high food import bills, an absence of accountability and the concomitant corruption in public life.

The NRC's responses to the above challenge was radical in some respects, that is, the repudiation of external debt and revaluation of the cedi, but also naive. As argued earlier, the first two years of the NRC registered average growth rates and some amount of macro stability. But after the success of the first years, the economy went into a massive nose dive. The success of earlier years, built partially on the back of good cocoa prices, also generated a structure of government expenditure partially geared at placating the power centres of the country especially the military, police and associated services. Once the cyclical cocoa price syndrome had reached a low ebb, the expenditure pattern became unsustainable. Expenditure grew rapidly in the Acheampong and immediate post Acheampong period while revenue stagnated, resulting in serious budgetary deficits. Total government expenditure had been around 20% of GDP since 1970. While acceptable during periods of buoyant revenue, this could not be maintained when revenue collapsed. Originating from this poor revenue position therefore, a budgetary surplus in 1970/71 fiscal year had by 1980/81, turned into a deficit that far exceeded the total revenue collected. The deficit equalled 91% of total expenditure and 14.6% of the gross domestic product, a level of dislocation that could only spell national bankruptcy. The overwhelming deficits were financed mainly by the banking system and thus capping the catastrophe with rises in money supply unmatched by any positive economic or social indicator.

The NRC established Regional Development Corporations for the then nine regions charged with pushing forward development in each corporation's catchment area. This could be interpreted as partly a reaction to the grumbling from the Volta Region; the ex-German colony, that it was being ignored in the distribution of resources for development. This also coincided with the serious downward slide of the economy. The corporations thus became embroiled in distribution of "consumables" [as shortages were registering in the economy], instead of marshalling the natural resource base of each region for agricultural, manufacturing and or industrial purposes. Where such ventures were attempted, no serious attention and supervision was provided. The corporations, with their dominant distributive role, became vehicles of patronage in an era of scarcity and social sycophancy.

As had become customary of all Ghanaian regimes, the NRC was not to be left out in the formulation of a development plan. A Five Year Plan was initiated in January 1974, with the establishment of a new National Economic Planning Council under the chairmanship of the Head of State. The Planning Council was to be serviced by a newly created Ministry of Economic Planning which was to act as the Secretariat. The new Five Year Plan, to be effective from 1975-1980, identified three recurrent and inter-related phenomena as the *bête noire* of Ghanaian economic growth and development. These were also said to be responsible for the static per capita income growth of the population. The three were identified as: the openness of the economy and a chronic balance of payments disequilibrium, unemployment [not excluding underemployment] and inflation. The significant item in the balance of payment argument as per the Plan, is seen in the link between domestic output and imports, with marginal propensity to import estimated at 28%. Unemployment was seen as a social evil and an economic waste, while inflation was recognised as distorting resource allocation and impacting negatively most on the economically vulnerable.

It needs be stated, however, that notwithstanding the near 'perfect' intentions and recommended responses to the diagnosis of the Ghanaian economy, Plan implementation was almost non-existant with fiscal, monetary and other economic disciplines totally absent. It is debatable whether the Five Year Plan even deserves a mention.

The NRC's and its later metarmophosis SMC[9] economic and political mismanagement during their period in office induced a 40% fall in real per capita income, leaving the population worse off than it was at 1970. The pattern of development policy revolving around heavy government intervention in industry, laxity in dealing with state supported projects, the use of state enterprises for political patronage, over-protection of manufacturing, currency over-valuation and general price relationships leading to a downturn in agriculture and exports etc., was more pronounced under the NRC/SMC than any other government.

A major lesson of the collapse of the NRC/SMC regime was the inability of the state to halt the economy from nose-diving into the doldrums after a fiscal acceleration [on the back of good commodity prices at the onset of the regime]. This is primarily due to the under-developed nature of Ghanaian agriculture, low productivity across sectors and the political ineptitude of the ruling elite. The leadership could have imposed a higher sense of fiscal and monetary discipline on the country. Secondly, a major programme on improving agricultural productivity and rural incomes should have been developed in the earlier days of boom.

Monetary and fiscal policy

If there was one particular policy area where the NRC and subsequent regimes prior to April 1983 under performed, this was it. Throughout the period 1972 - 1981, inflation averaged 55% per annum, a level of inflation that was extraordinarily high by any standards. This, without suitable adjustment to either currency values or increased productivity, led to a downward spiral of the real value of the cedi although the nominal exchange rate remained at one cedi fifteen pesewas to the dollar until September 1978. A palace coup staged by Acheampong's number two in government [Gen. Akuffo] took the tentative step of modestly raising the cedi - dollar exchange rate to two cedis seventy five pesewas, a rate that was no where near any reflection of the dollar/ten cedi shadow rate at the time (see Table 3.1).

The combination of inflationary pressures, an over-valued currency and dwindling ability of the state to meet demand for foreign exchange created a parallel market boom. Concurrently, import licences [Special Unnumbered Licence] were being issued by the Ministry of Trade in large numbers to traders without any hard currency support. This, *ipso facto,* led to increased disparity between official and parallel market rates as shown by table 3.1 below:

Table 3.1
Official and parallel foreign exchange rates and selected currencies
[1978-1983] cedis per unit

Currency	official rate	parallel market rate		
		sept 1978	oct 1981	march 1983
Sterling [UK]	4.50-5.50	16	75-85	110-120
Dollar [US]	2.75	10	40-45	70-80
CFA franc [1000]	8.50-11.50	36	120-140	200-220

Source: Council of State: Reviewing Ghana's Economy 1981, p.25, and Huq 1989, p.196.

The divergence between the official exchange rate and the parallel or shadow rate[10] had reached stupid proportions. By 1982, the dollar exchanged for sixty two cedis on the parallel market compared to the official rate of two cedis seventy five pesewas (Rimmer 1992, p.210). Thus there existed an implicit or *de facto* taxation of exports and an opposite subsidisation of imports caused by the dislocated cedi - dollar relations. Over-valuation of the cedi did not only reduce import capacity through its export effect, but simultaneously increased the demand for foreign exchange. The ensuing dysfunction between supply and demand was managed partly by external borrowing [often in the form of repayment arrears], but principally by exchange controls and licensing.

It might come as a surprise to many development professionals and economists that the above situation was allowed to fester unchecked. The explanation, if even partial, is found in the deep recesses of Ghanaian politics. The very idea of devaluation or floating of the currency had until the Economic Recovery Programme in April 1983, been an anathema in the depths of Ghanaian collective thought pattern. As in some other countries, devaluation was seen in terms of loss of national pride. The Busia regime suffered the fate of being kicked out of office by the military for attempting it. While the writer disagrees with the World Bank/IMF worship of devaluation, which is but one of the mix of economic tools available, in the developing world, there are times when devaluation, in conjunction with other instruments, is a needed step in correcting a currency out of alignment. The Council of State, established under the Third Republican Constitution, had this to say when faced with the review of the Ghanaian economy: "... the discussion of the value of the cedi has been characterised by undue emotion, and even fear...." (Council of State 1981, pp.23-24).

83

The PNDC[11] Secretary for Finance and Economic Planning [the supreme guru of the economy] in presenting the 1983 budget statement, commented on the inaction of the period thus:

> Against the background of high inflation rates in post 1978 period, maintenance of rigid official dollar/cedi rate resulted in over-valuation of the cedi against all major currencies. A number of anomalies follow from the over-valuation. Principal among these is the conferring of large and often illegal and untaxed profits on those who get access to foreign exchange (Ministry of Finance 1983, p.2).

Revenue

The revenue position of the state continued to deteriorate to dangerous levels of insolvency during the period under discussion. In 1981 and 1982, government current revenue was only 52% and 57% of recurrent expenditure respectively. The negative current account balance, in addition to the capital account balance, created intolerable levels of budgetary deficits in the range of four and seven percent of gross domestic product in the early 1980s. The seriousness of the deficits is highlighted by the simultaneous decline of both tax and non-tax revenue. The contribution of non-tax revenue probably experienced an even worse decline from ¢42m at 1970 prices in 1965 to ¢ 7.5m in 1982, with this arising essentially from the poor performance of public sector commercial enterprises (Huq 1989, p.3). If the fall in non-tax revenue was dramatic, the decline of the tax base was even more so. This had fallen to about 5% of the Gross Domestic Product with investment also falling below levels needed just to maintain the depleted capital stock.

Table 3.2
Government revenue and budgetary outrun in relation to GDP estimates 1972-1983

Year	(1) GDP estimate ¢m	(2) gov't revenue ¢m	(3) budget surplus ¢m	(4) ratio of (2) to (1) %	(5) ratio of (3) (1) %
1972	2815	392	-153	13.9	-5.4
1973	3501	584	-155	16.7	-4.4
1974	4660	805	-357	17.3	-7.7
1975	5283	815	624	15.4	-11.8
1976	6526	1075	-871	16.5	-13.2
1977	11163	1539	-1479	13.8	-9.1
1978	20986	2188	-1907	10.4	-9.1

1979	28171	3026	-1645	10.7	-5.8
1980	40995	3279	-4440	8.0	-10.8
1981	76655	4855	-4674	6.3	-6.1
1982	86451	5253	-3593	6.1	-4.2
1983	184038	10241	-4517	5.6	-2.5

Notes: Figures for revenue and deficits are calculated for the calendar years in 1982 - 1983, otherwise for fiscal years beginning in the year shown.

Source: Tables 4.4, 4.6, 5.4, 5.6, 6.4, 6.6, 7.9 and 7.10. World Bank: African Economic and Financial Data. Washington, DC 1989.

As revenues contracted relative to a declining GDP, and particularly from 1977, the deficits increased so much that they virtually matched revenues in size. The deficits were met largely from Bank of Ghana (central bank) credits, whose statutory limits on lending had earlier been amended to make government borrowing easier. Even the amended limits were often just ignored as the occasion demanded and by 1983, government deficits had reached 14.6% of GDP.

Money supply

As stated previously, the worst period of fiscal and monetary mismanagement occurred during this period when expansion of public demand was not met by increased output in the domestic economy, resulting in escalating inflation rates, a gross imbalance of external accounts, a steep rise in net credit to the government from the banking system to finance budget deficits [₵781m in 1977] and a jump in money supply from an average of ₵281m in 1971 to ₵ 1761m in 1977.[12] By 1979, the excess liquidity in the economy, caused essentially by government's deficit financing, had become so unmanageable that a demonitisation exercise had to be undertaken, the net result of which was to expropriate currency in private hands. This measure was again attempted by the new regime in 1982 in what Rimmer (1992, p.206) described as:

> blatant manifestations of a process of exploiting holders of money that had gone on for some twenty years, at first deliberately and later almost involuntarily, as governments debased the currency through 'inflation tax' - bidding resources from private to public use through the creation of additional purchasing power in favour of the public sector.

Within a twelve year period, money supply had increased from ₡305.4m in 1970 to ₡11439.5m by 1982 at a time when real GDP [and thus productivity] had fallen accordingly. More ominous was the amount of money outside the banking system [reflecting the lack of confidence in the system]; ₡ 150.7m as against ₡154.7m lodged with banks as demand deposits. This further escalated to ₡6957.2m in comparison to the ₡4482.3m in 1982 (see Appendix 2). The loss of confidence in the banking system was total (see appendices 1&2).

Productivity and investment

Productivity and investment are virtually two sides of the same coin. Any analysis of productivity in the medium to long term would thus have to take into the equation, investment levels. Investment here is not just limited to the acquisition or the upgrading of physical stocks, but must be defined to take account of investment in people viz. education, health and training as well as other aspects of social well being in the economy. Investment must also encompass environmental and legal infrastructure, all of which go to boost any given economy.

The performance of the Ghanaian economy as regards productivity cannot be separated from the pattern of development policy adopted by the founding fathers of the nation and probably mismanaged beyond comprehension by the NRC. Development policy revolved around heavy government intervention in industry [and for heavy, substitute indiscriminate], laxity in dealing with state and aid supported projects, the use of state enterprise for political patronage, over protection of manufacturing, currency over-valuation and general price relationships which imply a discouragement of agriculture and exports.

The industrial, agricultural and manufacturing decline in the 1970s was predominantly home bred. The global economy had acted to condition and limit the domestic economy's options as it had in several other developing countries but inefficient public policies and bureaucratic mismanagement had played the yeoman's role in the peculiar Ghanaian debacle. J. Ofori-Attah, a prominent Ghanaian economist writing on the period claimed "the sluggish growth in Ghana is due more to policy failures than to any inherent weakness of the economy" (Ofori-Attah 1975, p.29). The most important of such failures being the absence of a clearly defined development direction, along which the population can be mobilised. This particular failure is partly explained by the inability of the country to produce leaders who have the critical attributes of a sense of direction, charisma, ability to pursue the charted direction, nationalistic without being dictatorial and above all who can inspire the confidence of the population. Confidence of the population would serve as a bastion against the hardships and sacrifices that a dynamic nationalistic development path would throw up.

The fall in productivity cut across all sectors. Cocoa production, from its peak figure of 557,000 long tons in 1964/65 plunged to an estimated 100,00 tons in 1983/84. The cocoa sector, which once contributed 40% of government revenue, made a zero percent contribution in 1980 and actually incurred a net deficit in the budget of 1981/82.[13] Gold, the other major foreign exchange earner, consistently registered fallen output despite a relatively high trading price on the bullion market in the early 1980s. Production fell from 724,000 fine ounces in 1972 to 402,033 by 1978 and to an even lower 260,000 ounces by 1983.[14] The main causes, particularly in the case of gold, were a lack of new investment, inadequate forex allocation for spare parts, and general infrastructural decay. The infrastructural decay extended to other mining activities, being particularly pronounced in bauxite and maganese which both depend on the railways for volume movement.

The over-valued currency became a disincentive for exports. Smuggling across the borders to Togo, Burkina Faso and Cote d'Ivoire became more lucrative, even to small holders and traders. Within just a five year period, factory capacity utilisation had fallen from 53% in 1975 to 25% of installed capacity in 1980 (World Bank 1984, p.64). Tables 3.3 and 3.4 capture the decreased productivity succinctly.

Table 3.3
Major Ghanaian export items 1975 -81 (quantities tonnes)

	1975	1976	1977	1978	1979	1980	1981
Cocoa (1,000)	322	328	258	213	204	211	190
Cocoa prods (1,000)	19	22	21	12	25.0	23.2	14.2
Gold (grams)	15973	16416	15208	9747	11818	10820	10764
Timber (cub.meter 1,000)	615	499	539	629	-	-	-
Diamonds (carats 1,000)	2372	2308	2079	1476	1007	879	944
Maganese (1,000)	373	360	321	287	-	-	143
Bauxite (10,000)	320	219	250	293	203	223	150

Source: Kodwo Ewusi: The Ghana Economy in 1981/82: Recent Trends and Prospects for the Future. Legon Institute of Statistical, Social and Economic Research 1982, p 34.

The disincentive to cocoa production, brought about by an over-valued currency, falling world market prices, an inefficient and thus expensive Cocoa Board bureaucracy culminating in low producer prices, was manifested by the inter crop terms of trade going against cocoa in the domestic market as exemplified by Table 3.4.

Every other crop had recorded more appreciative price level changes, reflecting the high inflationary pressures, than cocoa. Maize for example, between 1970 and 1981, had its producer price shoot up from 177 to 15152 as against cocoa registering a rise of less significance. The situation is exacerbated by both cocoa and maize calling on the same quality of land in the southern regions of the country, thus leading to a preference by farmers of maize as against cocoa.

Table 3.4
Cocoa and food price indices (1963 = 100)

Item	1970	1972	1974	1975	1976	1977	1978	1979	1980	1981
Cocoa	133	167	250	267	333	607	1215	1822	2186	2915
Mize	177	261	304	378	862	1799	1835	2602	6275	15152
Cassava	155	239	288	441	938	2378	2216	2584	5535	11200
Plantain	146	195	295	379	772	2303	3574	3823	5610	8923
Cocoyam	207	294	457	548	1045	2725	3277	4055	6517	14135
Palm oil	144	215	334	471	690	1210	2810	3468	5120	-

Source: Ministry of Agriculture.

Decreased productivity was not just restricted to the export sector. The production of almost all principal crops except cotton seed, a relative new dimension to general cotton production, suffered in this climate. Maize production suffered a near 300% fall from 486,000 tons in 1974 to 172,000 tons by 1983, millet a 385% fall from 154,000 tons in 1974 to 40000 by 1983, with other crops such as sorghum, paddy rice etc. also recording dramatic downturns during the period as the table 3.5 indicates:

Table 3.5
Production of principal crops (thousand tons)

	1974	1975	1976	1977	1978	1979	1980	1981	1982	1983
1. Maize	486	343	286	274	218	380	390	420	420	420
2. Millet	154	122	144	125	93	149	66	73	90	40
3. Sorghum	177	135	189	131	121	158	106	142	150	56
4. Rice-paddy	73	71	70	109	108	93	62	79	90	40
5. Sugar cane	220	230	210	198	195	190	192	190	220	100
6. Yams	850	709	575	535	544	602	620	650	670	866
7. Cassava	1600	1900	1819	1811	1895	1759	1800	1850	1900	1729

8. Cocoyam	1510	1100	773	722	726	749	800	850	870	720
9. Cotton seed	1	5	5	55	4	4	4	4	4	
10. Cocoa bean	382	396	324	260	255	296	250	230	230	160
11 Coffee green	2	4	6	42	1	2	2	3	1	
12. Copra	11	11	6	77	7	7	7	7	7	
13. Palm kernel	33	34	32	30	30	30	30	30	30	30
14 Groundnuts	156	111	113	81	83	107	100	90	110	70

Source: UN: African Statistical Year Book 1984 part 2 p 11-7 Table 17.

Table 3.6
Index of agricultural production 1974 - 76 = 100

	1976	1977	1978	1979	1980	1981	1982	1983
Total agric. production	91	84	83	88	87	87	87	83
Total food production	91	84	83	89	87	87	87	83
Per capita agric prod.	89	79	76	78	74	72	69	64
Per capita food prod.	88	79	76	78	74	72	69	65

Source: UN: African Statistical Year Book 1985, pp. 12-8.

With a shrinking productivity base reflected in overall GDP which in 1980 was already a low $4,654m, [$4225m and $4037m for 1982 and 1983 respectively] at constant 1987 prices (UN 1984, p.16), monetary autonomy thus became a vehicle of squeezing the money economy and denying it of resources. The actors here therefore moved into activities of lower social profitability, into subsistence and into employment in other countries, the largest beneficiary being the booming Nigeria of the 1970s. Monetary autonomy also produced substantial divergence between the nominal exchange rate and the real rate determined by market forces - the parallel rate. The foregoing translated into a subsidy of the nominal exchange rate which widened as the economy deteriorated, with the largest subsidy occurring between 1975 and 1983.

The domestic savings rate of about 14.2% of GDP in 1970 had by 1982 tumbled to 1.4%, one of the lowest in Africa as the incentive of saving disappeared. At that rate, domestic savings, translated into domestic investment was inadequate to provide for normal depreciation requirements to maintain the status quo. Foreign inflows had unsurprisingly, dried up.

Table 3.7
Investment and savings (million cedis)

Financing of investment				as a % of GDP	
	GDI	NS	FS	DS	NS
1970	320	305	15	14.2	13.5
1975	673	681	-8	12.7	13.5
1980	2368	2053	315	5.7	5.0
1982	1148	1198	50	1.3	1.4

Notes:
GDI = Gross Domestic Savings
NS = National Savings
FS = Foreign Savings
DS = Domestic savings

Source: World Bank : Ghana: Policies and Program for Adjustment 1984, p.19.

Table 3.7 indicates that as a percentage of GDP, both gross domestic investment and national savings had declined sharply during the period specified. By 1982, virtually all of domestic product was consumed, with very little savings and thus no capital formation or accumulation. Lower savings here are attributable to a host of reasons, chief among them was the public sector's increasing ownership of all assets in the economy as well as the corresponding shift in national income in favour of public sector. The shift *per se* would not have had this crippling effect if the public sector had been efficiently managed and in the interest of the mass of the population instead of serving the interest of a ruling cabal.

The external sector

The politics, if not the economics of the external sector of the Ghanaian economy during this period of accelerated decline was set during the first few days of the January 1972 coup. At the beginning of Dec 1971,[15] cocoa prices had reached a new five year low in what had become the traditional price cycle (Card 1975, p.52). The psychological effect of this on the population as well as the coming to terms with the corrective devaluation announced the same month was worrying, even if one saw the devaluation as inevitable.

The fact that devaluation of the over-bloated currency could only marginally influence the supply side of the economy in the short term did not help. And as to the demand side of the equation, the effect of the devaluation would largely be insignificant on trade patterns and levels with major trading partners. But the same cannot be said of the largely unrecorded West Africa trade, particularly in sawn timber, salt, colanuts and live animals. The devaluation, subject to other corrective measures would also impact positively on the inter crop terms of trade within the economy.

On the 1972 coup therefore, Card commented "... once again, cocoa prices and the import-export sector had coalesced to produce political instability in Ghana, but in both cases, it was instability born of continued colonial economic relations rather than instability derived from the birth of a new order" (ibid.). The new leader in his maiden address to the nation, lambasted the Busia regime for not taking militant action, preferably suspending payments on external debts and rather bowing to international pressure. Col. Acheampong's regime therefore repudiated existing debts, thus indicating an independence of western political opinion and western governments. The playing of the nationalist card won the respect of the Ghanaian populace during the initial critical months of the coup. This approach differed considerably from the first military regime of the NLC [in which Acheampong served as a senior level appointee] which was eager to assure and court western popularity. It is also important to note the inherent contradiction since most of the debts under question were contracted by another left leaning nationalist regime under Nkrumah.

Although the Busia devaluation of December 1971 involved a 44% fall in the value of the cedi as against its fixed anchor of the US dollar, the NRC, even in rescinding the Busia decision, did not bring it back to its pre-devaluation level but pegged it at ₵1 to $0.78, involving an implied devaluation of 20%, notwithstanding the impression being created that the Busia devaluation had been rescinded.

The decline of the foreign trade sector was the most noticeable feature of the deterioration of the macro economy. In 1972, imports and exports each totalled about 25% of GDP. By 1982, imports had fallen to 2% while exports in 1983 were only 50% of the 1980 figure, a figure which was in itself, one of the lowest in the country's history (WB 1984, p.35). Based on 1970 levels, import volume had fallen to one-third, real exports earnings also shrinking by 52% and exports declining from about a quarter of gross domestic product to 4%. All these at a time when petroleum imports, in response to the OPEC price hikes of the era, had risen to account for half of export earnings (ibid. p.xvl).

Not only did exports fall both in prices and as a composition of GDP, but in the late 1970s and early 1980s, actual absolute volumes were also down, recording in 1979 - 1981, only half of the 1970 volume (ibid. pp.8-9).

Table 3.8
Merchandise exports (average 1978 - 1982)

	US $M	%
Cocoa	654.5	72.9
Timber logs and products	38.2	4.3
Gold	135.1	15.0
Diamonds	10.3	1.1
Manganese	9.6	1.1
All other goods	50.1	5.6
	------	------
Total	*897.8*	*100*

Source: World Bank 1984 P X.

Social and demographics

The nature of the Ghanaian crisis was such that the social fabric of the community could not be left untouched. The decline manifested itself in several ways on the social horizon, but in all its manifestations, the poor of the community were the worst affected.[16] Structures and institutions providing a cushion for the poor could hardly survive the onslaught of massive mismanagement and corruption by the ruling elite and its hangers on.

GDP per capita[17] declined rapidly and was in 1980, only 80% of its 1970 figure, leading on to a further depreciation of 63% by 1983. The figures here do not provide the whole picture but only a glimpse into the abyss. They do not take into consideration, the effects of a rising population on social and communal facilities nor the increasing polarisation of society. Gross domestic capital formation had also gone down drastically and by 1983, was less than one-third of the 1964 level.

The result of this state of affairs was the inability of both the state and the economy to support the essential socio-economic services that citizens had a right to expect by virtue of their contribution to, and membership of the community. In 1965, the population per hospital bed was 61,300, by 1980 this had jumped to 106,300. The figure for midwife per population had also jumped from 4,700 to 6,300. Even where an absolute decline had not taken place, increased supply was not commensurate with the new population levels.

Table 3.9
Statistics on education and health, selected years

	1965	1970	1975	1980
EDUCATION				
Enrolment in elementary schools (000)	1313	1400	1491	1858
Enrolment in secondary schools (000)	33.1	49.2	74.8	107.1
Enrolment in technical schools (000)	4.8	7.6	10.4	-
Enrolment in tertiary education (000)	3.4	4.8	6.0	8.3
N0. of trained teachers in primary & middle schools	14973	30350	44005	41669*
HEALTH (average 000)				
Population per hospital bed	61.3	- -	106.3	
Population per trained nurse	2.9	1.2	-	1.2
Population per public health	66.1	58.6	-	-
Population per midwife	4.7	3.0	-	6.3
Population per dentist	217.2	208.8	-	115.3
Population per doctor	13.4	12.8	-	7.1

Notes:
- data not available
* For 1981
Sources: CBS Statistical Year Book 1969-70 and Quarterly Digest of Statistics 1983, Ghana Education Service, Digest of Education Statistics, Ministry of Education, Ghana Education Statistics 1970 - 71.

A prominent feature of the period was rising unemployment. The contraction of the formal economy meant massive job losses, particularly in the private sector where a number of factories had been forced to close down for lack of foreign exchange support to import needed raw materials and spare parts. Agriculture also suffered from rural labour drifting into urban areas in search of non-existent jobs.

Table 3.10
Number of wage employees by industry (thousand)

Industry	1976	1977	1978	1979	1980	1981	1982	1983
Agriculture	67	66	76	74	69	68	66	64
Mining	24	22	23	24	21	19	18	18
Manufacturing	89	89	85	80	77	71	69	66
Construction	37	37	32	28	29	27	26	25
Electricity	3	15	16	16	16	16	17	17
Commerce	31	34	32	32	30	28	25	23
Communications	28	21	19	19	18	17	15	14
Services	192	191	198	210	203	206	195	188

Source: UN, African Statistical Year Book 1985 Part 2 Addis Ababa.

From table 3.10, all industries, except the relatively new electricity sector, employed less labour in absolute terms in 1983 than in 1976, a year that was not spectacular in itself. Communications for example, employed 28,000 in 1976. By 1983, this had shrank to only half the 1976 figure. The cataclysmic nature of this scenario is best appreciated when cognisance is taken of the increased labour supply in the economy as a result of thousands of school leavers joining the pool of labour.

Not only did unemployment rise by numbers, but real income levels fell drastically. The average worker's salary index in 1970 was 183.36 [1977 as base year] but within half a decade, this had regressed to only 38.02. Except for the very few Ghanaians with access to patronage handouts, the working population as a whole experienced unheard of deprivations. Tables 3.10 and 3.11 captures vividly this decline, with communications and manufacturing sectors and workers being the worst affected.

Table 3.11
Index of employee earnings (1970=100)

ITEM	1970	1973	1974	1975	1976	1977	1978	1979	1980	1981	1982
Minimum wage:											
Cedis per day	0.75	1	2	2	2	3	4	4	5.33	12	12
Index nominal wage	25	33.33	66.67	66.67	66.67	100	133.3	133.3	177.7	400	400
Index real wage	183.36	172.99	292.31	225.4	144.17	100	77.03	49.88	44.28	46.05	38.02
Average monthly earnings:											
Index nominal earnings	42.98	57.01	78.74	84.25	94.49	100	188.2	237.8	352	538.5	-
Index real earnings	315.26	295.85	345.25	284.3	204.33	100	108.7	88.96	87.73	62.01	-

Source: Central Bureau of Statistics.

The changes in the country's population in terms of growth, composition and urban - rural segmentation is worthy of note. These impacts severely on the provision of facilities for the population. From 8,611,000 in 1970, the population had reached 9,831,000 by 1975 and 10,734,000 by 1980. The dynamics of rural - urban migration as well as the increasing infantile nature of the population were further complications. In 1960, only 12.8% of the population was classified as urban, that is, living in localities with at least five thousand inhabitants. By 1983, the urban population had exploded to 38%, creating its own social and economic discomfigurations (UN 1984, p 11-1 Table 1).

The poor performance of the key agricultural sector as indicated earlier (see Table 3.5) created its ancillary problem of reduced food sufficiency. The country's food sufficiency ratio was 83 in 1964/66, 71 in 1978/80 and by 1982, this was only 60, and this in an agrarian economy. Concurrently, the country's ability to import was being sapped away by dwindling foreign exchange availability. So pronounced was the deterioration in food supply that it was estimated that the average Ghanaian family consumed at least 30% less food in 1982 than the same family did in 1970 (see World Bank 1984, p.58). At the commencement of the 1970s, the country was recording food surpluses in all "principal food crops except rice, but a decade later, she was experiencing large shortages for all crops except cassava" (ibid.).

The incubus of the Ghanaian polity during the period under discussion is best summed up by Rado. He wrote "The eleven years [1972 to 1983] are Ghana's nightmare......This period saw the recurrence of all faults of Nkrumah period of economic mismanagement, only magnified manifold." The state of the economy in particular, was therefore, the cumulative effect of a downward spiral which was in turn, resultant from the interactions of predominantly poor domestic policies and adverse external events. Large government deficits, induced excessively by the need to support an inefficient parastatal system to provide public sector employment, led to accelerating rates of inflation. At the social levels, poverty had began to eat deep into the social fabric as wages and other income forms failed to keep up with inflation and general cost of living. Within the rural constituency of the country, the cost of development and other social investments increasingly fell on communities as the ability of central government to provide these diminished.

The stage was therefore, set for another attempt at redeeming the Ghanaian economy from itself. This attempt, termed restructuring or structural adjustment, is the theme of the subsequent chapters of this book.

Notes

1   The ruling body headed by Col. IK Acheampong.
2   With the Armed Forces as the major beneficiary.
3   This did not affect the non-payment of income tax enjoyed by the military.
4   The increased money supply was in itself, generated by abnormal increase in government borrowing from the banking sector.
5   Which the Bank did not support and which the government later recognised as untenable, resulting in resumed negotiations and payments in April 1973.
6   The then Governor, who initially negotiated this understanding with the NRC, being retired in the process.
7   This pressure was felt even more on foreign exchange.
8   This pressure was felt even more on foreign exchange.
9   Supreme Military Council under both Gens. Acheampong and Akuffo.
10   March 1983.

11 Provisional National Defence Council was the ruling body that took over the administration of the state after the 31 Dec. 1981 coup.

12 Budget Statement 1978/79. Legon Observer (Legon) vol. 10 29 Sept no. 3 p.67.

13 See The Mirror, 30 April 1983. Accra.

14 See West Africa, 20 June 1983 p 1465.

15 The last month of the Busia regime.

16 See chapter 6.

17 Which although is not necessarily an efficient nor indeed effective means of assessing welfare or well being, nevertheless provides a broad standard of measurement.

4 A theory of structural adjustment

The last decade has witnessed the phenomenon of Structural Adjustment Programmes invading the African continent with widespread repercussions. By 1993, at least forty countries in Africa were engaged in one form of structural adjustment or the other. This chapter examines the history, character and application of Structural Adjustment in the broader African and, indeed, limited global context.

Structural Adjustment programmes of the World Bank [Bank] and the International Monetary Fund [Fund] have transformed the realism, if not the interpretation of African political economy. This transformation - from devaluation, privatisation to cost recovery and deregulation - has been effected not only in the economic sphere, but also the political. The hitherto near sacrosanct certainty of the centrality of the state and the seeming inevitability of development have been overtaken by the weakening of the state and the concentration on growth [as opposed to development], which in any case, has been most erratic.

In analysing or examining present day African economy therefore, scholars and practitioners alike will have to come out, if not abandon, the paradigmatic state-centrism of one party, military or one man rule that characterised the African State of the 1960s and 1970s. The spectacular responses and outcomes of droughts, food riots, informal sectors, gender development and adjustment conditionalities have critical long term implications not to be ignored. Adjustment [and conditionalities] have transformed not only the terms of trade [internal and external], but also the social relationships which underpin the terms of trade. As Shaw argues (1992), the very political economy of Africa, that is definitions and relations of state, class and community, has changed.

Still, on the broad front, the 1990s have seen the priorities and intensity of the range of elements including devaluation, deregulation, desubsidisation, liberalisation, privatisation etc. become a bit more variable from one country's political economy to the other. But this minimal flexibility, appropriately marketed by the Bank and Fund as great flexibility,[1] does not take away from the characterisation of most national packages, homogeneity, leading to "defaults" or backsliding on some conditionalities as political opposition in individual countries mount.

Historical

Africa and Sub - Saharan Africa in particular, has recorded the weakest economic growth rates, let alone development, of all developing regions of the world. Between 1965 and 1985, GDP per capita [even forgetting one's reservations about accuracy and meaningfulness], increased by less than one percent [1%] a year on average. Arising from this negligible GDP growth rate, a large number of African states had lower per capita levels in 1985 than they did at independence. For most Africans, real income in the 1980s was lower than in 1970.

The Structural Adjustment programmes of the Bank and the Fund in the late 1970s and early 1980s have come in for great criticism (Yeebo 1991, Herbst 1993, Helleiner 1990). A major element of this antipathy is the role of conditionality in the scheme of adjustment. Contrary to popular perception, the Bank has never advanced unconditional loans to developing countries, even during the era of massive project finance. If the Bank was financing a power project for example, some conditions, often involving pricing and management were involved. The case of the Volta Dam in Ghana is a pointer. However, the extent of policy conditionality was still project oriented or at worst sectoral/sub-sectoral in scope.

Three important considerations influenced the move towards Structural Adjustment Loans in the 1980s:

- The use of non-project or programme lending. Programme lending separates development finance from specific items of investment; it is given as general support to balance of payments to facilitate imports and hopefully, development.
- The combination of programme lending with policy change conditions.
- The broadening of these conditions from sectoral or sub-sectoral to national macro-economic level. Structural adjustment loans in the 1980s should therefore, be seen or defined in terms of "programme lending with policy reform conditions that are economy wide" (Mosley 1991, p.28). This form of lending has a precedent in the Bank's lending to India in the 1960s (see Bhagwati & Srinivasan 1975, pp. 83-172), where the Indian government,

having agreed to implement policy changes as part of the negotiation for a loan, abandoned reforms when results of reform proved unsatisfactory.

Even after India halted reforms, programme lending to support balance of payments continued from the Bank to India all through the 1970s [even if at reduced levels] and without conditions attached. Pakistan and later Bangladesh also enjoyed this facility within this period - on the grounds of geo-politics which called for parity of treatment - without policy change conditions. However, by the end of the 1970s, Bangladesh in particular, had attracted reservations of lending without policy changes, essentially because her policy environment was considered weak and unfavourable for development.[2] The dominant role of aid in the Bangladeshi economy provided good prospects for leverage, a factor not present in India or Pakistan. Even before the formal introduction of Structural Adjustment loans by the Bank, Bangladesh was at the receiving end of conditions relating to food policy arising from non-project lending by the Bank.

In the late 1970s and arising from perceived limits to the absorptive capacity of individual projects, emphasis changed from project to programme lending or giving in case of grants. The oil shocks of 1973 and 1979 had resulted in further deterioration of developing country position, thus increasing the erosion of even the broader policy environment. This had some effect on the success rate of projects and according to apologists for programme lending, necessitated a change of emphasis (see OECD 1984, p.221).

The introduction of programme lending combined with policy change conditions in Africa took off in the early 1970s after the Bank's Indian experience of the 1960s. The introduction [in case of Africa] and the revival, in the case of Asia, was not thoroughly thought out, but a panicky reaction to the October 1973 oil shock which produced serious deterioration of current account balances in several African states. Between 1973 - 1975 Kenya, Tanzania and Zambia were offered programme loans with policy changes conditions attached. These were principally, but not exclusively, changes to existing organisation and regime of agricultural marketing and prices. One programme loan was sanctioned for Kenya and two for Tanzania under this arrangement. In 1978, $150m was sanctioned for Turkey (Mosley et al. 1991, p.32) and was accompanied by a "*letter of intent*" indicating the Turkish government's determination to reform major aspects of its trade strategy.

However, the concrete idea of the Programme Loan had still not been accepted within the Bank at this stage, especially by the Executive Board. What probably tilted the scale was the second oil shock of May-November 1979. The phrase 'structural adjustment lending or loan' came into use at about this time. This also coincided with the political shift to the right in three major western powers.[3] This move to supply sided conservatism in economic policy strengthened the move towards SALs at the critical stage, although the right turn did not create the move in the first instance.

The role of some personalities in linking the Indian experience to mainstream bank instrument in the 1980s is extremely important. Ernest Stern, who was the Bank's Vice President for Operations and led the move to SALs had worked in South East Asia for USAID [involved in the Indian attempt] before joining the Bank in 1973. The Vice President's senior advisor on SALs between 1980 - 1983 was Stanley Please, who was on the Bank's team to India in the 1960s negotiations as fiscal economist. It is, therefore, most likely that the Bank's Indian experience, some critics say inadequate leverage, did affect both the introduction and design of SALs, with their strong emphasis on leverage.[4]

A theory of adjustment

A major problem of the study and critical analysis of adjustment is the absence or at best inadequacy of any cohesive body of knowledge that can safely pass as a theory of adjustment. This problem emanates from among other things, the conflicting ideological and idiosyncratic philosophies of the two major players - the Fund and Bank.

My aim therefore, in this section, is to attempt to provide from the evidence, what appears to be the theory impelling the Bank/Fund's policies. Adjustment programmes are at their basic, intended to improve *economic* management and thereby, raise the standard of living of the population in the medium term (see Nashashibi 1992, p. v). Thus the overriding consideration has been economic management. Exacting maximum economic efficiency from the macro economy has been the implicit goal of adjustment programmes in Africa. This is where the structural conflict between social welfare [which in itself can be a stimulus to increased productivity] and short term economic gains is manifested on the horizon. In the short term, per capita increases as well as GDP/GNP growth rates are the dominant factors, whereas educational investment and innovation, health delivery and job training have a longer gestation period but equally critical to long term development.

A critical problem of adjustment, therefore, has been deciding the mix between stabilisation [which is more IMF and short term driven] and structural reform instruments. While a greater dependence on structural reform instruments is preferable from the point of growth, the extent of the stabilisation instrument would be dictated by the urgency of bringing down the imbalance of the macro economy to a sustainable level. And even in the case of identifying which adjustment instruments to use, policy makers would still have to contend with which instruments have the effect of reducing the imbalance, preserving or promoting growth and protecting the poor. Accepting that the probability of a particular instrument achieving the three objectives is minimal, I still deem it important that the overall package achieves these objectives.

The critical conditions prevailing in a country must be paramount in the determination of which instruments [or composition of instruments as the case may be] and mechanism to adopt in the adjustment process. It must not be overtly ideological, although the adjustment process in Africa has been bedevilled with ideological definitions, as opposed to empirical ones. Adjustment is supply driven, on the lines of right wing economic conservatism of dominant western economic powers. Unfortunately, the weight of the stabilisation instruments in particular - in adjustment packages - has become dependent on external circumstances that determine the magnitude and sequencing of adjustment.

The project mode of lending, prior to SAL, reflected the then dominance of engineers within the Bank. It is almost second nature for engineers to see development as a sequence of projects, whereas economists tend to be more sceptical of the project mode. During the 1960s debate within the bank over project versus programme assistance, some economists raised a number of issues, one of which was the *fungibility*[5] problem. Project aid, it was argued, would also create a misleading sense of certainty of impact of aid on the development process. This was not seriously applicable to the post 1970 Africa where the oil shock and its ripples had reduced the ability of the state to marshal its own resources for project finance and thus were overly reliant on aid finance to have the capacity of creating the fungibility problem bank economists were so worried about. The project mode according to economists, was also problematic because the general macro-economic environment in which each project had to operate was often unaffected by the project and was not often favourable to project success. When economic policies are not well ordered, a number of consequences for projects arise.

The above is not to say that the Bank did not recognise the need earlier for some performance related criteria for project finance. It devised a way of linking project aid allocation to general indicators of economic performance, particularly with the International Development Association [IDA] funds where apart from population size, per capita GNP etc., an indicator of "performance" on scale 1 to 5 was incorporated in the allocation (Mosley et al. 1991, p.31). Economic performance was one of the factors shaping a country's quota of available funds which was operationalised in the form of project loans. From a Bank perspective, project aid suffered from being unable to respond quickly when confronted with external shocks. When large gaps opened between export earnings and import costs, quick financial support was not possible under project aid to smooth the path of adjustment. Premium quick disbursing aid was almost impossible, recognising the usual project finance gestation of about five years from conception, design and packaging to implementation.

The formal announcement of the new move by the Bank to make long term non-project assistance available to countries prepared to embrace economic policies regarded as necessary for growth [by the bank] was made at UNCTAD meeting in Manila in April 1979 by President of the Bank McNamara. This new direction was operationalised by the conversion of some existing sector lending to the new policy based lending, as for example, with the Philippines. This followed the Turkish 1978 programme loan pattern, although such lending was eventually repackaged as SECAL [Sector Adjustment Loan] from 1983 onwards.

The sectoral lending approach before 1983 was considered weak in leverage and these more omnibus structural adjustment loans [SALs] gave the bank entry to the top policy making levels in developing countries. This was to facilitate loans large enough to enable the Bank to pressurise decision makers [i.e. government ministers and high level civil servants] to switch to more orthodox economic models. The conditionality had to be economy-wide to both justify the large loans and also to be effective, considering the large loss of trade terms most African countries in particular encountered.

Contrary to the Bank's earlier stand that SALs and later SECALs were to be given only in cases when IMF stabilisation programme existed, a number of these were provided where no stabilisation programme existed. The Argentinean facility of $1.25bn in Oct. 1988 was one of such. Political pressure, particularly from the USA, was responsible for this and other such loans. If there is any one particular instrument both Bank and Fund have used to devastating effect in Africa, it has to be conditionality. This instrument has come under various guises and names, such as *leverage* and *policy dialogue*. Conditionality is expounded as the need "to increase the effectiveness, or productivity of capital resources supplied" by the twin institutions. Conditionality here referring to the 'negotiation' with recipient country of a set of changes in economic policy that the recipient must implement in return for a loan or grant.

Composition of adjustment

Adjustment programmes, as indicated earlier, have a number of components both from an institutional point of view and from the point of inputs such as facilities and design elements. From a design perspective, structural adjustment programmes have two major components; Stabilisation and Structural reform [often referred to as adjustment].

Stabilisation

The IMF singularly has the role [with borrower country] of designing and supervising stabilisation policies of indebted countries seeking Bank and Fund assistance. Stabilisation aims at reducing macro-economic deficits, reducing inflation and crunching out domestic credit expansion.

In pursuing the above, the IMF's posture, if not philosophy, has been that external disequilibria are always the outcome of excessive credit expansion (Bacha 1987, p.1457). From this position therefore, the Fund sees the cure for disequilibria in purging excessive demand. This approach to stabilisation has often been a major cause for strained relations with its twin institution, the Bank which the Fund has consistently regarded and treated as the junior institution. Stabilisation programmes often include three sets of policies (see Cornia 1987):

- expenditure reducing policies. These are aimed at curtailing domestic aggregate demand and consequently, imports.
- expenditure switching policies aimed at increasing supply of 'tradeables', that is export import substitutes, by switching productive resources [labour and capital] from non tradable to tradable sector. This is often induced by a change in relative prices and terms of trade of the two sectors, using instruments such as exchange rate adjustment, productive pricing, and by measures enhancing factor mobility.
- institutional reforms such as privatisation, trade liberalisation, fiscal reform, reform of financial markets, price and trade liberalisation, improving production incentives and stimulating savings and incentives.

It is important to note that, stabilisation is short term in nature, averaging about eighteen months in most cases.

Structural reforms

This is the second stage of structural adjustment programmes, although this stage can and is increasingly more so, run in tandem with stabilisation. Unlike stabilisation, structural reforms are medium to long term and aim at tackling the underlying disequilibria of the macro economy as a whole - and not just the balance of payments.

Structural reforms have come to involve the price incentive, the role of the state in production and productivity, public sector policy capacity, the banking system, internal terms of trade etc. Elements also include desubsidisation, privatisation, public sector reform, deployment of "excess" labour and or redundancies, export promotion, liberalisation of the macro economy, among others. Whereas the Fund has hegemony in stabilisation policies, the same cannot be said of the Bank in structural reforms. Until the mid 1980s, all medium and long term reforms were assumed to fall under only Bank competence, but with the establishment of the Structural Adjustment Fund and the Extended Structural Adjustment Fund by the IMF, this balance of power changed. Both Bank and Fund are now therefore, involved in structural reforms.

Facilities of adjustment

The key to understanding the complexity of adjustment programmes rests within the confines of a number of specific financial facilities provided by both the Fund and the Bank. These facilities or loans provide the means of imposing adjustment leverage on adjusting countries. The facilities are:

Structural Adjustment Loan (SAL)

Although the move to SALs began in the late 1970s, the formal announcement of the move to policy based lending was made in April 1979 at the Manila UNCTAD meeting. Even then, the Executive Board of the Bank did not approve of this until 1980. Even within the Executive Board, approval was not unanimous. Structural Adjustment Loans were justified in terms of the need "to assist countries ... prepared to undertake a programme of adjustment to meet an existing or avoid an impending balance of payment crisis" (WB 1988a, p.22). This meant SALs, at least at the time, were one off responses to exceptional crisis in balance of payments, but one that required a longer time than the IMF standby facility [SBA]. No country was also to receive more than five SALs at intervals between twelve to eighteen months (Mosley 1991, p.40). This however, had to shift. Since 1983 - when Ghana signed up, SALs have been increasingly defended as a means of persuading governments to change their economic policies, with internal factors being given more prominence as causes of poor growth performance.

Structural adjustment loans are also noted for their stringent conditionalities. But conditionality is irrelevant if both the bank and borrower are like minded on the need for reforms and the modalities of achieving such reforms. When however, real differences emerge or exist as to how to facilitate reforms, then does conditionality become relevant. Under this scenario therefore, SALs have become products of a bargaining process - so much money being exchanged for so much reform. Structural Adjustment Loans have been historically linked to the existence of IMF stabilisation programmes. This linkage was looked at by the bank in the 1980s with a view to de-constraining this link, particularly as conflicts with the Fund exacerbated. This re-examination resulted in the introduction of Sectoral Adjustment Loans [SECALs], first given to Pakistan in

1983 - 1984. SECALs were promoted as a relatively more flexible adjustment lending facility on a non IMF basis.

The other design faults of SALs, apart from the linkage to IMF stabilisation programmes, soon overtook the initial success of SALs, particularly the Turkish success stories.[6] These flaws were often located within the core bank philosophy and thus generated the need for SALs to be either reformed or replaced. From 1984 therefore, Sectoral Adjustment Loans became the main vehicle for the Bank's adjustment lending.

The Sectoral Adjustment Loan (SECAL)

Arising out of the Bank's dismay with SAL, particularly that of linkage with IMF stabilisation discussed in preceding pages, Sectoral Adjustment Loans were introduced in 1984. This was meant to provide for a more flexible system of adjustment lending on a non IMF basis. The first SECAL went to Pakistan in 1983 - 1984, continuing a trend of using the Indian peninsular to pilot such schemes. From 1984 therefore, SECALs became the main vehicle for bank adjustment loans, overtaking SALs in the process.

Sectoral adjustment loans themselves proved problematic, mainly because of the difficulty in securing an economy wide macro stability to enable a sectoral programme proceed on a sound footing. How do you for example, secure realignment in a sector when the economy as a whole is on inflationary spiral? The recognition of this problem drove the bank once again to do an about turn to using SECALs in conjunction with IMF stabilisation programmes. Returning to IMF stabilisation was not problem free either, with SECALs often blinding the Bank to overall macro economic perspectives. The Bank and the Fund attempted once more to resolve this in the late 1980s by producing two new innovations; the Policy Framework Paper [PFP] and the 'New Concordat' of 1989. The PFP was drafted by the IMF, and amended and agreed by the Bank and the borrowing government setting out an understanding of the economic situation of the borrowing country and policies necessary for stabilisation and adjustment (Mosley 1991, pp.52 - 54).

The Structural Adjustment Fund (SAF)

This fund, SAF, was established by the IMF as a result of the criticism heaped on its stabilisation programmes and partly from the reservations of its field staff working with borrower governments. The background to this is quite relevant to appreciating and assessing the effectiveness of SAFs.

When initial major macro economic problems were spotted in Africa at the end of the 1970s, the problems were viewed as temporary deterioration occasioned by the combination of recession in the industrial world and the poor terms of trade for raw material producers. It was accepted wisdom that these could be remedied, if not corrected, by stabilisation programmes drawing on existing Fund facilities such as Standby Agreements [SBA] and the Extended Fund Facility [EFF]. These were seen as adequate arsenal with which to combat the short term disequilibria rearing its head across the parapet. SBAs in particular were deployed in large numbers across many nations as a matter of urgency. Between 1980 - 1989 therefore, one hundred and eight [108] SBAs had been entered into between the Fund and thirty seven African countries.[7]

The Structural Adjustment Fund was established in 1986 by the Executive Board of the Fund in recognition of the inadequacy of SBAs and EFFs. This move also marked a significant shift in IMF thinking of external disequilibria. The medium to long term nature of the problem of disequilibria was recognised, adding a new dimension to the hitherto short term definition of the problem and response.

The shift to SAF was to provide concessionary lending to support medium term macro economic and structural adjustment programmes of countries eligible for World Bank assistance through its soft loan affiliate, IDA [set at $550 or less per capita income] and have long standing balance of payment problems. Each eligible borrower was potentially entitled to the equivalent of seventy percent [70%] of its quota. SAF loans carried 0.5% annual interest, beginning five and half years and ending ten years after each disbursement (Nashashibi 1992, p.2). A major consideration for obtaining the facility is the agreement of a PFP for the applying country.

The Enhanced Structural adjustment Fund (ESAF)

The Enhanced Structural Adjustment Fund,[8] like its predecessor the Structural Adjustment Fund (SAF), was created by the Fund to provide concessionary lending to the poorest countries [with per capita income of $550 or less] implementing adjustment programmes. But unlike the SAF, ESAF has a longer time frame and is specifically tailored towards 'structural' problems of these countries in the medium term.

The Extended Structural Adjustment Fund was introduced in 1987 to provide additional assistance to those countries whose programmes were deemed quite vigorous and thus deserving increased support. Its objectives, eligibility and basic procedural features, including PFP, parallel those of SAF. Differences between the two therefore, in addition to time frame, relate to monitoring and the strength of programmes as well as the access to and funding of, the facilities. A member may draw two hundred and fifty percent [250%] of its quota under the ESAF, although in exceptional circumstances [defined by the Fund], this may be bridged (see Mosley 1991, pp.54 -55).

The Policy Framework Paper [PFP]

While the Policy Framework Paper is not a 'facility' in the strict meaning of a loan, the agreement of a Policy Framework Paper has become conditional to a country receiving funds from the concessional Enhanced Structural Adjustment Fund [ESAF] and increasingly, for SECAL, from the Fund and Bank respectively (Mosley, 1991). The PFP is developed for a three year period by the Fund, the Bank and the borrowing country but with the Fund as the lead player. The Policy Framework Paper sets out the implementing authority's macro economic and structural policy objectives, priorities and how the authority [country] hopes to pursue these objectives and priorities over the three year period. Performance during a programme year is monitored by benchmarks that reflect the programme's key elements.

Financial benchmarks are likely to include and specify on a quarterly basis, monetary, fiscal and external debt variables. Structural benchmarks on the other hand, would include major institutional reforms such as in the banking sector and in public enterprises or on various aspects of tax policy.

Bank and fund conflicts

It is tempting to assume that conflicts between the two institutions are new, but they are not. Conflicts between the World Bank and the International Monetary Fund have been legendary and are as old as the institutions themselves. Such conflicts have reared their heads almost from the very beginning but by the 1960s, with most former colonies having attained nationhood, the need to resolve these perennial conflicts had become unavoidable. A Concordat was therefore reached in December 1966 between the two institutions that attempted to delineate the spheres of competencies of the institutions. The agreement gave the Fund responsibility and lead in "exchange rates and restrictive (trade) systems ...adjustment for temporary balance of payment disequilibruia, ... and stabilisation programmes." The Bank was to lead on "...development programmes and project evaluation, including development priorities." (Feinberg 1986, p.5).

But the big grey area of financial institutions, capital markets, domestic savings, domestic and foreign debt remained an overlapping responsibility (see Mosley 1991, p.36). In addition to the specific areas of joint competencies, there has always existed the more subjective - options, routes and responsibility for the development process. Whereas the Bank seems to have a broader remit, the remit is also largely 'unquantifiable', leading to greater reliance on subjectivity.

The Concordat of 1966 did not bring to an end, the Bank/Fund disagreements. The 1970s and 1980s witnessed the widening of these conflicts as many economies of developing countries took a battering. The Bank found the Fund very restrictive in its handling of its exchange rate remit. The Fund's over-enthusiastic wielding of the axe regarding public expenditure cuts also drew Bank displeasure. But the Fund's concerns were mostly in line with its own institutional priorities and ideology, particularly on balance of payments, deficit reduction etc. The problem was worsened with the introduction of the Fund's Extended Fund Facility in 1974. For the first time, a medium term element was introduced to the Fund's lending [EFF was on ten years duration], pushing the Fund into areas of development hitherto monopolised by the Bank, thus threatening the Bank with loss of institutional identity[9] (see Mosley et al. 1991, pp.51 -54).

The limitations placed on the Bank by its Articles of Agreement restricting it from advancing programme loans except in 'exceptional' cases also strengthened the hands of the Fund. To get around the limitations on the introduction of SALs, the Bank this time imposed another conditionality, but this time on itself! It made the disbursement of SALs dependent on the existence of a Stabilisation Programme between the borrowing country and the Fund conditional to receiving a SAL.

Structural Adjustment Loans further complicated Bank/Fund relations. The SALs moved the Bank into conditional programme lending and added conditionality to areas or situations where Fund conditionality was already in operation, creating the problem of cross-conditionality between the two institutions. These are essentially of two kinds:

I) Problems arising from the different nature of the two conditionalities. Fund conditionalities, as stated earlier, are quantifiable and precise, relating to macro - economic performance indicators already in place. Failure to meet conditions are serious and non-negotiable, resulting in a cessation of further financing until such is reinstated by the IMF Board. Bank conditionality, however, goes through the quantifiable to highly qualitative and thus performance or compliance becomes more complicated to judge. There is also a lot more negotiation as to compliance because of the large dose of quantitative indicators involved and non compliance may not necessarily draw the same reaction as would be expected from the Fund. A re-affirmation of good intentions by the borrower is often enough to escape sanctions. Political influence is often heavier here than with the Fund.

II) Problems arising from the need to harmonise the content of the two kinds of conditionality. Consistency poses a major problem for borrowers. Conflicting, or even contradictory advice from the Fund and the Bank, each mandatory and carrying some form of sanctions will be seen as double jeopardy conditionality. As a result of the differing institutional objectives of the Bank and Fund in their dealings with the Third World, each armed with its condition making power, each may easily either directly or indirectly require of the borrower country, action which frustrates the other. For example, the Fund's setting of values for key macro economic variables will notoriously constrain what can be done in the Bank's realm of micro and *meso* economic supply side changes [or changes to the internal terms of trade].

Critique

Structural Adjustment Programmes in Africa have achieved the unique distinction of being opposed by the [nearest one can find of a] totality of all African peoples whose governments are implementing these programmes. Only two other pervasive issues in the history of modern Africa have achieved the same level of notoriety this century - colonialism and apartheid.

The criticism, particularly from development practitioners - most of whom are the first to recognise the urgent need to restructure African economies, has been particularly directed at the model being promoted by the Bank and the Fund. The Bank/Fund model is so much ideology driven that, the objective conditions of the African continent has been marginalised, if not ignored in its articulation. A cardinal mistake of the Bank/Fund supported model is the over-generalisation of both the impact and incidence of reforms. Although the intensity and sequencing of adjustment have been tinkered with within the last five years, particularly between externally and internally induced changes, some commonalties still characterised all programmes in Africa:

1. Intense and incomplete adjustment has diverted almost all African political processes and economies away from longer term issues of development in industrialisation, ecology, infrastructure, technology; and indeed attention has been unduly devoted to short term issues, *viz.* Bank and Fund missions, Donor and Commercial Bank Consultative Group in Paris and London; generally external financial agencies and agenda determining internal processes and priorities.
2. The old distinctions between larger and smaller, industrialising and non industrialised, that is the Third and Fourth Worlds have been jettisoned for 'strong' and 'weak' reformers (see WB, 1994). More worrying is the fact that the new or novel distinction is determined, if not defined, by World Bank indicators and interests, that is, whether African countries have succumbed to Bank pressures and effected its policies or not. This newly created dichotomy, irrespective of the efficacy of the prescriptions, further complicates attempts at Regional Co-operation in the African Region.
3. Adjustment reforms have also transformed political economies leading to intense debates and domestic changes, irrespective of the 'correctness' or otherwise of reforms. A rare species is now the African middle class, the victim of the ongoing shift in social and power relations. The prospects for

unemployed and under-employed are worse than ever and only the very rich, or the well connected and internationally mobile can survive (Shaw 1993, p.70).

4. Adjustment serves to divert attention from development in the short term while undermining the resilience of the State in the longer term. The Bank/Fund claim of market forces leading to growth and development is not supported by history in this century. The Newly Industrialising Countries of this world are characterised by strong rather than weak states.

5. Although adjustment may in the short term lead to growth, this often repeated claim is unproven, at least in Africa. Results from the continent are ambiguous or even disappointing (WB 1994a). The Economic Commission for Africa on the results of adjustment wrote:

> any attempt to portray the economic situation currently prevailing in Africa in cosy terms, to minimise the impact of an adverse external environment and to depict the effects of structural adjustment programmes as having been positive, does not only detract from reality of the situation, but it is also cynical in the extreme (ECA Economic Report on Africa 1989, p.iii).

The continent-wide unacceptability of key elements and arguments of Bank/Fund adjustment[10] is epitomised by the divergences or counter-revolution as some have called this, between the Lagos Plan of Action (1983) that advocated for a form of economic nationalism that advanced self reliance through state managed programmes and the Bank's Berg Report (Berg, 1986) and particularly, the Bank's 1981 "Accelerated Development in Sub-Saharan Africa: An Agenda for Action."

Attempts in the mid 1980s to find some convergence between the broad African intellectual thought [represented in addition to ECA by bodies such as UNICEF, UNDP, WHO etc.] and the Bank/Fund did not succeed, which was not by itself surprising, recognising the gulf between the two positions, as the attack and counter attack represented by the Bank's "Africa: Adjustment and Growth in the 1980s" (1989) crashed headlong in direction and analysis with the ECA's "African Alternative Framework to Structural Adjustment Programmes for Socio - Economic Recovery and Transformation" (1989). The emphasis on 'growth' by the Bank and 'transformation' by the Economic Commission for Africa is at the core of the dilemma confronting African States in pursuing Adjustment. Must African State's continue their pattern of production [albeit more efficiently through the private sector] with a much more globalist aspirations as the Bank and Fund seem to advocate or transform not just production relations with the outside world but also the very outward oriented focus established by colonialism and equally pursued by the post colonial [if not the *neo* colonial] state?

The Economic Commission for Africa's criticism of the Bank/Fund programme as contained in its alternative framework zeroed on seven distinct grounds:

- The crucial intention of any adjustment programme should be *development*, and not growth. It asserts that while stabilisation responses may be necessary in the short term, they should take into account established historical contexts and conditions, particularly, the genesis and character of underdevelopment;
- Difficulties and deficiencies of current conditionalities result from a mistaken premise, that is inattention to underlying characteristics (see Shaw, 1993, pp.1-9);
- The disinterest of Bank/Fund in the social costs or dimension of adjustment, particularly education and health thus "endangering the fabric of the African Society" (ibid. pp.1-7);
- Current conditionalities have neglected several crucial issues and forces. For example, the informal sector, environmental protection, women's roles, regional co-operation, popular participation, adequate infrastructural provision etc.;
- Profound technological changes and sectors that have occurred elsewhere as well as the recognition of the fallacy of composition;
- Limitations of top-down change and call for "democratic development", that is, popular participation in planning and implementation as well as production and consumption;
- Intensity and homogeneity of most adjustment packages which fail to take into account, histories, ecologies, resources and performance.

Structural adjustment programmes have also attracted a lot of fire from the Basic Needs camp of development. SAPs have through cost recovery, created declines in literacy and well being levels in the short term (see UNDP, 1990). In the longer term, structural adjustment will negatively affect the generation and utilisation of technologies and skills that Africa [and all developing countries for that matter], would need to drag themselves from the pit of underdevelopment. Many underpaid professionals have had to divert attention to raising chickens etc. to supplement their earnings. UNICEF's State of the World's Children Report (1989, p.18) is at pains to point out that "a decade of achievement is threatened" as the pre-occupation with adjustment and debt draws attention away from the human factor. It warns that "policies which lead to rising malnutrition, declining health services and falling school enrolment rates are inhuman, unnecessary and ultimately, inefficient."

Structural adjustment conditions, combined with inflation and high population growth, has led to a precipitous and exponential decline in Basic

Human Needs satisfaction, primarily in health and education. Contraction in government budgets and the effects of devaluation have produced a decrease in facilities and opportunities while cost recovery has put these services beyond the majority's ability to utilise such services. The cost recovery policy has been particularly championed by the Bank which sees this as a key component of its programme (WB, 1988b).

The structuralist school of thought [and model] has probably been more articulate in its critique of SAPs. This school has particularly poured intellectual scorn on a key segment of the whole adjustment package, that is devaluation. Missaglia is probably the most stringent of the numerous critiques from this wing of the development debate (Missaglia 1993, p.223). Devaluation has three serious setbacks in a developing economy;

- It creates general price increases owing to the need to support the increased costs of intermediate import goods.[11] The consequent reduction in real wages will bring about a redistribution of income from workers to capitalists and so cause *ceteris paribus* a fall in aggregate demand.
- Devaluation on one hand allows exporters to make large gains while on the other hand, it inflicts higher costs on importers. Given the current account deficit in which most developing countries find themselves trapped, the overall effect is depressive.
- The probability of a decrease in demand will be greater if export elasticity is small in respect to prices. In primary commodity producing Africa, the elasticity tends to be small and so in just as many cases, devaluation leads to stagflation.

Devaluation in developing country setting is fraught with many dangers, both politically and technologically. Structuralists argue that in such settings, the elasticity of supply of exports and elasticity of demand for imports are too low to satisfy the Marshal Lerner condition, in which case, devaluation may worsen as opposed to improving the balance of payments (see Taylor, 1991).

A major weakness of the Bank's approach to SAPs in Africa that cannot be allowed to go unchallenged is the tendency for the Bank to attempt to duplicate its pioneering Asian experiences [or indeed experiments] in Africa. SALs, SECALs etc. were all pioneered or tested in Asia and implemented wholesale in Africa with very little regard to the peculiarities of the African economy.

There is also the criticism of the Fund over-killing demand in stabilisation beyond what is justifiable either from a balance of payment perspective or from a growth angle. The experience of Brazil and Mexico [both in 1983] supports this view. Whereas Brazil, under its agreement with the Fund over-fulfilled the balance of payments targets, it was still unable to meet either the fiscal or monetary targets set by the Fund (Bacha, 1987). In the case of Mexico, its current account for the same year displayed a surplus of US$5.5bn, instead of the Fund programmed deficit of $4bn (Cordova 1986, pp.319-390). It is important to note that Fund programmes tend to err in only one direction - mainly in establishing stricter domestic performances criteria needed to attain balance of payments objectives of their supported programmes.

By way of conclusion, it might be useful to ask why adjustment programmes in Africa are not working.[12] The most obvious counter is that adjustment remains problematic in impact because it is improbable in content. The content of most packages ignores the reality of the African socio-politico-economic condition as already argued and unless new models are developed with predominant African and country specific input, adjustment will continue to be enigmatic in impact.

In redesigning adjustment programmes, cognisance would have to be taken of the crucial role of the state in Africa. Although one recognises the need to hold the vampire state in Africa in check, we must recognise that the state can and does play other roles in the body politic other than that of the sucking vampire. And it is this productive and relevant role that has to be incorporated into adjustment and strengthened, not weakened. For as Nzongolia puts it, "No political economy is intelligible without the analysis of the crucial role the state plays in the economy" (Nzongolia 1987, p.20).

It must be accepted by policy designers and practitioners that social forces and the state tend to learn from each other and have particularly taken lessons from each other on how to subvert unacceptable consequences and costs. If models that encompass the African reality are not designed, social forces will find a way around whatever 'disciplines' the Bank/Fund would want to impose. It is equally in the interest of Bank/Fund credibility not to ignore this, for they ignore this experience at their peril. For Africa and those with the interest of Africa at heart, the bright spot on the horizon through the gloom is that the enlarged civil society, strengthened paradoxically from the adjustment process will defend and thwart unacceptable impositions under adjustment.

Notes

1   Such as the "new emphasis on human resource development" [World Bank, 1991].
2   The World Bank in particular was getting exasperated by its failure to significantly influence policy direction in the country.
3   UK in May 1979, US November 1979 and the Federal Republic of Germany in 1980.
4   Mosley and his colleagues have so powerfully established this connection [see Aid and Power, 1991 vol. 1 pages 27-29].
5   If aid finances a project which the implementing government would have undertaken anyway, aid or no aid, then the aid money is financing some other unidentified project beyond the control or knowledge of the aid agency.
6   With Turkey taking 35% of all SAL lending between 1980 - 84.

7   IMF Annual Surveys (various issues).

8   Occasionally referred to as the Extended Structural Adjustment Fund.

9   The seemingly insurmountable differences between the two institutions have led to the call since the late 1960s, for a merger of the two institutions. This was picked up again in the 1990s with John Smith, the late Labour Party Leader (Britain) returning to the theme of merging the two institutions in 1993. The call has been re echoed in 1995 (the 50th anniversary year of the institutions) by both Governmental and Non Governmental Institutions with the US Congress being the most vocal, even if for different set of reasons.

10 Most ably articulated by the Economic Commission for Africa.

11 Using the 'Kalecki' theory of prices, which states that every increase in variable costs will be reflected in the general level of prices as a result of the 'mark up' rule.

12 Or at least not working as well as Fund/Bank strategists would want us believe.

5 Stages in the management of Ghana's economic reform

There are a number of themes which need to be considered separately in the elucidation of Ghana's Structural Adjustment Programme and I will deal with them in turn in this chapter, to justify the conclusion drawn in this book. Any attempt at understanding, analysing or even challenging Ghana's Adjustment Programme, would be meaningless unless it is undertaken in the context of the pre - 1983 state of the economy. The state of the economy gives the programme its defining character. Thus, Ghana's programme is often cited, as the best and most comprehensively implemented in Africa (see WB, 1994b).

A clear account of the Ghanaian situation is not only desirable as a means of understanding how a specific country develops, but as portent for the rest of Africa and indeed the low income developing Third World. Ghana's SAP experience also mirrors in a major way, the current state of North-South co-operation in the development arena, with the key northern roles played by international financial institutions and other international development agencies such as the UNDP, UNICEF, UNFP, UNEP etc. It is therefore, useful to prefix this section with the question:

What was the specific nature of the Ghanaian economy in the early 1980s?

The preceding chapters have given detailed accounts of the erosion of the economy and social structures of collective welfare, particularly from the middle 1970s. What immediately follows, is therefore, only a recap of the degree of deterioration. Both adverse externalities and prolonged inappropriate domestic policies were at the root of this extended deterioration. The effects of worsening international terms of commodity trade, a succession of severe

115

droughts and an influx of over a million Ghanaian emigrants expelled from Nigeria[1] were compounded by a severely over-valued exchange rate.

For a country whose declared aim at independence in 1957 was the achievement of sustained economic development, it is extremely difficult to comprehend the set of policies pursued afterwards. A crystal ball was not required to foresee that the policies run counter to the declared objective. The gulf between declared intention and actual results aroused the classic conundrum: *"Why should responsible men adopt public policies that have harmful consequences for societies they govern?"* (see Bates 1981, p.3).

It is my intention here to examine both the immediate influences on the decision of the Ghanaian state to succumb to the Bretton Woods institutions and adopt their 'recommended' adjustment route as well as the stages or phases the implementation of adjustment involved.

External shocks

In 1982, a number of exogenous shocks, over which neither the government of the day or the Ghanaian state had any control, added to the problems of the polity. They influenced not only the move to macro policy reform, but also quickened the reform process itself. The worst drought this century in the country's history occurred in 1982-1983 leading to unprecedented food shortages. The same drought reduced the generation capacity of the Akosombo hydro-electric dam resulting in power rationing both to industries and domestic use. The water level had fallen below minimal levels requiring the closure of at least two potlines of the Valco smelter in Tema, whose total usage accounted for the largest portion of electricity generated. The effect of the loss of generating capacity was a further erosion of industrial capacity to a meagre 20-25% of installed capacity (Toye 1990, p.47).

The drought induced horrific bush fires, which although affected the whole country, seemed to have reserved its venom for the food producing middle belt of the country. The bush fires destroyed about one third of all farms, both food and export crops including cocoa. Food imports on a commercial basis had to be undertaken at a time when national coffers were literally empty. The overall effect on agriculture was devastating, recognising that agriculture provides about 65% of total employment in the country and is the largest contributor to the national product. No other sector, facing a similar adversity, could have induced the same level of mass impoverishment.

The 1979 - 1980 oil price rise further debilitated the economy by increasing the amount of scarce foreign exchange devoted to oil imports. The oil price increases also resulted in a global recession, thus forcing down the prices obtained for the country's raw material exports. Furthermore, credit facilities, traditionally extended by Nigeria to Ghana was also withdrawn in 1982, exacerbating the balance of payments crisis confronting the country.

Economic developments

The perilous economic position of the country was instrumental in determining the internal politics of the country. The disastrous state of the economy by April 1983 is reported in chapter three, but it is still worth reiterating some highlights of the decay. By 1982, real per capita income was lower by 30%, real export earnings by 52% and import volumes by 30% than in 1970. Depressed real wages had caused a large scale emigration of skilled workers (Heller 1983, p.36). One major source of the fall in real GDP per capita had been the persistent large government deficits financed essentially from Central Bank drawing and inflation. Inflation, conflated by exchange rates fixed over long periods, generated one of the most critical reductions in real exchange rates ever recorded. Table 5.1 indicates government deficits exploding from less than half a billion cedis in 1970 to nearly five billion cedis by 1982. The table also indicates that the real exchange rate in 1982 was less than 10% of its 1957 value, pointing to a grossly overvalued currency.

Fundamental to the economic collapse was a decline in real foreign exchange earnings generated in part by the fall in real exchange rate occasioned by an abnormally over-valued cedi. In 1972, the parallel market rate for the cedi was 28% greater than the nominal rate. By 1976, the cedi, still officially pegged at one cedi and fifteen pesewas to the US dollar; was 60% over-valued, compared to parallel market trends. In 1982, the market rate was 250% above the official of ₵2.75 to US$, that is, ₵61.6 to the same dollar (Wood 1988, p.122).

The cumulative over-valuation left the cedi with only about ten percent of its value at Independence in 1957 (Leith 1993, p.259). The government, unable to ignore the exchange rate policy debacle, implicitly threw in the towel by 1980, having lost control, by creating a system of Special Unnumbered Licences that allowed Ghanaians to import goods without formal state foreign exchange support. Potential importers were thus encouraged to bid for funds from the parallel market, even though the Exchange Control Act still made this illegal (Huq 1989, p.327).

The exchange rate maladministration affected all exports, but principally cocoa, the main export. Whereas timber exporters, for example, were able to manipulate their control of the export trade through dishonest and illegal means to offset the disincentive created by the over valued cedi, - cocoa farmers, because of the monopoly the Ghana Cocoa Marketing Board in cocoa exports, did not have any such means of offsetting their real loss of earnings. Cocoa production thus fell from the heights reached in 1965 - 1970 and, by 1983, volume production was only one- third of the 1965 figure. Real domestic producer price had even declined faster to only about 13% of the 1970 producer price. Bloated Cocoa Board expenditure equally played a role in the exploitation of the farmers [all of whom were rural based] by the state for the benefit of a parasitic urban elite in charge of state machinery (see Leith 1993, p 234). Indeed, it is argued (Herbst 1993, p.40) that the over-valuation of the cedi was central to the loss of market share in general and cocoa in particular from the 1970s. Exports were hurt by over-valuation, with the result that total exports in constant cedi in 1980 was only 52% of the 1970 figure (WB 1984, p.85).

Social developments

The deterioration of the Ghanaian polity was not limited to the economic sphere. The social consequences and implications were just as important, if not more in the Ghanaian case. By April 1983, the real purchasing power of formal wages was already very low, not only in terms of importables, but also in terms of locally produced foodstuffs and other necessities (Ewusi 1987, pp. 56-57 table 26).

The educational and health services had also ceased to deliver to the majority of the population due to shortages of inputs and breakdown of service infrastructure. By 1981, government expenditure on education amounted to less than 1.9% and on health, to less than 0.7% of GDP. These contrast to the average for all Sub-Saharan Africa of 4.6% and 1.6% respectively (UNDP/WB, 1989). Although the figures should be taken with utmost caution [as indeed all statistics on Africa], it is still an accurate representation of the extent of the decline. Simply put, health and education had ceased to deliver [down from its trail blazing days of the 1960s]. For the working man, survival became more dependent on emigration, accounting for the massive emigration to the new booming economies of countries like Nigeria and Gabon.

Political

The adoption of the April 1983 reform programme, dubbed the Economic Reform Programme [ERP], in line with its economic centred philosophy, was influenced by developments in the political arena, thus partly creating an enabling environment for reform. The specific occurrences were not always related, but collectively, served the same purpose. The initial option of the PNDC government was not for a 'market forces' led structural adjustment programme, but for a collectivist, national democratic and independent development. To this end, the government between January and June 1982, energetically courted financial assistance from the then USSR, Eastern Europe and Libya. Other than Libya, which made an initial token gesture of some food shipment and 500,000 barrels of oil [with promises of massive financial assistance if the Ghanaian government palyed ball],[2] nothing was forthcoming from this option. In fact, the rapprochement with Libya had a major negative consequence, since Nigeria,[3] the traditional source of Ghanaian oil imports, withdrew credit facilities to Ghana and insisted on down payments.

The leading advocates of an independent and anti- imperialist development path were from the left wing of the PNDC.[4] This faction held the dominant position in government during the early days of the regime. The failure of the radical left to secure external assistance from fraternal sources was a big blow to the national democratic development approach and was possibly, the single most important factor that threw Ghana into the laps of the International Monetary Fund and the World Bank. The left was further lumbered with the creeping acceptance by the general populace [outside of the radical intellectual sections] that the statism of the past had not worked.[5] Under Acheampong, Akuffo and Limann, inefficiency of governance had led the average Ghanaian to conclude that the lofty ideals of statism did not translate well in practice.

By the end of 1982 therefore, conditions of social chaos, the failure of the regime's foreign policy initiatives, the severity of the country's decline and the antipathy of the populace towards messianic solutions had compelled influential members of the government to acknowledge that the regime's preferred populist approach to national resuscitation was not viable. Even the most committed leftists in government had written off the possibility of getting the required assistance from the then Eastern bloc or Libya. Two other events reduced the left wing as a powerful political force to impotency [and thus as an anti - IMF bloc] - the murder of the three judges and the retired army officer and the failed coup attempt in November 1982.

The murder of the three judges and a retired army officer in 1982 sparked a wave of revulsion in Ghana. The crime, traced to a renegade unit of the shadowy security apparatus operated by the regime, was passed off as left wing anarchism, although the left was the first to publicly condemn the act and call for a full public enquiry. Two leading members of the ruling council, none of whom was associated with the formal left wing in the regime were implicated by the Commission of Enquiry set up to investigate the heinous crime. Notwithstanding this, the left suffered blame largely because the public could not or was unwilling to differentiate between the various shades of the left in the country at large. A failed coup attempt in November 1982[6] sealed the fate of the intellectual and organised left in government, reducing them to irrelevance in the power game. This paved the way for the right to take over both the economic and political direction.

The government, now under the control of its centrists and right wingers, set up a committee to chart a new direction for the national economy. It must be said that contacts between a small cadre of technocrats under the political direction of the right, had been made with officials of both the Fund and the Bank, particularly during the annual Fund/Bank meeting in 1982. This group informally raised the possibility of funding a major reform programme, which was seen as very encouraging by both the Fund and the Bank. Their encouraging response was probably what finally set the reform programme in motion.

To informed Ghanaians, the preparedness of the Bretton Woods institutions to favourably receive the proposed reform programme was not surprising. These institutions traditionally have had a disposition to favour what they refer to as 'strong' leadership; which in developing world, invariably means authoritarian regimes. The IMF had indicated in April 1981 that any new external assistance for the intended stabilisation programme of the Limann government [which many saw as long overdue] could only be provided if certain policy conditions were met or included in the programme. The conditions included devaluation, increased producer prices for cocoa, increased interest rates, increased repayments of debts [including by 1982 $580m arrears] and reduction in government expenditure, especially its payroll (Ray 1986, p.123). The Bank, approached at about the same time for an Export Rehabilitation Credit, also insisted on a major overhaul of the Cocoa Board in addition to some of the issues already raised by the Fund. But the Limann administration, held hostage by the experiences of the AFRC era and the vehement ideological opposition to any talk of devaluation,[7] procrastinated until the 31 December 1981 coup ushered in the PNDC. Ironically, a Fund mission was still in Accra on the day of the coup.

Character of adjustment

The peculiarity of Ghana's Adjustment Programme has often defied standard categorisation. A number of commentators such as Frimpong-Ansah, Leith, Toye, Herbst, Mosley, and Abbey have been unable to agree on whether it was an indigenous grown programme or a World Bank/IMF diktat. There is very little doubt[8] that the initial decision to restructure the Ghanaian economy was taken by the Ghanaian authorities. The deliberations of both the Committee of Secretaries and the Interim National Co-ordinating Committee of People's and Workers Defence Committees point to this direction.[9] The constitution of a small group of economists and other senior bureaucrats[10] to come up with a blueprint in 1982 was the first major move in the reform process.

The April 1983 Programme, announced by the PNDC Secretary for Finance and Economic Planning, aimed at a fundamental break with not only the PNDC's policies of the previous fifteen months, but also from the thrust of economic practice since independence with the possible exception of the short lived Busia period. In Botchway's words [the Finance Secretary],[11] this required "a complete overhaul of policy in areas of incomes and pricing, including pricing of foreign exchange" (People's Daily Graphic 25 April 1983, p.4). The Head of State further justified the government's position in a major broadcast. He stated:

> We have reached a critical stage in our history and we need to ask ourselves serious questions: Why has it become so profitable in this country simply to engage in trade instead of production? Why are the most productive and industrious people usually the poorest? Why do we make it less profitable for a person to produce maize here than for him to get an import licence to import it from abroad? Idleness and parasitism have become more rewarded in this country than production work... This is the time to reverse the process. (Government 1983a, pp. 4-5).

The same budget statement also raised the issue of a new relationship between the State and the economy. The Finance Secretary noted that "...the rigid enforcement of prices unrelated to costs of production is (not) a satisfactory basis for action" and rather affirmed that "pricing ... be based on production costs together with appropriate incentive margins" Dr Obed Asamoah [the Foreign Secretary] reflected that there was the realisation that some adjustment has to be made in the exchange rate of the cedi, but at the same time, there was some feeling in the country that success stories based on IMF devaluation prescriptions are hard to come by. But a full understanding of the development of Ghana's Economic Recovery Programme must be based on a careful examination of the pre existing political economy so as to appreciate two things:

- What it was that had to be stabilised and adjusted;
- To be clear how the decision to adjust was made and the involvement of both the Fund and Bank in the process.

The Programme was from the beginning designed with a series of partially overlapping phases;
  i) stabilisation,
  ii) rehabilitation of the economy

iii) economic liberalisation (WB 1984, pp.xvii & 73)

External support was to come from several sources; the IMF, the World Bank, bilateral aid donors and eventually, private foreign capital. Ghana's Adjustment Programme, in line with the programme of most other developing countries, can be seen as a by-product of the developments on the international scene. In some respects, those in charge may have been shrewd in anticipating what other governments only grudgingly felt forced into at much later stages. The election of Margaret Thatcher in the UK, Reagan in the USA and Kohl in the then Federal Republic of Germany represented an extraordinary development of a fundamental re-evaluation of the role of the state in not only the economy, but also in economic governance. The *dirigiste* state was consigned [at least temporarily] to the dustbin of history with critical repercussions on international financial institutions and other international development agencies.

The foregoing did not mean that there was no opposition to the reform programme and particularly, the role of IMF and the World Bank. But despite the political unacceptability of the expanded programme[12] to key constituents of the regime [students, labour and the intellectual left], the nature of the collapse of the Ghanaian economy made any further resistance to reform very difficult and by default, made the case for the programme.

The parallel market rate of the cedi [as an example of the state of the collapse], was almost twenty times the official rate (Herbst 1993, p.31), and very few goods were sold at the official price. The beneficiaries of such sales were the bureaucratic/political and military elite and those who served them. The devaluation and the lifting of price controls therefore had less real effect on prices since most people, except the few well connected, were already paying higher prices. Thus the first in what later became a series of devaluation, only confirmed what was already happening on the ground. The extreme poor state of the economy had unwittingly made the introduction of the Stabilisation Programme easier than would have been the case.

Stages of adjustment

The adjustment programme was staggered over a number of years with different components. Some of these components overlapped between periods and/ or sections thus making distinct divisions difficult, unworkable and unhelpful. Nonetheless, it is still useful to recognise these stages. The first critical stage, was dubbed the Economic Recovery Programme which was implemented in two instalments.

Economic Recovery Programme One (ERP I) was formally launched in 1984, although its implementation started earlier with the announcement of the April 1983 budget. This has created unnecessary confusion and most publications seem unable to make this distinction. The goals of ERP were many and varied. But ERP1 was essentially a stabilisation package and should be recognised as such. Being a stabilisation bundle, its thrust was predominantly "fire fighting". Its goals included:

- Shifting relative prices in favour of production, particularly exports;
- Restoring fiscal and monetary discipline;
- Initiating rehabilitation of the country's productive base and its economic and social infrastructure and restoring incentives for private savings and investment.

The Programme concerned itself with what was to be done immediately to tackle the proximate cause of Ghana's economic atrophy by:

- Changing the exchange rate to a level which would both restore an incentive to export and remove rents from foreign exchange;
- Tackling the government budget deficit.

ERP I was the ground breaker concentrating on the short term. It sought to create what was seen as the essential conditions for macro stability. These included exchange rate adjustment and cutting the huge government deficit to size by increasing tax income generation through the establishment of greater financial discipline in the public sector; and increasing the tax base of the economy to rope in aspects of the non public sector, especially the small to medium size private sector. ERP I was supported by among others, a one year standby facility of the IMF [1983 - 1984] and a second eighteen months standby facility [1984 - 1985]. These facilities were aimed at establishing a foundation for economic growth and a viable external payments position (Heller 1988, p.36). The Programme was also designed to get output rising and to export a higher percentage of that output; to control inflation and improve international credit worthiness and to rehabilitate the country's economic infrastructure.

The IMF played the lead role in providing additional resources during ERP1, providing about 60% of the $1bn. channelled to Ghana with the World Bank providing 13% and the rest coming from bilateral sources (Loxley 1988, p.24). This division of financial responsibility reflected the fund's lead role in macro economic stabilisation, narrowing the gap between official and parallel rates of the cedi, curbing inflation by cutting government aggregate demand, removing price controls and providing foreign exchange to ease import strangulation (see Toye 1990, p.52; Government of Ghana 1984).

Economic Recovery Programme - stage two

Economic Recovery Programme Stage Two was launched in 1987 for a three year period as a sequence to the ERP I and was a hybrid between stabilisation and structural reform. Reform was intended for both of medium and long term duration. ERP II was to ensure economic growth of around 5% per annum in real terms, stimulating significant increases in savings and investment, improving public sector management and placing the external sector on a sound footing (Gov. of Ghana, 1987b).

ERP II was also dubbed by some as Structural Adjustment Programme One [SAP I] - to indicate its adoption of structural changes and not merely economic stabilisation. The Bank of Ghana in particular, consistently referred to this phase of the Recovery Programme as SAP I. This reflects the emphasis of its managers on reform as opposed to ERP I which as indicated earlier, was a stabilisation programme. ERP II (or SAP I) was to:

a) establish an incentive framework that would stimulate growth at around 5% per annum;
b) encourage substantial savings and investment;
c) strengthen the balance of payments;
d) Improving resource use particularly in public sector, while ensuring fiscal and monetary stability;
e) implement the Programme of Action to Mitigate the Social Cost of Adjustment (PAMSCAD).

It was to increase public investment to 25% and domestic savings to 15% of GDP. Social expenditure was also to be increased considerably via the instrumentality of PAMSCAD (Gov. of Ghana 1987b, p.10).

Segments of reform

Within the general flow of adjustment, reform was conducted in the context of 'segments.' The state of decay, and thus the task of restructuring at hand was such that appropriate policy initiatives were worked out and implemented via a series of correlated segmentations. The analysis of the reform programme would, therefore, be undertaken along the lines of segmentation but with an overarching canopy.

The government's determination to place public sector reform high on the agenda was exemplified by the initiation of a Public Enterprise Reform Programme [PERP] in 1983 as a component of the broader and far reaching Economic Reform Programme. The reform aimed at privatising some state owned enterprises, and improving the efficiency of the remaining enterprises to be maintained in the public sector so as to salvage the huge losses that had become a feature of the sector. A major tool in this direction was the institution of a system of corporate planning and performance contracts. Under this innovation, state owned enterprises were to prepare corporate plans, negotiate performance contracts with the shareholder [state] and report quarterly on their operations, giving reasons for variations from agreed targets should these occur. The essence was to bring to bear on the public sector, private sector managerial ethos and practices.

State owned enterprises [SOE's], occupying a pedestal position in the economy, had so under-performed particularly in the 1970s and early 1980s that, the national economy had virtually become a hostage of their under performance. By the early 1980s, Ghana had in operation a total of 235 SOEs of which the state had a direct majority holding in 181 (Adda 1989, p.305). These accounted in 1980 for 50% of all formal sector labour force in comparison to the African average of 19% (UNDP & WB, 1989, p.166; Heller & Allan 1983, p.7).

These enterprises had grown both in size and numbers over the years because they have been convenient, both politically and economically for governments over the past and the creation of a number of them was for purely political reasons, performing poorly as commercial enterprises. The need to reform these enterprises was therefore paramount, if the macro economy was to be brought under efficient management and control. This need was made even more urgent by the increasing share of government expenditure incurred on non performing state owned enterprises.

In 1982, SOEs received 13% of all government expenditure in the form of subsidies, equity contributions, capital and grants (see Adda op. cit., p.307) but by 1983, this had ballooned to 25% as the cumulative under capitalisation of these enterprises became critical, thus needing billions of cedis in recapitalisation just to maintain production at existing poor levels.

The reform encapsulated the strengthening, both in the capitalisation and managerial terms of a core number of state owned enterprises[13] and the general strengthening of all SOEs with the short term aim of weaning them off state subsidies. In the medium term, all commercial enterprises were expected to pay dividends to the state as a shareholder. By 1990, subsidies and transfers, hitherto making up a quarter of all government expenditure, had fallen to 10%

while direct subsidies had virtually been wiped out as a result of the reform package. The elimination of direct subsidies to most state owned enterprises enabled the government to eliminate its expenditure deficit by 1987 even though general government consumption had grown from 6.5% of GDP in 1982 to 10.6% in 1987 as the need to attend to neglected infrastructure and other items of social capital had become unavoidable. The elimination of the government expenditure deficit has been widely celebrated by commentators but the government account went into another bout of deficit in the early 1990s when the combination of the cost of running the first elections in 1991 [since the start of reform in 1983], the slower than expected disbursement of overseas credits and the forced restraint imposed on labour cost, proved unsustainable.

The need for reform of public sector economies and social institutions as well as the promotion of a more accountable infrastructure of public administration is still as critical today as it was at the beginning of the Programme in 1983. The magnitude of the problem called for a long term approach. However, the state's ability to reform the public sector to save money, and raise efficiency while improving the welfare of the citizens is paradoxically limited by the state's ability to fund the reform programme. The minister for finance, in presenting the 1995 Budget to Parliament remonstrated that the state paid ₵27.9bn in End of Service benefits to workers in one hundred and seventy firms and organisations in 1994, including a significant portion to workers in state owned commercial enterprises which in the minister's words, " ...(had) throughout their existence, paid no return to government on its investment and some of which, even now owe billions of cedis to government in unpaid corporate taxes" (p.18). The government also paid ₵23.3bn to workers affected by redeployment, including ₵13bn to Cocoa Marketing Board retrenched staff during the same period (ibid.).

However, notwithstanding the efforts and successes of reform, SOEs have not found it easy to abandon the culture of unaccountability established over the years in their dealings with both the public and the state. State enterprises have continued, even if on a reduced scale, to ignore the realities of modern commercial practices as these relate to performance and returns on investment. The Finance Minister pointed this out before Parliament. "...What is even more worrying" he said:

> is the fact that some state owned enterprises have continued to draw extremely lucrative fringe benefits without due consideration for other priority obligations such as tax and dividends repayments and loan obligations... These state owned enterprises are advised in their own interest, to review these harmful practices and to rededicate themselves to the objectives for which they were set up. In the mean time, to underscore government determination to stop these practices, it has been

decided that henceforth, appropriate rates would be set for these organisations to pay every year to ensure that they contribute their fair share of revenue to government. (Budget Statement 1995, p.41).

Civil service reform

Critical to the Public Sector Reform generally was the reform of government machinery itself. The Ghanaian Civil Service, like other apparatus of the public service, had grown so large over the years that it was customary to see civil servants on the payroll without designated office accommodation! Messengers and clerks were hired at the whims and caprices of senior officers without any regard to establishment procedures and positions. It was thus not uncommon to find two messengers solely serving one senior official.

In designing and supporting Ghana's SAP therefore, the International Monetary Fund, through the various SAF and later ESAF facilities, pressurised the Ghanaian leadership to put increased efficiency and effectiveness of the civil service at the top of the reform agenda. This involved the reduction of civil service numbers, increasing salary differentials [to attract the right calibre of staff], restructuring pay and grading of management, and raising real remuneration.

Thus under the auspices of reform, 50,000 civil servants [including those of the education service] were made redundant[14] between 1987 - 90. A further 12% reduction in staff numbers of the civil service was made in 1991. By the end of 1991 therefore, 15% of the core civil service [excluding education service] had departed. This is in a country where the public service employs 50% of all formal sector employees. Equally critical for equity is the implied belief that pay differentials had to be widened between the lowest and the highest levels in the service to raise efficiency. Thus the differentials between the lowest paid civil servants and the highest paid widened from 5.7:1 before the reform to 10.5:1 by 1991 as part of the reform. The foregoing ignores the army of 'experts' hired as consultants to strengthen the civil service and whose emoluments are denominated and paid in dollars at going international consultancy rates. The World Bank argues that as at 1994, the Ghanaian civil service still remains one of the largest in Africa in relation to the country's population size and should therefore be further pruned down (Leechor 1994, p.167).

The civil service reform is built on the premise of overstaffing. What has not been tackled is the increased inequity created in the service as a result of the reform. Equally important is the question of what happens to the large army of redundant civil servants in an economy already wracked with unemployment.

A consensus had emerged by the middle of the 1970s that African SOEs had performed poorly and that with few exceptions, SOEs had revealed pervasive patterns of inefficiency, maladministration and financial liability.[15] Divestiture of state owned enterprises was thus seen by many policy makers as an appropriate response to this failure. What was not answered was whether SOEs performed poorly because they were state owned or because there existed fundamental weaknesses in their set ups. But the treatment of SOEs under structural adjustment programmes shows a fundamental belief that SOEs [particularly in Ghana] performed badly because they were state owned. It therefore becomes logical to assume that stripping them of that identity should solve their problems. This would be correct if the diagnosis of a statist virus is the entire, or even the main explanation for poor performance.

The proper approach to the diagnosis should be whether state ownership, as opposed to private ownership, fundamentally affects the constraints that determine poor performance in Africa. High on the agenda of the reformers was the divestiture of state enterprises. Beginning from 1985, the government decided to divest itself of the ownership and running of a number of these SOEs through outright disposal or privatisation, joint holding, leasing arrangements and the granting of commercial autonomy for those core organisations, eighteen in number, mainly in mining, energy, transportation, utilities and cocoa trade the government felt compelled to retain in the public sector (Tangri 1991, p.526).

An agreement was thus concluded with the International Development Association of the World Bank Group setting up a Divestiture Secretariat in October 1987 to this effect. The agreement also provided a credit line. On a formal note, the PNDC Secretary and Chairman of State Enterprises Commission [as well as the Divestiture Implementation Committee] in putting forward the case for divestiture on behalf of the government, assigned five 'basic' reasons for the government's programme of privatisation:

- The changing economic environment; that for many enterprises, the original objectives behind the creation are no longer valid;
- Effectiveness; that there is abundant evidence that SOEs are not as effective in serving their clients as the private sector. Privatisation, it was argued, would put SOEs under the test of the market place with the view of improving efficiency;
- Public Funds; Public ownership of SOEs placed enormous demand on government resources to manage and financially support various enterprises, resources the government no longer provide on the old basis;

- Management Styles: The Public Institutions operated using public resources. Decision making was said to be slow and management of these enterprises were strangers to taking risks; whereas it was claimed in a commercial milieu, adaptability to rapid changes in markets and technologies were essential.
- Fairness and equity: Many SOEs are said to compete directly with the private sector. In effect some businesses see their own tax moneys being used to compete against themselves. This, according to the government position, is hardly fair or conducive to the enterprise system that the government geared to establish.

Thus the Ghana government's approach to privatisation, according to the sector PNDC Secretary and Chairman of the SEC, is 'based on specific objectives designed to ensure the appropriateness of the SOEs, while encouraging a vibrant private sector' (Adda 1989, p.311) .

The recognition of the drain on fiscal resources by SOEs was as important as any of the fore mentioned factors in the move to divestiture. Indeed Herbst argues that privatisation in the Ghanaian case arose not from a fundamental rethink of state led industrialisation, but from a fiscal stand point (Herbst 1993, p.98). The ruling PNDC on its part, noted:

> a substantial part of central government expenditures have included transfers to cover losses of public corporations by way subventions... To check this enormous drain, government has undertaken a major review of the public sector and intends to reduce the burden on itself of such public corporations by divesting itself, wholly or partly, of some of their operations (Government of Ghana 1987, p.25).

Public enterprises incurred large deficits and in 1982 for example, the total operating deficit amounted to over three percent of Gross Domestic Product, that is about equal to the combined government expenditure on education, health, social security and welfare for that year (Berenchot,Moret & Bosboom, 1985 p 99). Budgetary support continued all through the 1980s, ranging from 10% of total government expenditure in 1982 to 8% of the same in 1986 (Adda, W 1989 p 306). The state's commitment to these enterprises did not end with budgetary support; indeed the support, even if by default, extended far beyond that. As at June 30, 1986, the state had on its books, loan guarantees to almost all of the commercial enterprises. Eighteen of these SOEs had outstanding liabilities emanating from these guarantees to the tune of ¢15.68bn owed to both internal and external creditors (ibid., p.307). Outstanding tax arrears were already standing at ¢2.5bn by the end of 1985 (ibid. p.306). The Ghana National Petroleum corporation's indebtedness to the Bank of Ghana, as a single example, stood at over ₵140bn at the end of 1994 (Budget Statement 1995, p.11).

Table 5.1
General structure of state owned enterprises in Ghana: public equity holding

Public equity (%)	Number of enterprises
100	93
50 -100	43
25 - 50%	39
Less than 25	15
Total	190

Source: Adda 1989, p.306.

However, the drive towards divestiture was moderated by the state's ability to meet the retirement benefit and similar obligations to public sector employees who became redundant once such enterprises are sold or liquidated. In 1988 for example, it was estimated that the state's obligations amounted to over a hundred billion cedis, nearly Ghana's total internal revenue collection for the year. The end of service benefit of at least 40,000 people leaving the public service in fiscal years 1988 and 1989 from parastatals alone amounted to ₵10bn - ₵16bn ($71m - $79m). While rudimentary attempts were made to retrain some of these workers, the very ideology of divestiture in Ghana was more of 'getting rid' of public sector employees and the state was not prepared therefore to re engage the affected even after retraining. With the powerful incentive of getting a job after retraining removed, most workers recognised the futility of going on a government retraining scheme and opted to collect their severance benefits.

The nature of divestiture in developing countries, not excluding Ghana, makes the measure a very difficult one and not just from a politico - social angle but also from a technical point. Tangri, whose work on divestiture is one of the most authoritative, sees divestiture as 'technically one of the most difficult of all adjustment measures.' The scope of skills needed to prepare SOEs for divestment have consistently been high, with Ghana being a good example. (Tangri 1991, p.528). Divergence's in the estimation of assets between the state and potential investors alone can have serious impact on the state's ability to carry through a divestiture programme. Notwithstanding the above, a number of divestitures have taken place while a number more of such are planned for 1995 including the sale of substantial shareholding in Ghana

Commercial Bank, the Social Security Bank, the National Investment Bank etc.
Table 5.2 shows the extent of actual divestiture.

Table 5.2
Divestiture proceeds

Year	Mode	Number of firms	Cedi value (m)
1989/90	Outright sale	3	1,280.3
1991	Sales of shares	8	2,004.6
	Lease	3	171.0
	Liquidation	22	274.4
Total		36	3,730.4
1991	Outright sale	7	8,020.6
	Sales of shares	3	205.4
	Joint ventures	3	2,275.6
	Liquidation	2	0
	Total	15	10,501.6
1992			
	Outright sale	4	1,920.0
	Sale of share	5	5,490.8
	Joint venture	2	4,181.4
	Liquidation	2	0
	Total	13	11,592.2
1993			
	Outright sale	2	2,290.0
	Sale of share	2	321.0
	Joint venture	3	3,920.0
	Liquidation	5	0
	Total	12	3,920.0
	Total cedi value	76	32,355.1
Approximate (US$)			73.8
1994			
	*Total		2,733.0

Source: Divestiture Implementation Committee.
* 1995 Budget Statement

Fiscal reform

At the heart of most adjustment programmes favoured by the International
Monetary Fund in particular, has been fiscal policy reforms. Such programmes,
according to the Fund, are directed at stabilisation of the fiscal regime as well

as restructuring the regimes (see Nashashibi 1992 p 1). The tax base in Ghana, prior to Adjustment, like in many other developing countries tended to be very narrow, excluding relatively important sectors of the economy that may not be fully monetised or encapsulated into the formal economy, such as large segments of agriculture and services (Tanzi, 1987). Tax avoidance, as the findings of the Citizens Vetting Committee[16] set up by the PNDC government in 1982 proved, was prevalent in large segments of the formal economy, particularly in the trade sector as well as among self employed professionals such as lawyers, medical practitioners, accountants and property owners.

Ghana's fiscal policy since 1983 is said to have been 'aimed at correcting the fiscal imbalances, reforming the tax system to augment revenue collection and to enhance economic incentives, increasing public and private savings, and rehabilitating the economic and social infrastructure' (Kapur 1991 p.29). The foregoing was built on a growth oriented strategy that was seen as cardinal to the whole adjustment programme. The strategy called for an increase in savings from the public sector so as to make room for higher investment. This was also aimed at achieving greater efficiency in public resource management through improvements in allocation and implementation of public investment, in the structure of the revenue system and revenue mobilisation and in the allocation of government current expenditure as well as the reform of state owned enterprises.

Revenue At the root of Ghana's fiscal policy since the launch of the Economic Recovery Programme in 1983 has been the maximisation and efficiency of revenue collection by the state. Bringing the country's fiscal programme into balance would have ordinarily warranted a cut in expenditure as well as efforts to increase both the collection and efficiency of collection of revenue. But the peculiar circumstances of the Ghanaian economy made this undesirable. Apart from in 1982 and 1983 when total expenditure as a percentage of Gross Domestic Product was lowest (see Table 5.3), government expenditure, particularly capital expenditure has gnerally been on the increase so as to bring back from the brink, the country's economic and social infrastructure. Critical to the revenue issue, is the direction of the of both direct and indirect taxes.

Table 5.3
Central government expenditure and net lending 1980-1991

	1980	1983	1984	1985	1986	1987	1988	1989	1990	1991
Economic classification										
[In percentage of total expenditure and net lending]										
Total Expenditure	96.7	97.2	97.1	95.6	96.4	95.5	96	96.2	96.4	96.9
Current Expenditure	82.2	89.4	84.9	80.3	83	75.3	74.1	72.8	75.1	74.7
Goods and services	48.4	47.9	56.9	57.4	57.5	56.5	56.7	54.8	54.5	54.2
Wages and Salaries	28.5	24.7	19.2	30.3	35.7	33.6	33	30.8	31.2	30.4
Other Goods and services	19.9	23.2	37.7	27	21.7	22.9	23.7	24	23.4	23.8
Interest payments	12.8	14.5	12.5	10.6	15.5	9.9	8	9.2	10.3	10.7
Subsidies and transfers	21	27	15.5	12.3	10	9	9.4	8.8	10.2	9.8
Capital Expenditure	14.4	7.9	12.3	15.2	13.4	17.3	19.9	18.7	18.3	19
Special Efficiency						2.8	2	4.7	3	3.2
Net Lending	3.3	2.8	2.9	4.4	3.6	4.5	4	3.8	3.6	3.1
In Percentage of GDP										
Total Expenditure										
Current Expenditure	19.1	8	9.9	13.3	13.8	13.7	13.7	13.9	13.5	14
Capital Expenditure	2.9	0.6	1.2	2.1	1.9	2.5	2.8	2.7	2.5	2.8
Total Ependiture and Net lending	20	8.2	10.2	14	14.3	14.3	14.3	14.4	14	14.5
Memorandum Items:										
Capital expenditure [broad]		0.6	1.9	3.3	5	5.4	5.8	5.1	5	5.9
Total Expenditure [broad]		8.2	11.1	15.4	19.2	19.1	18.9	18.9	18.1	19.3
Functional classification										
[In percentage of total central government expenditure]										
General Public Services	21	26.4	24.9	21.3	20.8	19.3	22	19.3		
Defence	6.3	4.6	6	7.5	6.5	6.5	3.2	3.1		
Education	17.1	20.4	20.2	18	23.9	23.9	25.7	24.3		
Health	6.4	4.4	8.6	9.8	8.3	8.3	9	10.1		
Social Security & welfare	7.2	4.3	4.2	5	5.3	6.4	6.9	7.3		
Housing and Community Amenities		1.7	2.1	2	1.9	1.9	3.5	2.6		
Other Community and Social services	3.1	1.8	2.2	1.5	1.7	1.7	1.5	2		
Economic Services2	22.7	21.6	18.9	23.8	15.4	18.6	17.9	16.9		
Interest on Public Debt	13.2	14.9	12.8	11.1	16.1	10.4	8.3	9.5		
Special Efficiency						2.9	2.1	4.9		

Notes:
1. Data for 1975 and 1980 are on a fiscal year basis (year ending March); from 1983 onward the fiscal year coincides with the calendar year
2. Includes services for agriculture, forestry and fishing, mining, manufacturing and construction, roads, and other transport and communication. Other transport and communication services

Source: Ishan Kapur et al. 1991, p.311.

The essence of fiscal reform, at least on the revenue side, was to increase both the volume and efficiency of revenue collection while establishing a greater amount of equity by expanding the tax base. To this end, efforts were

133

made through various administrative reforms as well as putting tax collection on top of the political agenda. One of the most distinguishing moves of the new PNDC administration on seizing power on the last day of 1981, was to constitute two powerful committees, the Citizens Vetting Committee [charged with bringing to book all those who had evaded their tax obligations] and the National Investigations Committee, with the remit of investigating and bringing to book, cases of economic crimes.

In addition to the above, a National Revenue Secretariat was set up [headed by a PNDC Secretary] to oversee all aspects of collection and administration of the tax regime. As part of the overhaul of the revenue machinery, the former Central Revenue Department was reorganised into an autonomous service agency and renamed Internal Revenue Service, outside the direct administrative control of the civil service. The other major revenue collection body, the Customs and Excise Department, was also reorganised with an eye for greater efficiency and autonomy. It thus became the Customs, Excise and Preventive Service with improved conditions of service to go with its new profile.

The operation of the new fiscal regime under adjustment has had a positive effect on increasing the revenue share of GDP. This increased from the low 4.6% of GDP in 1983 [itself a slight improvement on the 4.1% of 1981] reaching a peak of 13.8% of GDP in 1991, thus equalling the 1975 level (See table 5.3). Whereas the improvement has been considerable, beginning from its low base in the early 1980s, the revenue percentage of GDP is still lower than the Sub- Saharan Africa average and much lower than the total African average of 14% and 21% respectively (Kapur 1991, p.29).

The composition of revenue has also within the adjustment period altered, with individual and export taxes becoming less significant than they were. For example, individual tax constituted 8.6% of total revenue and grants in 1983 but in 1991, its ratio had declined to 5.2%. Export duties provided 28.6% of government revenue in 1983 but by 1991, this had also gone to 10.3% (see table 5.3). Corporate tax and petroleum tax have increasingly become important sources of revenue. Petroleum tax's contribution to government revenue had reached 21.7% by 1991 from a position of zero in 1984 (ibid.).

The simplification of the collection process for taxes through the establishment of a uniform rate for most imports increased the efficiency of the collection process. This reduced the opportunities for the use of discretion by individual tax officers, removing from the administration, a major area of abuse. The formal abandonment of Import Licensing with the introduction of a system of foreign exchange auction further decreased the paper work associated with the administration of import duties and another critical avenue for patronage and corruption. Another important outcome of the exchange rate reform was to increase the real value of import duty collections, for the higher exchange rate meant a larger local currency value of imports on which duty was payable.

Import duties thus increased from 2.7% of GDP in 1983 to 5% in 1991, having previously touched 6% in 1987 (Table 5.3).

Direct taxes In the area of direct taxes, emphasis was placed on the lowering of corporate taxes from the existing 55% in 1984 to 45% for businesses in agriculture, manufacturing and exporting and from 55% to 50% in 1989 for the remaining firms other than those in banking, insurance, commerce and printing. In 1991, further reduction from 45% to 35% for firms in agriculture, manufacturing, real estate, construction and services was announced, creating an environment more conducive to private savings and investment [Ishan Kapur 1991 p 33]. The rationale behind the reduction was to expand the general tax base and reduce the burden on the small base that has historically borne the burden of taxation.

Indirect taxes The reform of taxation under ERP was all encompassing, thus indirect taxes were not spared in the fiscal reform process. The major reform in this sphere took the form of the abolition of excise duties on products other than petroleum, beverages and tobacco, with the revenue loss compensated by an increase in the standard general sales tax from 10% to 20% and subsequently to 25% before being reduced first to 22.5% in 1989 and to 17.5% in 1991 (IDS 1994 p 58). In discussing indirect taxation, the increasing use of petroleum tax comes in for special attention. This form of tax has come to play a very important role in raising funds for the treasury. This rose from 1.5% of total government revenue [inclusive of grants] in 1985 to 21.7% by 1991 (see table 5.3).Indirect taxation now seems to be the preferred form of taxation adopted by Ghanaian fiscal authorities with the introduction of a Value Added Tax[17] as part of the 1995 budget statement. How this is going to fundamentally change the tax composition of government revenue is yet to be known, but evidence points to this form of tax becoming a very useful form of raising taxes in the years to come, notwithstanding the initial problems collecting VAT in a not totally monetised economy.

Government spending

During the period of decline, government expenditure, particularly, capital expenditure, plummeted from 4.5% of GDP and 19.5% of total expenditure in 1975 to a paltry 0.6% and 7.9% respectively by 1983 (Kapur et al. 1991 p 29). As part of the general trend of serious decline in government expenditure, spending on health, education, social security and welfare over the same period fell from 8.7% of GDP to 2.3% of a fast shrinking GDP.

The fall in government expenditure had a serious impact on civil and other government service wages. The fall was evident from annual wage rate increases of about 35% and an inflationary rate of 73% induced qualified professionals to leave the service, further disabling the fiscal authorities' ability to manage the system. This was particularly manifested in the relatively high percentage of taxes collected from salaried workers in comparison to private sector workers, the self employed, particularly of professional people because of the relative ease and difficulties of collection respectively.

However, the efforts of revenue collection and other fiscal policy options brought about an increase in available resources, leading to higher government expenditure, particularly capital spending, which increased from 0.6% of GDP in 1983 to 2.8% by 1991. As a percentage of total government expenditure, capital spending increased from 7.9% in 1983 to 19% in 1991 (see Table 5.3). This level of spending was needed to rehabilitate and expand economic infrastructure, having been neglected to the level of total collapse during the years of decline (see Nashashibi 1992, p.27).

Stages of fiscal reform

Fiscal reform under adjustment can be broadly divided into three overlapping phases. In the first stage [1983 and 1984], the government responded to the inherited fiscal deterioration by relying on expenditure cuts and the restoration of tax base to generate increased revenue. In stage two, covering 1985 to 1986, the objectives of fiscal policy were broadened to include fiscal rehabilitation and expansion of basic economic and social infrastructure. The third stage, beginning in 1987 emphasised further strengthening of economic incentives, particularly for private savings and investment and 'promoting equity' (Kapur et al. 1991 p 31). As indicated earlier, the stages overlapped and were not as distinctive as they appear. The three stages would now be discussed in turn.

Stage one

Restoring discipline in government finances was said to be one of the major aims of the ERP as a whole and not just fiscal policy at this stage. Thus from a fiscal perspective, the first year of the fiscal adjustment saw the budget deficit reduced from 6.3% of GDP in 1982 to 2.7% through largely a contraction of government spending from 10.2% of GDP to 8%. This was lower than even the budgeted 9.5% of GDP and was necessitated by a shortage in government revenue. The expenditure cut in turn created a government borrowing reduction from 4.3% of GDP to 2.3%, 1982 against 1983 (ibid.). The 1984 budget benefited from the impact of the exchange rate adjustment on receipts from cocoa taxes [ibid.] as well as import duties. To minimise the hardship of these fiscal policies on the average citizen during phase I, the PNDC, true to its populist credentials, made discretionary tax changes by raising the lowest taxable income tax brackets and also reduced the marginal income tax, creating in the process, a lower average effective tax rates for personal income tax. Revenue/GDP ratio also did rise in the course of this phase to 8.4% in 1984 from 5.6% in 1983, while direct budget deficits [minus expenditure financed from external sources] also came down (ibid.).

Stage two

The second instalment of the government's fiscal reform programme was introduced in the 1985 Budget Statement with emphasis shifting from rehabilitation to growth. Government capital spending was targeted at expanding public investment through the Three Year Public Investment Programme. This phase built on the progress made during the first phase. This duly necessitated a stepped up mobilisation of domestic revenue. Exchange rate adjustment contributed to higher revenue from international trade. Increased economic activity on its part yielded more tax revenue from domestic goods and services as well as corporate taxes. Total government expenditure and lending increased from 10.2% of GDP in 1984 to 14% in 1985 (see Table 5.4) led by increases in capital expenditure as well as outlays in remuneration. Capital expenditure increased from 1.2% of GDP to 4.2%. In the last year of the second stage, government expenditure was reined in, in line with revenue shortfalls.

Stage three

Fiscal policy was broadened after 1987 to encompass the efficiency and equity of the tax system. This period was also devoted to the strengthening of tax administration. This included increased efforts to strengthen incentives for private sector tax payers and generate a greater tax awareness and compliance, including all segments of the corporate sector. Aside of reductions in corporate tax rates at this stage, there was also the sharp reduction in capital gains tax to 5%, while income from mergers and acquisitions and publicly traded shares were exempted from capital gains completely. 'Withholding taxes' on dividends were also reduced from 30% to 15% in 1991 (Kapur. 1991, p.33). All these were geared at creating an environment more conducive for private savings and investment.

Fiscal deficits

Ghana was running a budgetary deficit of about 6.3% of gdp in 1982, which was itself lower than the 1980 figure of 11% of GDP (see table 5.4).

Table 5.4
Measure of central government fiscal deficit, financing and government savings 1975-1991, as % of GDP

	1975	1980	1983	1984	1985	1986	1987	1988	1989	1990	1991
Narrow surplus or deficit1											
Including grants	-7.6	-11	-2.7	-1.8	-2.2	0.1	0.5	0.4	0.7	0.2	1.9
Excluding grants	-7.6	-11.1	-2.7	-2.1	-2.7	-0.7	-0.3	-0.7	-0.8	-1.3	0.4
Broad Surplus or deficit											
Including grants			-2.7	-2.3	-3	-3.3	-2.4	-2.8	-2.1	-2.4	-1.2
Excluding grants			-2.7	-3.1	-4.1	-5.5	-5.1	-5.3	-5.3	-5.5	-4.4
Financing (narrow balance)	7.6	11	2.7	1.8	2.2	-0.1	-0.5	-0.4	-0.7	-0.2	-1.9
Foreign (net)		0.9	0.4	0.7	1	-1.1	-0.2	0.2	0.3	1.3	0.9
Borrowing			1.1	1.9	2.8	2.6	3.2	4	3.8	3	2.2
Repayments			-0.7	-1.2	-1.8	-3.7	-3.3	-3.8	-3.5	-1.8	-1.2
Domestic (net)	7.6	10.1	2.3	1.1	1.2	1	-0.4	-0.6	-1.1	-1.4	-2.8
of which:											
Banking system	7	3.8	1.4	1.1	0.9	0.5	-1	-0.9	-1	-1.1	-2.1
Government Savings2											
[narrow basis]											
Including grants	-1.9	-8.1	-1.8	-0.3	0.5	2.5	3.7	3.8	4	3.2	5.1
Excluding grants	-1.9	-8.3	-1.8	-0.6	0.1	1.7	2.9	2.7	2.5	1.8	3.6
[broad basis]											
Including grants			-1.8	0.1	1.1	4	5.5	5.2	5.7	4.9	6.8
Excluding grants			-1.8	-0.6	0.1	1.7	2.9	2.7	2.5	1.8	3.6

Source: Kapur et al. 1991, pp.33-34.
1. Negative number indicate a deficit.
2 Calculated at the difference between total revenue and current expenditure including special efficiency.
Note. The official Ghana budget is constructed on a 'narrow' basis, ie. excluding capital expenditure financed through external project aid, as well as corresponding project grants and loans but including foreign programme grants. The 'broad' basis on the other hand, include capital expenditure financed through external project aid.

The PNDC, on coming to power in 1981, clamped down on government expenditure as well as demanding tax arrears, particularly from the private professional class, be paid with penalties. The coercive state apparatus being deployed to effect this. The deficit was therefore reduced to 2.7% of GDP in

1983 (IDS Bulletin [1994], 25:3 p.59). The narrow deficit [including grants] then shifted into positive in 1986, growing to 0.7% of GDP by 1989 before settling down to 0.2% of GDP by 1990 (Kapur 1991, p.36). This deficit reduction occurred against a background of increased government consumption expenditure growing from 6.5% of GDP to 10.6 [1987 vrs 1982]. The reduction has been much celebrated by some commentators [e.g. J Clark Leith & Michael Lofchie] but the government account went into heavy deficits again in the early 1990s when the forced 'restraint' on labour cost proved unsustainable in the run off to the November 1991 elections. There has been some confusion on whether government deficits actually did decline [and creating a surplus of 0.7% of GDP as claimed by Kapur and his IMF colleagues] (1991 p.36).

This confusion clears if the element of programme grants, virtually non-existent in 1983, but which had become a major source of revenue, reaching 1.5% of GDP by 1990,[18] is taken into account. This extra source of revenue made it possible for targets for the 'narrow' balance to be achieved. The broad deficit, including grants, however, remained stable between 1983 - 1990 fluctuating between 2.1 and 3.3% of GDP.

From the foregoing, it is tempting to conclude that Ghana's fiscal reform programme was an unbridled success. The IMF in particular has been over the top in awarding its usual 'success' tag to the programme [an award that seems to automatically come to Ghana from both the Bank and the Fund] (ibid. p.29). The Ghanaian authorities on the other hand, have been more cautious. The Minister of Finance [who had been in the seat since 1982] in presenting the government's 1995 budget statement to Parliament acknowledged that:

> while the reforms [fiscal] undertaken since 1986 have improved collection and introduced some professionalism in the tax administration, the basic issue of voluntary compliance is still far from satisfactory. Incentives, educational programmes and administrative penalties have not been able to raise tax compliance to levels comparable to other economies. The thrust of the programmes of revenue institutions this year would be to achieve a higher level of tax compliance still (Budget Statement 1995, p.38).

Monetary policy

The general objectives of monetary policy in developing countries are usually related to money and credit control, price stabilisation and economic growth. It is argued that for developing countries, price stability is the most important task of monetary policy. This is said to be so because developing countries, particularly the least developed countries [LDCs], generally suffer higher rates of inflation than developed countries.[19] However, the particular peculiarities of the Ghanaian problem required radical measures that did not necessarily conform to the ordinary prescriptions of monetary policy.

The new monetary policy that came into effect in mid-1983 as part of the ERP, was formulated "in conjunction with the IMF" (Bank of Ghana 1992, p.206) with the objective of restricting the growth of money supply within quantitative terms. "This was done by preparing annual programmes based on the banking systems monetary survey in which quantitative performance criteria were set under IMF guidance as well as surveillance" (ibid.). The policy and its implementing measures required a range of instruments and institutional reforms to be effective. The thrust of monetary policy from 1983 - 86 [ERP 1] was to reduce the growth of money supply from annual average of 40% between 1975 and 1983 to a range of 10 - 15% by 1986. Towards this end, the Bank of Ghana introduced various policy measures relating to interest rates and credit with the aim of encouraging the mobilisation of domestic savings and channelling the flow of credit to the most productive sectors of the economy.

The traditional instruments of monetary policy prior to reform have been quantitative ceilings on domestic asset creation of the banking system and reserve requirements. These were specified in the form of definite bank ceilings on credit and other assets of the banking system and sectoral credit ceilings. Other instruments included the discount rate on government paper and borrowing and lending rates, all of which were determined administratively by the Central Bank.

Monetary reform was a kingpin in the adjustment process. ERP II recognised that "... successful implementation of ERP II on a well functioning and broadly based financial system mobilising and efficiently channelling resources into productive activity" (Ghana 1987b, p.23). The Central Bank in particular, was revolutionised in the way it operated and handled monetary aspects of the reform agenda. Monetary policy under adjustment is best looked at under specific sub-topics:

Banking and allied institutions The reform of the banking sector was given a very high profile in the government's monetary policy. It had been recognised over the years that Ghanaian banks had been consistently under performing and needed to be revamped and re-oriented to achieve national development objectives. The ERP II thus recognised that "... successful implementation of ERP II depends on a well functioning and broadly based financial system mobilising and efficiently channelling resources into productive activity" (Ghana 1987b, p.23). ERP II expected of the financial sector, improved performance in two basic areas:

- The efficiency of the system was to be improved;
- The financial sector as a whole needed to be restructured.

But even before the formal launch of the Financial Sector Adjustment Programme in 1988, the banking system had been undergoing major restructuring aimed at creating a sound and efficient financial base to support the economic recovery programme. This was to do away with the root cause of Ghanaian banking and financial regression which ranged from inappropriate macro economic policies to poor accounting and management policies (GCB, [QED] vol. 13 no. 3 & 4 p.1).

The government decided in 1987 to tackle the issue of banking sector under performance by appointing a private sector/world bank group in 1987 to conduct a diagnostic study of the banking sector. The study revealed that many banks were financially weak, unprofitable, illiquid, undercapitalised and in a few cases [such as the National Savings & Credit Bank], technically bankrupt. The causes of the distress was attributed by the study to:

- rapid changes in the macro environment under ERP;
- past political interference
- poor management practices.

Efforts to liberalise trade and other economic activities under ERP coupled with the continuous adjustment of exchange rates to reflect underlying economic conditions exposed many of the banks' corporate customers to foreign exchange risks and made them unable to service their maturing obligations, which in turn increased the non performing loans of the banks and adversely affected their liquidity and capital adequacy ratios.

Since the causes of the banking sector's distress were largely due to exogenous factors, the state's approach to the problem was broad based, policy oriented and directed at the totality of the financial system. The Financial Sector Adjustment Programme [FINSAP] was therefore initiated in 1988 and was supported by IMF and the World Bank with a credit of SDR 72, 000,000 and other resources from the Swiss and Japanese governments. The objectives were stated as follows:

- Enhance the soundness of the banking sector;
- Improve deposit mobilisation and increased efficiency in credit allocation;
- Develop efficient monetary and capital markets;
- Improve mechanisms for rural finance.

The Programme of Action designed and implemented as part of FINSAP included:

- A review and revision of the legal framework and environment for banking;
- Improved supervision and external audit of banks including improving bank of Ghana supervisory skills and effectiveness through training to apply internationally accepted audit and accounting standards.
- Restructuring banking institutions, after identifying problems and weaknesses of each bank, through preparing and implementing short term turn around restructuring plans.

Institutional reforms under FINSAP The Financial liberalisation exercise, which FINSAP signalled, could not be brought to fruition without institutional reform. Thus institutional reform was to be undertaken as part of the exercise. FINSAP aimed at strengthening the financial institutions, expanding the scope of services and improving the efficiency of financial intermediation in the country. Reform policies adopted were to enhance the soundness of banking institutions, increasing their capital base, restructuring their portfolios, upgrading their management and improving the regulatory framework and the development of money and capital markets.

The fulfilment of the capital and money market development aspirations involved the establishment of a Discount House in 1988, the licensing of a number of new commercial and merchant banks including the Ecobank, Continental Acceptances Ltd and the Meridian Bank. The Ghana Stock Exchange was also established in 1990 in pursuance of this objective with an initial market capitalisation of $30m, but which had increased to $803m by June 1994 (African Economic Digest 12 Sept. 1994, p.11).

To strengthen the financial sector, a Non - Performing Assets Recovery Trust was set up by the government to take over the portfolio of Non - Performing Assets of State Owned Enterprises and by so doing, the government relieved the banks of the burden of carrying these non - performing assets on their books. Most of these non - performing assets in the form of loans and other such facilities were guaranteed in the first place by the state. The First Finance Company Ltd was also established by the government as part of the broad financial sector restructuring as a venture capital company to raise funds from foreign and local sources for investment in potentially viable enterprises (GCB [QER vol. 13 nos. 3&4] p.2).

The institutional rationalisation also involved the consolidation of existing state owned banks with the aim of making them more efficient and viable. Thus the National Savings and Credit Bank, described earlier by the diagnostic team as technically bankrupt, was absorbed by the Social Security Bank in May 1994 (BS 1995 p 44). Furthermore, the state's shares in Ghana Commercial Bank,

National Investment Bank and the Social Security Bank are scheduled for floatation with the state selling off 60% of its 100% shareholding in each bank as a means of encouraging private sector involvement in the ownership and operation of these banks (Budget Statement 1995, pp 44-45).

Implementation of the first phase of FINSAP was substantially completed by December 1990 ahead of schedule. Bank of Ghana purchased non - performing assets from the banks at the cost of ¢52bn under the programme to recapitalise as well as taking off these non realisable assets off the books of the banks.[20] The purchase cost was covered by the issue of FINSAP bonds to the banks for ¢30.2bn while the balance was set off against obligations owed to the government or the central bank by the banks. Two categories of FINSAP bonds were issued;

- State owned enterprises non-performing assets [loans] were replaced with a series of bonds with five year maximum maturity and an interest rate of 12% percent per annum;
- Private Sector Enterprise [PSE] non - performing assets with the banks were replaced with bonds of maximum maturity of ten years negotiable in the second market but only discountable with the central bank at the discretion of the latter. These do not automatically qualify as secondary reserves asset and may be redeemed pre-maturely at the discretion the Bank of Ghana.

Policy related banking reform As part of the diagnostic team's report, each banks, rather than the central bank, were authorised to determine their borrowing and lending rates. Sectoral ceilings, which had hitherto been used by past governments to direct credit to priority areas of the economy, such as the 20% mandatory lending to agriculture, was also abolished (GCB, [QER vol. 13 no. 3-4] p.1).

Other restructuring measures included the injection of cash equity into some banks, conversion of long term loans due to government and the central bank into equity and the assumption of all foreign credit obligations of the banks outstanding prior to the launch of ERP. Measures were also introduced to upgrade and improve the banks'policies, procedures and systems. Boards of Directors and Managing Directors of all distressed banks were changed and the banks' operational management capacity strengthened. Phase II of FINSAP was also put in place to address corporate sector distress and the revamping of the executive capabilities as well as systems not of the commercial and development banks, as has been the case in Phase I, but of the central bank.

Policy reform included a new legislation, PNDC Law 225, which was passed in 1989, paving the way for effective reform of the banking sector. Under Law 225, the reserve requirements of banks was reduced from forty - sixty percent of total deposit liabilities to 42%, thereby releasing extra resources for investment and loans (GCB, QER vol. 3 & 4 1990, p.2).

Credit/money supply

The burden of financing the large government deficits of the 1970s and the early 1980s created a credit squeeze for the private sector. The state, unable to access commercial and other private credits, came to rely almost exclusively on bank credit. Increasingly, this had the effect of crowding out the domestic private borrower. In 1970 for example, the government's overall share of domestic credit was 49%, but in 1982 and 1983, this had ballooned to 70.63% and 89.6% of all credit in the banking system respectively (see Table 5.5). With the government taking up such credits, it was not surprising that real interest rate were negative 13.2% and 11.7% respectively.

Table 5.5
Selected indicators of economic performance

	1982	1983	1984	1985	1986	1987	1988	1989
Real GDP growth	-61	-2.9	7.6	5.1	5.2	4.8	6.2	6.1
Inflation rate	22.3	122.8	39.6	10.4	24.6	39.8	31.4	25.2
Exchange rate cedis/dollar	2.75	27.87	35.99	54.37	90	192.37	202.34	300
Parallel rate	120	97	100	145	218	175.3	292.29	365.44
Cocoa exports ('000 tons)	163.4	148.9	171.8	195.8	198.6	218.9	221.1	282.1
Producer price ('000/ton)	12	20	30	56.6	85.5	140	174	186
% of FOB receipts to farmers	38	24	25	24	28	37	40.1	43.6
Gold production ('000 ounces)	330.5	281.3	288	299.6	292	323.5	383	421
Government revenue & grant as percentage of GDP	5.1	5.4	8.3	11.8	14.4	14.9	14.5	15.9
Gov't exp. as % of GDP	10.8	8	10	14	14.3	14.3	14.2	15.2
Revenue as % of GDP	1	0.7	1.5	2.1	1.9	2.5	2.8	2.8
Overall deficits as % of GDP	5.4	2.6	-1.8	-2.2	0.1	0.5	0.4	0.8
Minimum wage (cedis per day)	12	25	35	70	90	112.5	120	170
Real minimum wage	0.33	0.31	0.31	0.57	0.59	0.52	0.43	0.48
% change M2	42.4	42	39.1	62.7	53.7	50.4	43.1	29.4
M2/GDP ratio	19	12.8	12.3	16	16.5	17.1	17.7	17.8
Government borrowing as % M2	70.6	89.6	48.2	50.1	35.1	17.6	6.3	-3.9
Nominal Interest rate	8	11	14.5	16.5	18.5	21.5	17	21.5
Real interest rate	-13.2	-11.7	0.31	0.57	0.59	0.52	0.43	0.48

Source: Bank of Ghana.

On credit policy, it was recognised that the main cause of rapid monetary expansion and high inflation rates before the onset of the Economic Recovery Programme was government borrowing. The credit policy was therefore geared primarily to curtail government borrowing and dependence on the banking system to finance budgetary deficits. Government credit was to be kept under tight control. Quantitative performance criteria were set to ensure financial discipline. For the rest of the economy, credit was to be re-directed in favour of the productive sector. This was a departure from previous practise when internal trade and service sectors absorbed 22% of credit to the private sector.

The above, combined with the previous crowding out effect of government borrowing, was said to have starved the productive sector of funds. All sectors of the economy were allocated credit ceilings initially [with the priority productive sectors adequately catered for]. However, the banks experienced a situation of excess liquidity when the favoured productive areas failed to take up its credit allocation as a result of the under capacity arising from previous neglect. The banks got round the problem of excess liquidity which threatened their profit margins by paying very low rates on deposits while charging high interest rates on lending.

The newly introduced sectoral credits proved a failure and were abolished in 1988 to give way to bank specific ceilings only to be abolished in 1992 in favour of further liberalisation of the financial markets to levels never experienced in the country's banking history. This further move included deregulation of interest on both deposits and borrowing. Market forces were to determine the direction of interest rates in the new climate. It is however, worth asking how effective in the national interest is the market in determining interest rates when the market itself, assuming classical theory even holds valid, is seriously imperfect. The Finance Ministry must exert a major influence -both externally and internally - on the adjustment of interest rates.

Interest rates/money supply

A new flexibility, which had hitherto been absent from Ghana's interest rate administration was introduced to ensure positive interest rates as well as provide incentive returns for development. The policy came into effect in October 1983 with all interest rates being raised by the government by 35 - 40%. This brought the savings deposit rate from 14% to 19%. This was aimed at achieving positive real interest rates between 1985 and mid 1986. The spread between key deposit and lending rates was narrowed while interest rates for priority sectors were adjusted to bring them almost to par with regular lending rates. In September 1987, the liberalisation was further deepened when the maximum and minimum lending rates were abolished, enabling banks to set their rates. A weekly auction for government paper was also introduced to help the market determine the discount rate. What I have tried to documents is the practice adopted by Governments to conform with both international market developments and conformist advice from the international finance agencies.

Devaluation/ exchange rate

The devaluation route becomes more dramatic when juxtaposed with the background of historical antipathy. Refusal to devalue had become a political sticking point, treating the cedi exchange rate as a matter of national pride (Richards 1989, p.79). Rather than reform exchange rates in the face of balance of payments problems, Ghanaian governments, as is the case with most African governments, have historically found it easier to administratively control imports. Unfortunately, administrative control in practice has often led to an over - valuation of the local currency and its exchange rate. Dependence on administrative instruments minimises the need to adjust exchange rates to reflect the differences between domestic inflation and inflation rates of major partners. In a perverse way, this encourages the ever increasing over - valuation of the exchange rate because the more over - valued the currency, the more largesse the government is able to bestow on its selected few who gain access to official foreign exchange.

In the years since Busia's overthrow, - after that administration taken the decisive steps to adjust the cedi exchange rate - [see chapter two], the exchange rate was left untouched while the economy experienced serious inflation, resulting in severe over - valuation of the currency. In 1972 for example, the parallel market exchange rate was 28% higher than the nominal rate. By 1976, with the cedi still valued at ¢1.15 to the US dollar, the parallel rate was ¢2.9 to the dollar, expressing a 60% over - valuation by the official rate. By 1982, the cedi had fallen to ¢2.75 to the dollar at the official rate but the parallel rate was a high ¢61.6 to the dollar, an over valuation of 22.4 times the official rate (Wood 1988, p.122).

On previous fears and links between devaluation and coups, e.g. Acheampong overthrowing Busia and the Limann's administration's overtures to the IMF/WB partly responsible for the overthrow of that regime by the PNDC, Dr. Abbey, the leading technocrat of the reform programme noted:

> Procrastination of successive governments over a prolonged period in refusing to adopt appropriate stabilisation policies destroyed the country's economy, giving the widespread belief that a stabilisation policy, especially devaluation of the exchange rate inevitably conjured up threats of a coup in Ghana. Consequently, a succession of governments had held on until the bitter end before attempting any sort of stabilisation

policy so that economic conditions were particularly bad when they finally did make policy changes (Abbey 1987, p.4).

It must be recognised that African economies, including Ghana's , are so open, with exports and imports routinely accounting for approximately 40% of GNP[21] in many countries. Thus changes in the exchange rate have a very broad effect on the economy as a whole. The control of exchange rates has therefore been historically important in providing goods to political clients and therefore making its reform even more difficult. The PNDC, once it had decided to go in for the reforms, summed up the position on devaluation of the cedi thus:

> Foreign exchange is a scarce resource in Ghana and if official banking system fails to recognise its scarcity premium, an avenue is provided for racketeers to extract rents. Providing foreign exchange at rates well below the actual transaction prices really means that the government is subsidising such racketeering.[22]

A Bank of Ghana official summed up the effect of devaluation on the collective psyche when he claimed "Devaluation is war. You have to have a strategy."[23] The PNDC's ability to implement its devaluation objective with relatively little resistance from a population that has been known to be vehemently anti devaluation, is probably a tribute to the regime's strategic brilliance. Yes, the regime had a number of favourable elements going for it, including co-opting the more radical left wing element of the body politic into its fold. Once the internal debate had been settled either by the power of argument or the use of brute military force in driving the radical left into exile, there was very little potent opposition to the deal.

Of the elements going for the PNDC as mentioned in the preceding chapter, the *de facto* price levels of importables and to some extent foodstuffs reflected the market value of the cedi and not the official rate in the period leading up to the ERP. Thus the initial devaluation was from the point of price level changes, not significant. But the history and near mythology associated with devaluation in the Ghanaian body politic still had to be tackled. And it was here that strategic brilliance was displayed by the Ghanaian leadership.

Rather than announce formal devaluation, the government in April 1983 introduced a system of bonuses for exports and surcharges for imports, creating a *de facto* weighted average exchange rate of about ₵25 to the dollar. This compared to the standing ₵2.75 to the dollar and which had been static since August 1978, notwithstanding an annual inflation rates averaging 60% in between. The system of bonuses and surcharges was to persuade recipients of foreign exchange to turn over their proceeds and provide finance for the bonuses/surcharges regime.[24] Although this approach did not please the IMF, who argued that the strategy was tantamount to the introduction of multiple exchange rates, which in the eyes of the Fund was an unacceptable transgression of its fastidious code, and that the system was going to be difficult to administer, the Ghanaian government stuck to its strategy.

The government's position was that this was an essential first step, mindful of the psychological effect of the word devaluation on the populace. The strategy was therefore pursued for six months until October 1983 when the government felt embolden enough to formally peg the cedi to ₵30/$. Price controls, hitherto ineffective, were thus abandoned at the same time. I have given this illustration in some detail to suggest how management of national economies in Africa must sometimes diverge from advice of powerful influential financial agencies - to protect national popularity but also play an integral part in the democratic evolution and accountability of world economy and social development.

Once the taboo of devaluation had been broken, the government found it possible to adjust the rate on three occasions, with the nominal rate rising to ₵50/$ in December 1984. Periodic devaluation began to have effect on domestic prices, particularly the three relatively small devaluations of 1985, which further depreciated the cedi by 20% (Leith 1993, p.269). At the end of 1985, real exchange rate stood at 57, using 1957 as a base year [100] (see table 5.6). In June 1986, a further devaluation of 50% was announced in the budget, raising the nominal exchange rate to ₵90/$. This was said to be aimed at improving returns to exporters.

Table 5.6
Indicators of change in the Ghanaian economy

	1982	1983	1984	1985	1986	1987	1988	1989
INCOME AND PRICES								
1. Real GDP (cedis b, 1985 prices)	316	318	326	343	361	378	402	
2. Real GDP/capita (cedis, 1985 prices)	27,55	26,68	26,346	26,969	27,654	28,243	28,430	
EXTERNAL SECTOR								
1. Merchandise exports (US$,m)	607	439	566	632	773	827	881	807
2. Merchandise imports (US,m)	589	500	533	669	713	952	993	999
3. Current account balance (US	-109	-174	-39	-134	-43	-97	-66	-98
4. Nominal exchange rate (US$/cedi, avg.)	0.3636	0.2899	0.0283	0.0185	0.112	0.0068	0.005	0.0037
5. Real exchange rate indicator								
[cedi/SDR, 1957=100]	9	14	40	57	88	123	133	141
6. Real producer price of cocoa (1963=100)	31	14	17	23	34	37	49	43
GOVERNMENT SECTOR								

1. Government expenditure (cedis, b)	9.704	15.175	27.485	47.89	73.327	106.987	149.88
2. Government revenue (cedis, b)	4.856	10.242	22.642	40.311	73.626	111.046	153.791
3. Deficit (-) or surplus (cedis, b)	4.848	-4.933	-4.843	7.579	0.299	4.059	3.911

Sources: IMF International Statistics, for all but line II.6: Ghana Cocoa Board, for line II.6.

By the middle of 1986, the task of constantly raising exchange rates had become politically daunting and a system of auction[25] was inaugurated in September 1986 which pushed the responsibility of adjusting the exchange rate to "market forces" and the central bank. An amount of foreign exchange was made available each week and bids were accepted from importers and other users of foreign exchange. The interaction between the bids and the amount available become the rate for that week. This removed 'responsibility' from government and also got the IMF off the back of the Finance Ministry as to when and how much the next devaluation should be. But of course, it placed power in the hands of bidders who could effectively distort prices in favour of their interests - which were not coincident with the national or indeed stable international interests.

In February 1988, foreign bureaus were established to mop up the foreign exchange available from the parallel market and other sources and informal sectors. Private operators were licensed by demand and supply. The bureau rates and the auction then began to converge and by August 1990, the bureau rates were within 5% of the auction rate, although by the end of January 1995, the bureau rate was ₵1080/$ while the Bank of Ghana sold to other banks at ₵980/$, a 9% differentiation.[26] The effect of this was gradually to institutionalise financial power against various trading interests, as opposed to manufacturing and allied interests, in the Ghanaian economy. The use of devaluation as a major policy tool of monetarism is probably the most prominent legacy of adjustment on the Ghanaian psyche within the last decade.

Growth

A major feature of the Ghanaian economy since the early 1970s has been the role of growth in first the decline, and later the resuscitation of the economy. The Ghanaian economy experienced an overall decline in GDP in the pre-ERP era. The decline was accompanied by shifts in types of economic activity. Growth rates, in agriculture and industry became even more negative in the late 1970s to the early 1980s. The negative growth recorded in the key industrial and agricultural sector was accompanied more devastatingly, by a shift to trading and government consumption. In 1979-1981, for example, the share of retail and wholesale trade in GDP rose from 14% to 26% in addition to the growth of formal trading related activities, a significant growth in parallel market growth. Transactions that had hitherto gone through the books via the formal sector increasingly left the latter and became largely unreported. The parallel market thus became a very significant sector of the economy as the formal economy deteriorated. In a study of this phenomenon, May found that, by 1982, the parallel market had grown to about 32% of GDP (May 1985).

A Growth oriented fiscal policy was adopted from the very beginning of the ERP. After the stabilisation phase of the early ERP years, ERP II became very focused on growth. The strategy was given enhanced backing via the instrumentality of the IMF's SAF/ESAF facilities drawn between 1987-91. This approach involved increases in public sector savings to leave room for higher investments. The savings were to be achieved partly from greater public resource management through improvements in allocation and administration of public investments in infrastructure and revenue mobilisation, and reform of state enterprises.

The goals for ERP II were to ensure economic growth at around 5% per annum in real terms, stimulation of significant increases in savings and investments, improvement in public sector management , and placing the public sector on a sound footing (Gov't of Ghana, 1987b). To give practical impetus to the growth strategy, government capital expenditure [including foreign financed capital] rose from 1.9% of GDP in 1984 to an average of 5.3% of GDP for the 1988-1990 period. The growth strategy generated an average of 5% growth in GDP between 1983-1991 (Kapur 1991, p.4) while between 1992 and 1993, a good agricultural performance led to a growth of 5% (ISSER 1993). By 1991, therefore, the Ghanaian economy was 40% larger than it was in 1984 (Lecher 1994).

Financing of Ghana's adjustment programme

The most critical elements of the adjustment programme has been the availability and accessibility of external funding to the reformers and reforming sectors. From a low point of 0.6% of central government revenue and grants at the start of the programme in 1983, such grants became a prominent feature of government revenue, reaching 10.4% of all revenue and grants by 1990 (Kapur 1991, p.30). The success or otherwise of the programme hinged on such credits, during the critical first decade of the programme. The significance of external funding at the launch of the programme is appreciated more if one recognises the perilous state of the country's debt position. Ghana's external debt stood at 105.7% of GDP at the end of 1982 [27] (Sarris & Sham 1991, p.3).

The IMF played the lead role in providing external resources for the adjustment programme during the first three year period - the ERP I. The fund provided 60% of the $1bn channelled to supporting the programme between 1983-1985 (Loxley 1988, p.24). The Fund's support was essentially made up of a one year stand-by facility in 1984-85 aimed "at establishing a foundation for economic growth and viable external payments position" (Heller 1988, p.36). The World Bank provided 13% of funding during this phase while bilateral donors made up the rest.

The lead responsibility of the Fund during ERP I reflected the fund role in macro economic stabilisation, narrowing the gap between official and parallel rates of the cedi, curbing inflation by cutting government aggregate demand, removing price controls and providing foreign exchange to ease import strangulation (Toye 1990, p.52). The Bank on the other hand, concentrated on programme aid to support balance of payments and projects lending to support rehabilitation. (See Table 5.7).

Table 5.7
Grants and loans 1983 - 1991 (US$m)

	1983	1984	1985	1986	1987	1988	1989	1990	1991
Capital Inflows:									
ODA*	110	258	224	358	437	499	569	629	622
Medium term debt	114	170	153	133	109	118	56	51	35
IMF	340	218	124	38	149	210	188	131	62
Total	564	646	501	529	695	827	813	811	719
Payments:									
Debt	125	115	248	251	182	208	184	123	122
Interest	82	101	106	105	126	142	118	106	105
IMF	16	4	0	22	174	255	184	111	66
Arrears	0	208	57	4	71	30	45	25	0
Total	223	428	411	382	553	635	531	365	293
Net position#	341	218	90	147	142	192	282	446	426

* Overseas Development Assistance.
# The (effective) realisable inflow of funds.
Source: Jeffrey Herbst 1993, p.20.

The table above [5.7] indicates a high level of IMF funding in the early years on the recovery programme. Indeed, the IMF commitment of $340m in 1983 was the highest level of assistance extended to Ghana during the whole period.

When the ERP II was launched in 1987, the Fund took a secondary position to the Bank in financing the programme, recognising that the programme had moved from stabilisation to structural reforms. As the table above indicates, the

Fund's commitments were progressively stepped down while official development assistance and medium term financing, in which the IDA of the World Bank Group and the core Bank itself played leading roles respectively.

The peculiar short term nature of the Fund's commitments created its own problems for the pursuance of ERP II. To ameliorate the high levels of repayments arising from the Fund's commitments in Phase I, Ghana was invited to draw on another newly introduced facility, the Enhanced Structural Adjustment Fund. The ESAF was timely, for it had a ten year loan period [moving the Fund to medium to long term financing, a field which had been an exclusive Bank preserve] with a five and a half year period of grace and substantially lower interest rates.[28]

While the Bank's SALs and Sectoral Adjustment Loans therefore relieved the economy of pressing payments schedules and also provided needed funding for infrastructural resuscitation, the Fund's willingness to make available to Ghana progressively cheaper money enabled the economy to stop short of being choked to death under the burden of a heavy repayment schedule. As an example of this, in 1985, out of the total inflow $501m as development assistance, only $90m effectively came into the economy as repayments stood at a colossal $411m.

The post ERP II saw attempts geared at consolidating the various funding options available to the country. Emphasis continued to be placed on capacity enhancing of economic infrastructure. This had led to public investment increasing from the negligible levels at the beginning of the programme to 8.2% of GDP in 1991.[29] For the period 1989 to 1993, a total of $4129.5m was pumped into the economy by way of disbursement. This figure is exclusive of direct foreign investment in the private sector (OECD 1995, p.96). Total grants for the same period amounted to $1967.5m with ODA loans also coming to $2062.3m (ibid.).

Table 5.8
Official aid flows from OECD to Ghana 1989-1993

	1989	1990	1991	1992	1993	1989	1990	1991	1992	1993
			Disbursement in US dollars							
1. TOTAL RECEIPTS NET						2. TOTAL ODA NET				
DAC COUNTRIES										
Australia	0.7	0.8	0.6	0.4	0.4	0.7	0.8	0.6	0.4	0.4
Austria	8.1	2	2.3	1.4	0.5	8.1	2	2.3	1.4	0.5
Belgium	0.6	0.1	13.8	1	0.6	0.1	0.2	2.2	0.7	0.6
Canada	38.6	27	38.8	37	32	39.8	28.4	39.9	38.7	29.2
Denmark	3.7	3.2	3.5	6.1	13.5	3.7	3.2	3.5	6.1	13.2
Finland	0.1	0.5	2.3	0.6	1.6	0.1	0.5	2.3	0.6	0.2
France	9.6	19.7	28.3	72.9	23.2	10.4	11.7	23.6	43.9	23.6
Germany	47.9	96.7	116	32.7	48	47.2	66	124.7	24	51.2

Ireland	0	0	0	0.1	0.1	0	0	0	0.1	0.1
Italy	9.9	-8.7	15	18.9	4.1	14.5	10.5	12.4	17	4.2
Japan	97.9	73.3	115.1	69.5	22.2	97.9	71.9	116.1	71.3	83.1
Netherlands	21.4	39.2	15.7	46.5	16	20.7	24.8	15.1	41.5	17.8
Norway	-3.1	-9.7	12.8	4.3	-2.4	0.5	0.6	12.8	1.6	0.6
Spain	1.5	3.2	0.5	0	0.1	1.5	3.2	0.5	0	0.1
Sweden	11.9	0.9	1.6	2.5	3.6	6.5	2	2.5	2.1	3.6
Switzerland	5.4	3.7	11.6	0.7	1.2	5.4	3.7	11.6	0.7	1.2
United Kingdom	241.3	36.9	134.2	126.8	138.5	71.9	22.3	53.8	55.5	36.9
United States	27	13	25	27	45	23	13	25	27	42
Total	522.5	301.9	536.9	448.5	348	351.9	264.9	448.6	332.7	308.5

MULTILATERAL

AfDB	28	36.2	19.1	15.2	1.5	-	-	-	-	-
AfDF	2	2.9	4.1	23.5	21.6	2	2.9	4.1	23.5	21.6
CEC	22.3	27	28.4	65.9	59.8	19.6	20.1	27.1	62.1	60.9
IBRD	-9	-10	-12	-12.1	-13	-	-	-	-	-
IDA	146	184	195	167.6	201.5	146	184	195	167.6	201.5
IFAD	0.2	1.4	1.8	1.3	1.6	0.2	1.4	1.8	1.3	1.6
IFC	2.3	97.1	18.1	10.1	92.7	-	-	-	-	-
IMF	165.6	61.6	159		-11.4	165.6	61.6	159	-	-11.4
UNDP	8.7	8.3	11.5	9.4	7.4	8.7	8.3	11.5	9.4	7.4
UNTA	1.4	1.5	1.6	1.3	1.5	1.4	1.5	1.6	1.3	1.5
UNICEF	2.5	2	2.9	4.1	4.4	2.5	2	2.9	4.1	4.4
UNHCR	0.2	0.2	0.6	0.6	4.3	0.2	0.2	0.6	0.6	4.3
WFP	17.4	10.4	14.1	6.3	15	17.4	10.4	14.1	6.3	15
Other multilateral	2.8	4.2	4.3	3.5	3.2	2.8	4.2	4.3	3.5	3.2
Arab agencies	-2.8	1	2.6	4.2	-0.7	-2.8	1	2.6	4.2	-0.7
TOTAL	387.5	427.7	451	300.9	389.4	363.4	297.4	424.6	283.9	309.3
Arab countries	2.2	1.1	8.9	-0.3	3.4	2.2	1.1	8.9	-0.3	3.4
CEC+EU	358.2	217.4	355.4	371.1	303.9	189.5	162	262.8	251	208.6
TOTAL	912.2	730.5	996.8	749.1	740.8	717.6	563.4	882.1	616.3	621.2

3. ODA GROSS
DAC COUNTRIES
4. GRANTS

Australia	-	-	-	-	-	0.7	0.8	0.6	0.4	0.4
Austria	7.6	-	-	-	-	0.5	2	2.3	1.4	0.5
Belgium	-	-	1.6	-	-	0.1	0.2	0.5	0.7	0.6
Canada	0	0	0	0	0	39.8	94.9	39.9	38.7	29.2
Denmark	0	0	0	0	0	5	3.2	3.5	6.1	13.2
Finland	0	0	0	0	0.1	0.1	0.5	2.3	0.6	0.1
France	8.5	6	11	25.8	7.4	3.7	6.4	14.9	21.1	19.7
Germany	31	22.4	28.9	5.1	30.7	16.2	275.4	141.4	23.5	24.9
Ireland	0	0	0	0	0	0	0	0	0.1	0.1
Italy	13.5	8.6	10.6	4.4	1.3	1	1.9	1.8	12.6	2.9
Japan	69.8	4201	79.2	49	52.1	28.1	29.8	36.8	22.3	33.5
Netherlands	8.8	11.5	2.4	26.3	8.5	11.9	13.3	12.7	15.4	9.5
Norway	0	0	0	0	0	0.5	0.6	12.8	1.6	0.6
Spain	1.4	3.2	0.4	0	0	0.1	0.1	0.1	0	0.1
Sweden	0	0	0	0	0	6.5	2	2.5	2.1	3.6
Switzerland	0	0	0	0	0	5.4	3.7	11.6	0.7	1.2
United Kingdom	1.8	2.6	0.5	1	0.5	75.7	25.8	59.4	60.5	41.2
United States	7	7	1	0	0	21	8	162	27	42
TOTAL	149.3	103.3	135.6	111.6	100.5	216.3	468.7	505	235	223.4
MULTILATERAL	327.8	264.8	387.3	209.4	240.7	51.5	42.1	47	84.8	92.5
Arab countries	7.2	6.1	12.7	3.2	2.8	0	0	0	0.5	0.6

CEC+EU	65.9	58.7	71.8	67.6	55.8	132.3	341.9	246.2	199.6	168.9
TOTAL	484.3	374.2	535.6	324.1	344.1	267.8	510.8	552	320.4	316.5

Source: OECD, 1995 Geographical Distribution of Financial Flows to Aid Recipients, Development Assistance Committee.

The Fund and the Bank have supported Ghana's programme more generously than the programmes of many other countries. For example, in 1993, another Structural Adjustment Fund facility [SAF] of SDR 143.5m was approved for Ghana by the Fund only to be replaced with the relatively more generous ESAF in April 1994, bringing Ghana's inflow from the Fund in 1993 alone to SDR 388.55m. There is no doubt that having projected Ghana as the star pupil of adjustment in Sub Saharan Africa, the Bretton Woods twins were prepared to go the extra mile to sustain and confirm their success story.

The dependence of Ghana's programme on external funding unwittingly destabilised the reform effort. The destabilising influences included the long term sustainability of the programme once external assistance ceased or even became no longer available in the same quantities. Then there is also the increased debt burden inherent in such non grant borrowings.

Despite the multiple resourced 'aid' programme, the country's economy has not achieved stability. This is best illustrated by an account of the rapid growth of its overall debt. The country's long term debt in 1970, for example was $520m, increasing to $1,162m by 1980. By 1993 the debt overload had tripled to $3,378m. Total national debt had also increased from $1,398m in 1980 to $4590m by the end of 1993 (WB 1994, World Debt Tables: p.182). Table 5.9 gives a good account of the country's debt position as at 1993 [in US$m].

Table 5.9
Ghana's external debt

	1970	1980	1986	1987	1988	1989	1990	1991	1992	1993
Total debt stocks (EDT)		1398	2742	3280	3076	3332	3799	4249	4312	4590
Long term debt (LDOD)	520	1162	1768	2292	2236	2390	2734	3021	3158	3341
Public & publicly guaranteed	510	1152	1730	2262	2204	2357	2701	2987	3123	3341
Private non guaranteed	10	10	38	30	32	33	33	34	35	37
Use of IMF credit	46	105	786	867	762	737	745	834	740	738
Short-term debt		131	189	122	78	205	320	394	414	474
of which int. arreas on LDOD		5	18	22	23	39	56	37	41	54
Official creditors		4	16	18	19	31	45	19	18	26
Private creditors		1	2	4	4	9	11	19	22	29
Memo: principal arrears LDOD		5	37	55	55	74	77	77	83	101

Official creditors		3	31	44	41	44	51	40	43	62
Private creditors		2	6	11	14	29	26	37	39	39
Memo: export credits			269	326	267	306	411	410	402	301

TOTAL DEBT FLOW

Disbursements	44	249	416	515	618	561	483	609	397	387
Long term debt only	42	220	378	367	401	384	418	449	397	322
IMF purchases only	2	29	38	147	217	177	65	159	0	66
Principal repayments: Total	39	106	117	299	418	338	250	186	186	168
Long term debt only	14	77	84	110	142	155	134	108	122	101
IMF repurchases only	25	29	33	188	277	183	117	78	64	66
Net flow n debt on debts	5	143	295	186	156	333	332	515	227	267
of which short term debt			-4	-30	-44	110	98	92	16	47
Interest payments (INT)		53	110	116	127	115	106	109	115	109
Long term debt	12	31	45	56	71	62	57	63	75	73
IMF charges	0	4	52	50	47	43	37	29	20	14
Short term debt		18	13	10	9	10	12	17	19	22
Net transfers on debt		90	185	70	28	218	226	406	112	157
Total debt service paid (TDS)		159	228	415	546	453	356	295	301	277
Long term debt	26	108	129	166	213	217	190	171	197	175
IMF repurchases and charges	25	33	85	238	324	226	154	107	84	81
Short term debt (interest)		18	13	10	9	10	12	17	19	22
Total debt service due						483	364	319	291	287

Source: World Bank , 1994: World Debt tables: External Finance for Developing Countries 1994-95.

The very short term nature of earlier IMF financing, particularly, the Extended Fund Facility and other Standby arrangements created serious debt servicing problems for the macro economy. Between 1987 - 1989, an average of 58.3% of all exports went to service debts due, most of which were due to the IMF for both current obligations and arrears. As the table below (table 5.11) indicates, the non-IMF debts due for the period under discussion only averaged 26.26% of exports. By 1991, however, the debt service ratio had declined to 30% in 1991 and 23% in 1992 including IMF and arrears (WB 1992, pp 219-220).

Table 5.10
Ghana's debt ratio (debt as percentage of exports)

	1984	1985	1986	1987	1988	1989
Excluding IMF	32.1	46.8	37.0	26.3	27.5	25.0
Including IMF	36.3	53.4	46.5	51.9	59.2	46.2
Including IMF arrears	46.4	61.8	46.9	55.0	67.3	53.6

Source: WB: Ghana: Policies and Issues of Structural Adjustment Report no. 6635 - GH, Washington 30 March 1987. Table 16 & Bank of Ghana Reports.

Labour

The labour market, or better still, the position and role of labour has proved to be one of the most contentious and complex sectors of the structural adjustment programme both from a political economy perspective and even from one of pure hard core economics. The adjustment programme impacted on labour and labour relations in a number of ways, including changes in the nature and character of job security, wage rates and earnings, relationships between capital and labour, and the role of labour in the decision making process both at the levels of the factory floor and national. The foregoing occurrences follow from the many different dimensions of the adjustment programme itself such as:

- The reallocation of factors across sectors arising from changes in the relative prices of goods and services;
- The direct reduction of public sector employment as part of the attempt to control government deficit and excess aggregate demand;
- The reduction of excess demand in general;
- Changes in particular labour market intervention such as the minimum wage policy and;
- Changes in relative factor prices due largely to changes in cost of capital and imported inputs.

It has to be said that as a result of the complex interaction of issues, the labour market part of Ghana's reform programme is far from being an exact blue print. The inbuilt political dimension further makes labour policy difficult to disentangle. The significant redistribution of income that has gone hand in hand with the adjustment process has left losers aggrieved and winners uncertain about the permanence of their improved situation. ERP1, recognising the political trip wire nature of labour relations, skirted round the issue. It took the ERP II [1987] for the government to formally and concisely address the issue of labour's functions and lack of such functions, in the adjustment process.

Under the heading of 'Human Resource Utilisation and Labour Mobility,' the principal focus was on the civil service. The problem of labour supply and demand was starkly put thus:

> An aspect of the long period of economic decline ... [was that] ... the Public Sector came under increasing pressure to take on additional personnel beyond what they needed to operate efficiently. In the result, ... it is a common sight in public services to find people reading newspapers endlessly and engaging in lotto "arithmetic" throughout the day. This overstaffing also had the effect of making resources unavailable to improve conditions, especially pay for those who do work. (Ghana 1987, p.17).

The solution proffered by the backers and movers of the adjustment programme to the identified problem of excess labour involved;

- The redeployment of public sector employees;
- Elimination of distortions in government wages and salaries.

The continued employment of thousands of public sector workers [most of whom are under-employed], has presented a daunting challenge to a Ghana government facing severe budgetary constraints. But once the government had made up its mind on cutting down the excess labour of the public sector, a Public Administration Restructuring Committee and a Manpower Utilisation Committee were set up under the Ministry of Labour in 1983 to work out the implementation of a retrenchment programme. Not surprisingly, the two committees had representatives of the World Bank and their consultants, Peat Marwick and Mitchell sitting on them.

The Manpower Utilisation Committee estimated that 20% of the total workforce in the public sector, excluding the parastatals, was under employed and that 31,700 of these could be retrenched without affecting public sector efficiency (Yeebo 1991 pp.203-204). Some 12,000 civil servants were removed from the payroll in 1987 alone, and about the same numbers going in both 1988 and 1989. The compensation structure in the civil service was also changed to reflect the new market ethos of public policy. The differential contribution of various grades of the civil service became more apparent with the government insisting "... It is the government's view that it is better to have a small well trained and well paid civil service with a consistently high level of productivity" (Ghana 1987, p.18).

One of the earliest targets of both MUC and PARC was the Ghana Cocoa Board. The Board was an obvious candidate because of the large number of employees on its payroll, and its strategic position in the economy.[30] An outcome of the deliberations of the two committees was the drawing up and implementation of a five year plan by the Board "aimed at substantial net reduction of employees per annum" (Owusu 1989). In April 1984, the first batch of workers, [6000] were retrenched. By June 1989, the staff strength of Cocoa Board had fallen from over 100,000 in 1982 to 43,000 (ibid.).

Effects of labour market developments

The accompanying macro economic effects of the revaluation of exchange rates and the subsequent inflationary spiral created a liquidity crisis for a number of firms; both in private and public sectors. This undermined the ability of some these companies to continue production or even pay their workers. African Timber and Plywood Company Ltd., a one time timber giant at Samreboi [state owned] for example, was unable to pay its workers for more than ten months in 1986 and the government eventually had to close its operations after persistent complains by the workers.[31]

Employment security suddenly became a thing of a bygone era for workers as hitherto "safe" jobs became "unsafe" overnight. Under the state owned enterprise reform programme, about 45,000 workers were laid off between 1985 - 1989 and another 10,000 laid off through liquidation and the transfer of ownership of some state owned enterprises (Tait Davis 1991, p.987).

Table 5.11
Public sector retrenchment 1982-1989

Organisation	Workers retrenched
Cocoa Board	57,816
Civil service/Education service	17,200
State Construction Corporation	1,000
Black Star Line	1,000
Ghana National Trading Corporation	2,000
Post & Telecommunications	500
Department of Civil Aviation	150
CIMAO Project	500
Other Parastatals	27,000
Total	107,166

Source: Zaya Yeebo 1991, p.205.

The climate of retrenchment was not limited to the public sector. Private companies, such as VALCO took advantage of the industrial climate to dismiss 625 workers in late 1982. This was most likely, to test the political climate of acceptability and see how far they could go, as subsequent developments at their Tema plant were to prove. The government, having rode, as some might claim, to power on the back of the workers, turned anti labour in its desire to attract foreign capital and took the side of international capital in disputes. These disputes were mainly with organised labour and the work place Committees for the Defence of the Revolution which the same government had created in its radical populist phase.[32] Such conflicts occurred at among other places, Pioneer Food Company,[33] GTP [where Unilever is a dominant shareholder], . Allied Food Ltd .

The PNDC's attitude change to labour restructuring was the direct outcome of the adoption of the ERP. The regime in its first ten months [coinciding with the dominance of the radical tendency in government] had a very pro-worker approach to labour disputes. When VALCO fired the first salvo in 1982 by retrenching the 625 workers mentioned earlier, the government unequivocally put its authority behind the workers (Zaya Yeebo 1991, p.203). The height of the governments 'betrayal' of labour came at the 1984 Donors Conference in Paris [organised by Fund/Bank] when the Ghanaian authorities accepted the Conference diktat "to impose a definite condition about substantial cuts in labour as a way to reduce wages and salary bills." The government also decided to evaluate all jobs in the public sector "with a view to redirecting all excess personnel at all levels into more productive activity in agriculture and community works." (Poku Adaa 1985). Zaya Yeebo[34] argues that while the external influence could have dictated the regime's approach, the decision makers in the PNDC after the ousting of the radical left in late 1982, shared the sentiments expressed at the Donors Conference (op cit. p.203).

The culmination of all the above on both organised labour and individual workers, including smallholder farmers, was to erode living standards at a time when the macro economy was being trumpeted as doing well. "Life has continued to be terrible for workers. There is no money in the system as the IMF devaluation has wiped out the purchasing power of the cedi. There is food now but people do not have the money to buy. The government that said that the coup of December 31 was a revolution for the workers and masses is now running the country like a business," complained the then Secretary General of the Trades Union Congress (Yankey, 1985).

It is therefore, not surprising that workers' morale, including that of the civil service, was at its lowest ebb in the country's post colonial history. The civil service has downed its tools on at least five occasions between 1991 and 1995 to protest at the loss of real earnings. And this coming from a hitherto docile civil service, epitomised the marginalisation of labour under adjustment.

Industrial peace has thus become a thing of the past in the public sector as the effects of adjustment continues to bite.

The stages of the Ghanaian adjustment programme as enumerated above, were informed by both external pressures and some degree of internal choices. But what stands out in comparison to other African programmes is the seeming determination of the Bank and Fund to have their '*success*' story. The Ghanaian programme is, therefore, unique in how it was resourced, even if the conditionalities and interpretation of the African experience by these two institutions were no different from their usual straight jacket policies.

Notes

1 Adding about twenty percent to the working population.

2 This involved demands unacceptable to the revolutionary and nationalistic regime of the early 1980s.

3 Nigeria's antipathy to anything Libyan was the consequence of the belief at that time that Libya was destabilising the West African sub-region.

4 The Provisional National Defence Council (PNDC) itself being a coalition of various interests in the Ghanaian polity.

5 Or more correctly, had not been effectively and efficiently applied.

6 Seen by many as a last ditch attempt by a small faction of the left.

7 The Youth wing of the party was the most vocal in its opposition to any downward revaluation of the cedi.

8 The writer was a leading operative of the government of the PNDC from Jan. 1982 to September 1989.

9 Minutes of the Joint Meetings of these two bodies during the period, and which I have had the privilege of reading.

10 This group came to be known as the Akuse Group after the hydro town of Akuse, where a secluded government guest house was put at their disposal for their deliberations.

11 Cabinet Ministers were formally titled PNDC Secretaries.

12 As opposed to the initial self reliant programme discussed earlier and which did not take off for lack funding.

13 The exact number of these remains uncertain but ranged from twelve to eighteen as various official documents differed.

14 'Retrenched' in adjustment parlance!

15 See John R Nellis, 1986, Public Enterprise in Sub-Saharan Africa. World Bank Discussion Paper No. 1 and Roger Tangri, 1991, "The Politics of Divestiture in Ghana", *African Affairs* 90 p.523 for a detailed exposition of this.

16 later renamed Office of Revenue Commissioners.

17 The government was forced to drop the VAT regime within three months of its introduction as national opposition to the tax mounted. However, the government has not given up on the need to introduce this form of taxation.

18 Thus enabling a higher level of domestic spending.

19 See Ghatak, Subrata, 1995, Monetary Economics in Developing Countries, New York. St Martins Press p.143 for a detailed discussion of this.

20   These were all state owned banks. The two major private sector banks then operating in the country, Barclays and Standard Chartered, were not providing advances for state owned enterprises. For that reason, they did not carry SOE generated non - performing assets in their books.

21   Calculated from World Bank, 1989, Sub - Saharan Africa: From Crisis to sustainable growth. Washington pp 221 & 240.

22   Quoted in the People's Daily Graphic, 8 January 1987.

23   Quoted by Jeffrey Herbst 1993 people 38.

24   This semantic wizardry enabled an influential Member of the PNDC, Mrs Aana Enin to tell market women that the cedi had not been devalued, since the official rate was still pegged at ¢2.75 to the dollar at that time.

25   The Bank of Ghana made available a stated amount of foreign exchange and bids were invited from purchasers through their primary banks. The bids, through a complicated laid down formula, then determined the exchange rate for the week.

26   This figure was supplied by the Chief Executive of the London Office of Ghana Commercial Bank during an interview with the author.

27   Translated to US $ at the parallel market rate.

28   West Africa, 19 - 25 Sept. 1988 p 1737 " Ghana's New Deal with the IMF."

29   WB, 1992, Trends in Dev. P 218.

30   There was the widespread belief (later confirmed by the government task force on 'ghost workers' that a number of these employees only existed on payrolls.

31   Ghana Newsletter, Published by Ghana - Dutch Committee, April/May 1986 no. 20.

32   Workers and People's Defence Committees were set up in January 1982 to "defend" the Dec. 31 'revolution' both in the community and in the workplace. The nomenclature of these committees was changed to Committees for the Defence of the Revolution (CDR) in 1983 but with the same mission statement.

33   The parent company being the US multinational - Star-Kist Incorp.

34   Zaya Yeebo was the first Secretary (minister) of Youth and Sports in the PNDC government of 1982. He was also a key player in the militant tendency within the PNDC and resigned his position in protest against the right wing turn of the regime in late 1982.

6 Agriculture and other sectoral problems

Agriculture has traditionally been the major backbone of the Ghanaian economy, whether from the point of view of contribution to GDP, exports, employment or simply social welfare. In 1984 for example, the broad agricultural sector accounted for 51% of GDP and 57% of employment with cocoa alone accounting for 60% of all earnings (WB 1984, p.58). Crops, other than cocoa, also provided 62% of the value added in agro processing in the same year. In a survey by GATT covering the period 1983 - 1990, agriculture accounted for 44% of GDP (GATT 1992, Vol. 1 p.14). Although the relative significance of agriculture in the Ghanaian GDP has declined, it is still the most important single sector in the economy. In 1990 for example, out of the country's total merchandise export earnings of $871m, cocoa and timber alone accounted for $449m.[1] By the early 1990s, the sector still provided 43% of GDP, 50% of export earnings and 70% of employment (WB Ghana 1992a p.29).

Even though cocoa stands out in agricultural exports and for this reason would be given a separate treatment in this chapter, its significance within the sectoral GDP is rather modest. Cereals and root crops alone accounted for 62% of agricultural GDP in 1988. Cocoa only accounted for 18%, livestock 7% with fisheries trailing at 3%.

One of the major functions of the nation state in developing countries in the post war period has been to meet the requirement of national food security. National food security denotes the ability of a nation to feed its inhabitants adequately from its own resources at all times. This need in Ghana has become particularly critical after the 1983 drought experience. The nation was historically fairly able to meet its basic food, especially root crop and cereal requirement up to the mid 1970s. This ability has however, been compromised since 1975. Table 6.1 makes this graphically clear. The table shows that even in the traditionally strong sub-sector of cereal production, the country now has to import substantial quantities of cereals to meet the demands of a population growing by about 2.5% per annum. And even worse in terms of volumes and domestic ability, is the importation of other food varieties. Food and live animal imports had therefore doubled to about 17% of total imports by 1986 (see table 6.1).

Table 6.1
Agricultural imports 1975 - 1987

Year	Imports of FLA at official rate (US$m)	Value of real cereal imports (US$ mill.)	Value of total merch. imports (US$m)	Proportion of food imports to total imports (%)	Value of total merchandise exports f.o.b. (US$m)	Proportion of food imports to total merch. exports (%)
1975	91.3	29.8	791	11.5	728	1.5
1976	103.3	15.1	862	12	779	12
1977	83.1	14.6	1038	8	891	8
1978	95	44.8	1114	8.5	895	8.5
1979	64.9	18.3	882	7.4	1066	7.4
1980	87.8	40.7	972	9	1104	9
1981	89.9	32.8	1021	8.8	711	8.8
1982	100.5	19.9	631	15.9	641	15.9
1983	353.7	31.2	539	65.6	439	65.6
1984	123	26.4	681	18.1	566	18.1
1985	123	16	727	16.9	632	16.9
1986	133	10.1	780	17.1	773	17.1
1987	NA	37.7	NA	NA	NA	NA

Source: adapted from Sarris & Shams 1991 p. 19.

The tragedy here being that the increased food bill, for an agricultural economy, has been at the expense of machinery and other industrial capital items needed for increased domestic production.

Causes of decline

The causes of the decline of agricultural productivity in Ghana are myriad, but for the purposes of this section, I shall concentrate on two broad based causes, since these two have determined the course of agricultural reform since the introduction of the country's reform programme in 1983. It is also important to keep in perspective that agriculture is estimated to have 'grown' by negative

1.2% from 1970 - 1980 (WB 1984, p.3). The average index of food production per capita, using 1969 - 1971 as base period [100], declined to 82 by 1979/80. The level of agricultural production in 1982 was therefore lower than in 1970 while population per sq. km of agricultural land had increased from 104 in 1960 to 181.6 in the late 1970s without generating any positive impact on food production (ibid. P.27).

Fiscal policy on agriculture

The World Bank is probably the most vociferous of the institutions who squarely put the blame for the decline in annual agricultural growth on the high rate of agricultural taxation in Ghana (see WB 1994a, p.77). The Bank argues that African farmers have faced the world's heaviest rates of agricultural taxation. The taxation, according to the Bank comes in the form of producer price fixing, export taxes on agricultural inputs and indirectly through over valued exchange rates, high levels of industrial protection which the bank argues raises consumer prices for farmers (ibid. p.76). While the Bank's assessment on industrial protection may be exaggerated, one cannot dismiss the validity of the Bank's analysis pertaining to Ghana. In a study by Schift, Maurice and Alberto Voldes (1992), Ghana, Cote d'Ivoire and Zambia were found to be taxing their farmers 70% more than the average agricultural taxes in the developing world as a whole.

Inappropriate and inefficient direct state participation

Ghana's attempt at formal state policy for agriculture has a long history. The most significant attempt at policy reform in the colonial period was the Watson Commission Report, set up to investigate the causes of urban riots in 1948. The Commission reported that life in the colony was dependent on food supply, but both policy and producer interest was geared toward export production, and more so cocoa, to the neglect of food crops by especially the then fifty year old Agricultural Policy (Sarris & Shams 1991, p.12). The first post colonial government concentrated largely on urban development and large scale state owned farms, much against the traditional contours of the country's economic base. By the middle of the 1960s, it was clear that the attempt at large scale agriculture had failed, just like the colonial experiment in Gonja had failed decades earlier. According to Sarris and Sham, the "... ministry of Agriculture no longer had responsibility for helping small scale farmers. Between 1961 and 1965, the bulk of development expenditure went to the socialised sector even though its contribution to aggregate production was less than 1% ..." (ibid.).

State farms, as pointed out in chapter two, had become the focus of agricultural policy. These farms became a part of the problem through the disproportionate percentage of resources devoted to such activities as well as their woeful performance, arising from the high levels of political patronage resulting in incompetent appointments. The main effect of the state's direct involvement in agriculture was the total neglect of the small holder private base, the golden fleece of Ghana's economic development.

The tragedy is that subsequent governments from 1966 to 1981, irrespective of their ideological orientation, retained the State Farms policy and only made cosmetic changes in the managerial set-up often involving just nomenclature. These state units tended to favour large scale, capital intensive modes of production over small farm units. This tendency, went in tandem with increased emphasis on industrialisation as the way forward to national development.

The culmination of all the above and a serious failure in 1982/83 farming year produced the worst food shortages in Ghana since the shortages of the inter war period. So severe was the 1982/83 famine[2] that, the decline in agricultural productivity pulled GDP down to levels lower in historical terms than in the 1960s (ibid. p.20).

Agriculture under adjustment

Agricultural reform, apart from exchange rate adjustment and cocoa price reform, started very late from a sectoral perspective, that is, five years after the ERP1 was launched. Reform, when it came, was geared towards reducing the role of public enterprises in production, pricing and distribution of agricultural inputs and outputs (Leechor 1994, p.171). Reform also entailed divestiture and in some cases, the liquidation of state owned farms, processing plants and agro chemical manufacturing companies such as the Abuakwa Reformulation Plant that produced chemicals largely for the cocoa industry

The mid term review of ERP1 showed that the agricultural sector, particularly the Ministry of Agriculture and its institutions were ineffective in playing assigned or expected roles largely because it had been neglected over the years. A programme to tackle short term adjustment issues, as such issues affect the sector was put in place and part of the programme [partly funded by the World Bank], the Bank undertook an Agricultural Sector Review[3] which highlighted the main elements of a strategy to promote agricultural development on a sustainable basis. The above report led to the launching of $53.5m Agricultural Services Rehabilitation Project [ASRP] in 1987.

The project was primarily geared at strengthening the capacity of the public sector to support research and extension services, irrigation and policy planning, and monitoring, evaluation and co-ordination, and to make the investment necessary to expand agricultural production. The ministry of agriculture was to be rehabilitated so as to be in a position to give effective support to agriculture through its implementation capacity. At the base level, the project had three inter linked objectives:

- to strengthen the institutional framework for the formulation and implementation of agricultural policies and programmes;
- to improve delivery of public sector services to agriculture, that is, extension, research, irrigation and veterinary services;
- to improve the procurement and distribution of agricultural inputs by privatisation (Sarris & Sham 1991, p.14).

The 1983 - 1985 period witnessed a number of ad hoc measures designed to overcome the neglect of agriculture and the food shortages caused by the drought of 1982/83 as well as the effects of the expulsion of a million Ghanaians from Nigeria. The major objectives of these measures were to mobilise all available human resources [returnees and rural and urban unemployed][4] and other resources to increase the production of major staples;[5] to reclaim abandoned cocoa farms; and to replant cocoa and other farms devastated by the 1983 bushfires (ibid. pp.12-13).

The adhoc measures yielded dividends in production figures leading to higher than planned results. For example, maize production, which reached an all time low of 141,000 m/t in 1983, increased to 574,000 m/t in 1984, dropping to 441,000 m/t in 1985. It must be noted that the high output of 1984 was the result of 1983 shortages which galvanised the whole country into taking steps to assure food security. The increased output did not result from the adhoc policy initiatives *per se*, but from the human instinct for survival. The absence of substantive policies in place in 1984 allowed market forces to bring the price of maize down from ₵10,000/100 kg in 1983 at official prices to about half the figure in 1984 (ibid. p.13).

The need for a national agricultural policy became critical in 1985 as the bumper harvest of 1984 and the subsequent fall in prices led to a decline in production levels, as the maize figures above exemplified. The absence of adequate and viable post harvest handling facilities and an economic framework environment that makes for consistent prices for producers were major areas that exposed the policy vacuum. In 1986 therefore, a new agriculture policy document *'Ghana: Agricultural Policy - Action Plans and Strategies, 1986 - 1988'* (Ghana, 1986) was formulated and approved by the government. Its main objectives were:

- self sufficiency in production of cereals, starchy staples and animal protein food, with maize, rice and cassava as priority in the crops sub-sector in the short term;

- maintenance of adequate buffer stocks for price stabilisation and food security during periods of seasonal shortfalls and major crop failures;
- self sufficiency in the production of industrial raw materials such as cotton, oil palm, tobacco, groundnuts etc. for agro based industries;
- increased production of exportable crops, cocoa, pineapples, coffee, sheanuts, ginger and kola;
- improvement in storage, processing and distribution systems to minimise post harvest losses;
- strengthening most of its activities including decentralisation by shifting operational responsibility from headquarters to regions;
- improving existing institutions and facilities such as the agricultural research centres, credit facilities, marketing facilities etc. and
- ensuring adequate returns to farmers, fishermen, distributors and processors. Incomes must be high enough to raise productivity in Ghanaian agriculture to levels comparable to those prevailing internationally.

The major difference between the 1986 programme and those before it was the specific emphasis on small scale farmer as the engine of reform. As part of the reforms, the government's direct involvement in grain purchasing and storage, and more importantly, the marketing of cocoa [limited at this time to internal], cotton and oil palm is being reversed and privatisation of most government processing and storage capacity, the privatisation of input supply, the freeing of cotton marketing, the freeing of international trade in palm oil, coffee, sheanuts and the introduction of the private sector in domestic cocoa market.

It must however, be recognised that the World Bank's approach to agriculture and agricultural productivity, more than any other external body or agency, has been market oriented, as has the thrust of its general programme of adjustment. In its key document 'Ghana 2000', the prospects for agricultural growth are examined by asking four fundamental questions:

1. What are the basic constraints on the supply side?
2. What are the policies and infrastructural provisions that limit the transmission of market signals to producers?
3. What sectors are likely to provide growth beyond that generated by domestic demand?
4. What should be the priorities for public policy in the face of the opportunities and constraints inherent in the agricultural sector? (ibid. p.29).

How the above address the lack of markets and low world prices cited often as the main constraints to agricultural growth is, however, not clear. The free market is hardly, in a developing country, able to answer the question of adding value, increased productivity and food security without government direction and intervention.

Notwithstanding the foregoing, the relatively good agricultural results in some crops, such as maize and millet, is ascribed to good weather and rainfall rather than to policy.[6] However, other crops have persistently experienced low production levels including plantain, most nuts, fruits and vegetables falling within this category. The aspects of structural adjustment that have positively affected agriculture seems to be more accidental than direct. Road construction, availability of spare parts for vehicles and agricultural machinery etc. are derived from the overall macro environment as against the specific agricultural policy (Kraus 1988, p.109). The significance of this assertion is manifested when it is realised that the most important cost factor affecting the ability of subsistence farmers to enter the market economy is transport cost (WB 1992, p.35). And yet, feeder road density in Ghana only averages 89 meters per square kilometre. This is roughly equal to that of India in 1951 (ibid.). The poor state of feeder road maintenance further cripples the road network by making a high percentage of such roads unusable during the rainy season. Only about 3,300 km out of the total 21,300 km are said to be in good condition, that is, usable all year round, with sixty percent[7] being unusable for parts of the year (ibid.).

The agricultural sector's growth between 1987 - 1991 averaged less than 2%, against the 1990 Medium Term Agriculture Development Strategy's target of a 4% growth rate. The performance even after 1991 did not improve. In 1994 for example, broad agriculture only recorded a 1% growth rate (1995 BS, p.4). The official explanation for this non-performance included 'less than favourable rainfall pattern during the major cropping season, particularly in the forest belt' (ibid.). This statement, probably more than any other, underlies the lack of success of agricultural reform since the launch of Ghana's Economic Reform Programme in April 1983. That rainfall is still the major determinant of agricultural output is an indictment.

Table 6.2
Agricultural contributions to GDP 1980-1993

	1980	1985	1991	1992	1993
Percentage of GDP	57.9	44.9	48.6	48.6	47.3
Average annual growth	-1.3	1.9	4.7	-0.7	2.8

Source: World Bank, Trends in Developing Economies, 1994 p.194.

Constraints, challenges and the future of agriculture

The need to get agriculture on an even keel for development cannot be overstated. Providing 43% of GDP, 50% of exports and 70% of employment in 1990 (Ghana 1992a, p.29), it is the dominant sector of the economy and thus if a high growth is to be achieved in the Ghanaian economy, then the sector has to be central to any such growth.

Notwithstanding the attempts at restructuring over the past decade of adjustment, Ghana's agricultural performance has not only lagged behind other African countries during this period, but has also lagged behind other sectors in the internal market. Whereas between the period 1987-1991 Nigerian agriculture grew by an average of 4% per annum, Ghana's grew by only 2% (WB 1994b, p.147).

A number of reasons have accounted for the relative poor performance of agriculture under structural adjustment. The upgrading of agricultural infrastructure has been slow, particularly rural feeder roads and critical links with the external market. As argued in the preceding pages, transport cost is the single most important item in linking the rural agricultural producer to the market economy. The slowness of opening up the rural areas through feeder roads has, therefore, become a major obstacle to increased productivity. Just as critical, [if not more than the feeder roads], has been the continual dependence of Ghanaian agriculture on rainfall for cropping. Rainfall has become the predominant factor for agricultural output (Kapur 1991, p.50). The growth in agricultural output in 1993 for example, was largely attributable to good rainfall, with output increasing from -0.6% in 1992 to 2.5% (ISSER, 1993). Attempts at irrigation as a way of lessening the dependence on weather have not been successful largely because of institutional weakness at the Irrigation Development Authority. Also contributing to the lack of success is the 'Green Revolution' attitude of mega projects adopted. Irrigation schemes have invariably been gigantic - Tono, Asutware, Vea, - with very little adaptation to the needs of the small holder farmer who has been and still is the backbone of the Ghanaian agriculture.

Price volatility of products has historically been one of the constraints of careful agricultural planning by farmers as Table 6.1 shows. If therefore, agricultural productivity is to be seriously addressed,[8] the issue of price stability has to be given more careful attention than has been the case in the past. How this can be squared with the new ethos of letting the markets decide prices has to be worked out one way or the other. If the state is unwilling to jettison its externally imposed free market doctrine, an answer should be found to create an enabling pricing environment without effective state intervention.. It is ironic that agriculture is one of the areas most protected in the industrialised West and yet, Ghana, like most developing countries, is being asked to pull down the barriers of protection. The Bank insists that the future direction of the public sector in agricultural marketing is for the state to stay out and concentrate on creating an enabling environment. This is to be done through infrastructure provision and facilitating private traders and producers through the "improvement of marketing standards, common facilities and trade regulations" (WB 1992a, pp.34-35).

The dependence on market forces is already costing the country dearly. Since the privatisation of fertiliser sales in 1989, fertiliser usage in the country has declined from 40,000 tons in 1988 to 23,000 tons in 1991. The removal of state subsidy, through the introduction of profit margins, has raised fertiliser and other agro chemical prices beyond the reach of most small scale farmers. A similar trend is noticeable in the use of chemicals by the cocoa industry (ibid.). It must be recognised that Ghana's soil is said to be geologically old and leached of their original nutrients. Soil erosion, soil fertility loss and deforestation have been estimated to cost as much as 4% of the gross domestic product per year (ibid. p.32).

The need for price stabilisation in agriculture, particularly for food crops, is made more urgent by the overall deterioration in agricultural terms of trade within the economy. This is not withstanding the fact that the real domestic prices of some commodities such as cocoa, has improved over the adjustment period [ibid. p 30]. And "...given that most of the poor live in rural areas and depend on agricultural activities for most of their income, the deterioration in terms of trade indicates that rural income may have fallen during this period, further exacerbating poverty in the rural areas" (WB 1992a, p.31).

The dash for growth in broad agriculture is also limited by environmental considerations, particularly in the timber sector. The government continues in this subsector to make increasing use of export restrictions on lumber in an effort to promote greater domestic value added in timber processing industries, such as plywood manufacture and for environmental reasons (GATT, 1992, p 112).

The critical constraint to growth in agriculture, according to both the Ministry of Agriculture and the World Bank, lies in the growth of effective demand. The Ministry's analysis indicates that only 13% of Ghanaian agricultural output is captured in value enhancing activities, compared to 80% in developed economies (ibid. p.34). This analysis may be on the low side, because of the sizeable portion of some cereals, e.g. maize that goes straight to *banku*[9] preparation without the intermediation of mills. The analysis is however, still valid in that there is still a lot of room for agro processing as a means of enhanced demand and food security.

For agriculture to achieve the sustained growth it is capable of achieving, as the relative good growth rates of some non-traditional agricultural exports such as pineapples, banana and mangoes indicates, then three key conditions must be met:

- The growth in the wider economy would be reflected in a growing demand for agricultural products through functioning markets;
- That favourable conditions are maintained for the growth of competitive agricultural exports and agro processing and;
- The institutions concerned with generation and dissemination of agricultural technology are revitalised and provided with the resources, not only to bring about increase in agricultural productivity, but also to prevent the further degradation of the natural resource base.

The sluggish performance of the agricultural sector, other than in 1984, clearly manifested by agriculture's negligible contribution to national economic renewal and expansion cannot be allowed to continue. Out of the about 40% expansion in the Ghanaian economy between 1984 - 1991, agriculture accounted for only 5% (Leechor 1994, p.170). To permit this trend to continue unchecked in the lead sector of the economy would be to put an unacceptable albatross around the neck of the Ghanaian economy. The poor performance of agriculture has another worrying repercussion on general food prices and inflation. As table 6.3 shows, there is the urgent need to give serious attention to agricultural productivity as a weapon in fighting inflation. An increased output, arising especially from increased productivity as against increased acreage, would tend to pull down or hold prices and establish macro stability from the angle of general price level changes for the economy.

Table 6.3
Agricultural output, food prices and inflation 1983-1991
(annual % changes)

	agric output	food prices	national consumer price index
1983	-8.0	144.8	122.8
1984	15.4	12.0	39.6
1985	-1.7	-11.9	10.4
1986	0.2	20.3	24.6
1987	-0.3	38.5	39.8
1988	6.0	34.1	31.4
1989	5.2	25.1	25.2
1990	0.0	40.2	37.2
1991 Jan -May	-	17.7	24.6

Source: Kapur 1991, p.51.

Cocoa

Both the historical and present day contributions of the cocoa sub-sector calls for attention hence the necessity of examining this sub-sector outside of broad agriculture. Cocoa has been the single biggest contributor to tax revenues for over a generation. Despite gold leaping ahead of cocoa as the country's leading export earner from 1993, cocoa still provides the largest single source of revenue. In the 1994 fiscal year for example, despite a lower than projected crop size, cocoa export duty amounted to ₵133.2 billion, providing more than 10% of all government receipts from all sources in that fiscal year (BS 1995, p.7). This occurs because about 25% of the export price of cocoa is appropriated by the state as export tax alone (WB 1992a, p.34).

Cocoa has over the years become the state's leading milk cow. The state's share of cocoa proceeds increased from 18% in the early 1960s to over 50% in the late 1970s, even when the size of the crop had fallen (Zurick 1994, p.2). Cocoa's uniqueness to the Ghanaian polity is unsurpassable even in the last decade of this century. Unlike gold mining, which now accounts for 45.2% of the country's export earnings (BS 1995, p.9) and is firmly established in the hands of multinational corporations, cocoa production is totally indigenous and therefore, suffers very little, if any, leakage from the Ghanaian economy. Largely because cocoa production is small holder based, it provides more jobs as well as a spread of ownership and equity in the economy. By being small holder base, and as opposed to the predominantly plantation style of neighbouring Cote d'Ivoire, the cocoa subsector is able to provide jobs for about 265,000 farmers and their families [and not counting the Cocoa Board bureaucracy] in Southern Ghana.

The attempt at restructuring the cocoa sector, however, preceded the adjustment programme. The government of the Third Republic under Limann recognised the need to reform and rehabilitate the sector and in conjunction with the World Bank, appointed KPMG Peat Marwick Management Consultants to undertake a study of the industry in 1981. However, the Third Republic was brought to an abrupt end via a coup d'estat in December 1981 before it could implement the proposals contained in the Report and which it had accepted in principle.

The PNDC, once it had decided on the ERP in 1983, appointed the same consultants on the basis of their 1981 work, under the terms of a World Bank facility, as advisors to the Cocoa Board with the remit of helping the Cocoa Board's management achieve the desired improvements marked out in their 1981 report. A team of twenty-five consultants from KPMG Peat Marwick therefore landed in Ghana in 1984 under contract to cover all areas of the Cocoa Board's operations.[10]

A key element of the cocoa sector reform package was the issue of prices paid to farmers. The government, while acknowledging the low level of prices paid to producers, was worried that the tax margin on cocoa would be drastically reduced [with balance sheet consequences] if farmers were paid a percentage of world market prices.[11] The effect of such an infusion of liquidity on inflation was worrying. Against this fear was the recognition of the fact that, responsible for the falling cocoa production from the all time high of 572,000 tons in 1964/65 crop season to 150,000 tons in 1983 had been the total inadequacy of prices paid to producers. This amounted in 1984 to 10% of world prices based on parallel market rates (see table 6.4). Ghana in the process lost its position as premier cocoa producer to its neighbour Cote d'Ivoire in 1976 and is currently, only the third largest after Brazil.

Table 6.4
Cocoa producer prices and the development of real
income 1957-1988

Year	nominal producer prices ₵/ton	barter terms of trade of cocoa	income terms of trade of cocoa	PRODUCER PRICES US$/ton Exchange Rate official	parallel
1957	276	231	164	386	-
1960	220	171	151	308	308
1961	220	167	195	308	308
1962	220	153	169	308	308
1965	182	85	128	255	278
1966	152	63	70	213	71
1970	294	111	122	288	170
1974	487	109	101	428	181
1978	1599	47	33	1056	178
1979	3314	64	42	1205	212
1981	5333	31	21	1939	203
1982	12000	58	35	4363	194
1983	16667	36	17	4832	218
1984	25417	39	16	719	212
1985	45073	63	29	834	300
1986	70800	80	46	787	373
1987	112500	91	38	732	-
1988	152500	94	62	757	-

Source: Cord Jacobeit, 1991 p.224.

The initial increases in producer prices in real terms induced increased purchases by the Cocoa Board. Farms almost abandoned as a result of uneconomic prices previously offered were brought on line and new farms burnt during the bush fires of 1982/83 were replaced with improved varieties by farmers encouraged by the new prices. Between 1984 and 1988, therefore, the nominal prices of cocoa increased fivefold. This was partly in fulfillment of the government's own agenda but the hand of the World Bank cannot be ignored. As a condition for a structural adjustment credit from the Bank, the government was to provide cocoa farmers with 55% of the world market price by the 1988/89 purchasing year (Commander, Howell & Seini 1989, p.112). This target was not however, achieved and still has not been met largely because of the deterioration of world cocoa prices and the need by central government to retain some reasonable level of receipts from the sector. The producer price is now about 45% of world market converted at the high and more realistic exchange rate. This compares very well with the past, such as in the 1978/79 crop year when farmers were paid less than 30% of world prices converted at the artificially low rate. Considering that the latter was a real foreign exchange price of less than 60% of the real price in 1957, producers in 1978/79 received effectively, less than 18% of world prices (Leith 1993, p.272).

It is however, one sided to examine the issue of prices from only the perspective of the state and the producer. Equally critical is the influence of the world market, dominated by chocolate and other consumer interest from the western industrialised world. Even the world bank, the supreme believer in 'free markets' acknowledges that the real price for cocoa on the world market dropped by about 70% between 1970 and 1990 (WB, 1994a, p.77). Between 1987 and 1990 alone, a 40% fall in the price of cocoa was recorded on the world market (GATT 1992, p.15)., leaving Ghana with reduced export receipts, not withstanding increased volumes and thus the state needing to hold on more to these receipts for general as opposed to sectoral development programmes.

Under such circumstances of world price instability, it has become difficult implementing a medium, let alone long term plan of adequately compensating producers for their labour. The sustainability of the whole cocoa industry in the long term is under a dark cloud with the continuing fall in world prices conditioned by increasing output set against a static demand. The increasing dependence of chocolate manufacturers on artificial additives within the Single European Market and thus further taking away market share from cocoa, has to be recognised.

Crop husbandry

Almost all of Ghana's cocoa is grown on relatively small farms ranging in size from less than one acre to about fifty acres, providing about six tons of cocoa beans on the largest of such farms (Zurick, 1985, p.2). The small holding nature of Ghana's cocoa is singularly responsible for the good husbandry practice that had given the country's cocoa the quality premium rating it attracts on the world market.

The drought and bushfires of 1982/83 that destroyed many older cocoa farms gave the Cocoa Services Division of the Cocoa Board a unique opportunity to start from scratch in many growing areas. Trained CSD technicians utilised the opportunity to educate farmers to replant healthier and more disease resistant Bonsu varieties which produce seeds in only three years, compared to the traditional five years of the Tetteh Quarshie, Amazon or T14 varieties (Mikell 1989, p.219). The CSD, in conjunction with the National Mobilisation Programme,[12] provided seedlings free of charge to farmers needing to replant their burnt farms.

Institutional reform

Of the various reforms of the cocoa industry, none has probably been as incisive and as far reaching as the reform of the Cocoa Board bureaucracy itself. The Board had grown from a small regulatory and advisory body to a labyrinth organisation involved in all aspects of cocoa production, from the actual growing through buying, collection, storage and selling. By 1981, the staff payroll of the Board had grown to around 115,000. In tandem with its payroll growth was increased inefficiency of its management (Zurick 1994, p. 1).

The consultants appointed by the government in 1981 pointed to the obvious over staffing of the Cocoa Board and the need to cut down on staffing levels. By the end of 1985, staff levels had been forced down to about 80,000 through natural wastage, freeze on employment and elimination of what the Ghanaian authorities called 'ghost workers'.[13] A tighter payroll administration had seen to the elimination of most of these ' ghost workers'. Another 17,000 staff were made redundant in 1986, reducing Cocoa Board employees to 63,000. Further retrenchment had by 1991 reduced Cocoa Board staff to about 40,000.

The streamlining of the operations of the Board's operations included moving the Board away from some of its previous functions. A good example of this was the transfer of the Board's feeder road programme to the Department of Feeder Roads of the Ministry of Roads and Highways. The Board hitherto constructed and maintained a network of feeder roads and bridges in its operational areas to support cocoa evacuation from and extension services in such areas. Under the reorganisation, such functions were consolidated in the general feeder roads programme of the Department of Feeder Roads.

Another major area of restructuring of the Cocoa Board was the internal marketing of cocoa. The Board began to license private buyers to internally buy the produce from farmers. The World Bank has pressurised for this since the late 1980s. The privatisation of internal marketing, apart from being in line with the broad ideological direction of the adjustment of the Ghanaian economy, was also meant to bring down the marketing cost of Cocoa Board from the 17% achieved in the 1990/91 crop year to a comparable figure of 10% as pertains in Brazil and the Far East (WB 1992a, p.34). In the 1992/93 crop season, the five private buying companies licensed were accountable for 20% of internal purchases (WB, 1994c, p .192).

Restructuring of the cocoa sector has not been without challenges. The reform of Cocoa Board in particular has proved more difficult than anticipated partly because of the built in resistance from the Board bureaucracy. With unemployment increasing within the formal economy, the bureaucracy, after the first tranche of layoffs, became unsupportive. There was also the inadequacy of resource provision for the execution of the large number of redundancies entailed in the exercise. Not enough funds were available to pay the end of service benefits of the tens of thousands of workers being laid off. The Board and thus the government had to unilaterally decide to pay such terminal benefits by installments, contrary to acceptable labour market practices of the country. The fact that the government in 1988 had to resort to the use of military and police armoured personnel carriers to disperse protesting aggrieved workers was indicative of both the lengths to which the government was prepared to go to force down its reform programme on workers and the brute force needed to implement aspects of adjustment that are anti-people and anti labour in particular.

At the macro and global level, the fallacy of composition[14] had become a disincentive for increased production. Even the World Bank concedes that the fallacy of composition is real and operational in the global cocoa trade. The expansion of cocoa exports from Ghana and Nigeria under structural adjustment as well as similar increases from Brazil, Indonesia and Malaysia, has contributed to depressed world prices for the crop (see Husain 1993, p.6).

Mining

Mining occupies a very important position in the Ghanaian economy and has done so for decades. The country's mineral holdings include bauxite, gold, maganese, limestone, diamond, salt etc. But it is in gold mining that the country is particularly recognised, having been christened the Gold Coast during the whole of its colonial servitude and producing up to 800,000 ounces from 80 mines up to the second world war.[15] Gold accounts for 80% of the country's total mineral exports and is only second to South Africa in gold production in Africa.

The mining sector, and particularly gold, suffered severely in the years of economic decline as new investment dried up in this capital intensive industry at a time when existing machinery needed replacing as they became obsolete and unworkable. Since the state effectively controlled all mines either by majority ownership as was the case with the then Ashanti Goldfields Corporation[16] or outright ownership as was in the case of the State Gold Mining Corporation operated mines at Tarkwa, Prestea and Konongo, private resources were unavailable to take off the burden of investment. From a high point of 1.2m oz. [34 tonnes] produced in 1961, output had fallen to below the 300,000 ounce mark by the middle of the 1980s, when the ERP began to focus on the mining sector (AED 7 Nov. 1994, p.22). Bauxite, another important mineral in Ghana's export trade, had also seen exports fall from an impressive 325,200 tons in 1975 to 170,000 tons by 1985 (UNIDO 1991, p.135).

Economic and regulatory environment

Once the government had decided to address the obstacles to mining sector productivity and growth as part of the broad ERP, it set itself the task of creating an enabling environment for the sector. This was an implicit recognition that the existing environment was either hostile or at best, not conducive to attracting and maintaining the needed level of investment by the private sector in mining.

Creating an enabling environment for the mining sector begun with re-assessing the legal framework. The Investment Code of 1985 and the Minerals and Mining Law of 1986 were instrumental in creating a body of legislation under which the mining was to prosper. The legal and tax reforms inherent in the two laws opened up the mining sector to private prospecting and management while ensuring that the state automatically kept a ten percent golden handshake in any new mining venture in the country in addition to retaining the option under the Mineral Law to increase its stake to twenty percent on a participation basis. A royalty, based on operating profits is also payable. The corporate tax rate of the mining sector was also reduced to 35% (Africa Business 1995 No. 197, p.28).

Mining was also an early beneficiary of deregulation and market liberalisation. For the lead product -gold, liberalisation has included the internal buying and selling of both gold and diamonds by private sector agents licensed by the Precious Minerals Marketing Corporation.[17] Small scale gold mining, popularly known as 'gallamsey' and hitherto illegal although prevalent and whose proceeds as a result of its illegality was smuggled to neighbouring countries, was made legal and encouraged to sell its output to the licensed agents for a competitive price.

In the case of Ashanti Goldfields Company Ltd.[AGC], the largest operation in the sector and accounting for about seventy-five[18] percent of total gold production, the government, in its capacity as the then majority shareholder, negotiated and guaranteed an initial $160m facility from the International Finance Corporation of the World Bank Group for the rehabilitation of its operations. By 1989, five more similar packages had been put in place for Ashanti Goldfields and the Ghana National Petroleum Corporation with the bulk of such investment going to AGC (Alderman 1994, pp. 40-41).

To further enhance the operations of AGC, particularly its ability to raise equity capital from both the Ghana and London Stock Exchange, the government undertook a flotation of the company in both Accra and London. The government, to kick start the floatation, off loaded a proportion of its 55% shares in AGC leaving it with only 31.3% while Lonhro, the technical managers of the company and until now the minority shareholder also reduced its share holding from 45% to 43.1% and in the process became the largest single shareholder. The flotation valued the company at nearly $2bn. and raised $450m. for the government of Ghana.[19]

The new environment has attracted a number of firms, 180 by mid 1994 to Ghana's gold and diamond subsectors (AED op. cit.). In 1990 for example, a new major $100m. goldmine Bogoso, a joint venture between Billiton International, the International Finance Corporation and Ghana Government producing 120,000 ounces of gold annually by 1993, had come on line (ibid.). Firms from South Africa,[20] Canada, Australia and the US have particularly been active in this new gold rush.

Productivity and output gains

The gains that have been achieved in the course of the reform of the mining sector has been remarkable, especially in gold mining and prospecting. At the forefront of this achievement has been Ashanti Goldfields Company. Beginning from an output of 240,000 ounces in 1985, the company is now on target to produce one million ounces of gold in 1995 (Africa Business May 1995, p.13), having invested a total of over $600m since 1986 (ibid.). The company's pre tax profits for its financial year ending Sept. 1994 amounted to $112.4m, making it the most profitable company in Ghana (Africa Business, March 1995 p 27). Gold earnings, accounted for 24% of the merchandise export of the country in 1990 (1991 p 3) but by 1994, had earned the country $548.6m, that is 45.2% of total merchandise export in 1994 (BS 1995, p.9).

Table 6.5
Value added to GDP by mining sector

Year	1982	1983	1984	1985	1986	1987	1988	1989	1990
Value	7.6	-14.4	13.5	6.5	-3.0	7.9	17.8	10.0	10.5

Source: Various.

178

Table 6.6
Mining output (thousand tons)

Year	Bauxite	Maganese Ore(gw)	Diamonds carats	Diamond industrial	Diamond gem	Gold ore ore (kg)
1982	64	160	684	616	68	10280
1983	70	173	340	306	34	8601
1984	49	287	346	311	35	8923
1985	170	316	639	576	60	9311
1986	204	259	586	498	88	8950
1987	195	254	465	400	65	10228
1988	287	231	620	465	155	11631
1989	347	334	494	370	124	13265
1990	381	314	515	386	129	16840

Source: UNECA, African Statistical Year Book vol. 1 1990/91.

The productivity gains were not limited to gold. As table 6.6 indicates, maganese production and export had more than doubled from 160,000 tons in 1982 to 314,000 tons by 1990, even if by 1993, production had fallen to 285,000 tons in 1993 (AED 7 Nov 1994, p.22). Bauxite production had also been brought back from the doldrums within the adjustment period. Table 6.6 records production as having risen from 64,000 tons in 1982 to 381,000 tons by facilities with assistance from the multilateral sources.

Aluminum is another mineral that has prospered significantly under the reform programme. Production shot up from 48,500 tons in 1985 to 163,500 in 1988 (UNIDO, 1991 table 3.13 p 135). Aluminum has had the added advantage to the Ghanaian economy of increasing its value added as well as linkages from 1975 when 94.8% of output went to exports, compared to 1988 when only 76.9% of a higher output was exported (ibid.) with increasing output being used as raw material in the building industry.

It must be emphasised however, that not all minerals achieved the same amount of productivity gains. Diamond mining for example fell from 3.2m carats in 1960 to 442,000 carats in 1987 and to only 300,000 carats in 1988 (Synge 1995). The government in 1993, allowed De Beers of South Africa to acquire a 40% stake in Ghana Consolidated Diamonds, the state owned producer[21] together with Lazare Kaplan International of USA with another 40% equity holding and leaving the government with twenty percent share holding. A production and management agreement with De Beers and Lazare Kaplan is expected to raise production levels to about a million carats by the year 2000.

The future of mining

The future of the Ghanaian mining industry, particularly gold looks bright. The outlook of gold prices in the 1990s according to the World Bank "has slightly improved from that which prevailed in the late 1980s" (WB 1992b, p.236). Gold would therefore continue to be a high earning area for the Ghanaian economy. However, this goal would be realised only if the country begins to place more emphasis on gold related processing and manufacturing activities such as jewelry market and more critically, build a refinery in Ghana.

The need for a refinery becomes more justifiable as Ghana heads for the two million ounce per year production target in 1996 (Synge 1995, p.439). A refinery would create the necessary linkage to other sectors of the economy and introduce new industrial skills into the macro economy. The value added component of the sector would also dramatically jump up and make the gold sector even more profitable for all. The World Bank's Trends in Developing Economies (1994c, p.192) survey indicates that value added in mining increased by 9% per year for both 1992 and 1993. The building of a refinery to process Ghanaian gold[22] also would give added impetus to Ghanaian industry in general and the mining and jewelry industries in particular.

Ashanti Goldfields Company has since 1994, established a subsidiary company, Ashanti Explorations with a $30m equity capital, following its own floatation, to prospect for gold in other African countries. The company, which has all the potential of becoming an African transnational, is currently licensed to explore in Guinea, Mali and Eritria (see African Business, May 1995, p.13).

The mineral sector, building on the success of the floatation of AGC on both the Ghana and London Stock Exchanges, is now in a position to raise relatively low cost capital for further investment. Such floatations, enabling the company to make forays into the Ghana and London equity markets, provides a spur for the economy as a whole. The $1.6bn value placed on the company during the valuation enabled an additional $450m to be pumped into the Ghanaian economy in new shares of the company.

Industry under adjustment

Critical to the outcome of the adjustment programme in Ghana is how industry, particularly manufacturing, fares in the grand scheme of things. It is obvious that the primary sector, particularly agricultural exports, cannot sustain either an export led growth or provide the necessary levels of linkages crucial to internally consistent development. Even the World Bank concedes[23] that the drastic fall in cocoa and other agricultural prices makes any dependence on the traditional sector unattractive. Neither does gold export, except as a refined final product, hold much promise as a basis of sustained development.

The onus is, therefore, on manufacturing, rather than quarrying or mining to lead the way to a sustained internally consistent and capacity enhancing development. Up until the adjustment programme, industrialisation in Ghana has been largely state led, as the large number of state enterprises discussed earlier in this chapter indicates. From the state led industrialisation of the First Republic through the partnership between state and private sectors of the National Liberation Council and the Second Republic to the present, the Public Sector has been the dominant player in Ghanaian industry. Except for the presence of some multinational corporations such as Nestle, Unilever, Coca Cola, Star Kist, BP, Shell to mention a few, all major industrial units have essentially been state owned. The indigenous Ghanaian private sector has been largely at the level of micro, small and medium scale enterprises.

The economic decline of the late 1970s and early 1980s therefore had a devastating effect on Ghanaian industry, and particularly manufacturing. What exacerbated the consequences of the general decline was the dominance of the state sector. The state sector is often cut off from access to private capital both on the local and international markets. Therefore, once the state becomes impotent [as the results of its own fiscal problems] to pump in the needed liquidity, units operating within this environment become paralysed. State owned industrial units, reflecting the generality of Ghanaian industry, was extremely dependent on foreign exchange for its inputs (Steel & Webster 1991, p.5). Once the macro economy became unable to provide the level of foreign exchange support needed, large scale industrial capacity became idle.

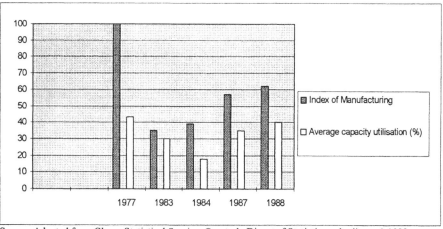

Source: Adapted from Ghana Statistical Service, Quarterly Digest of Statistics vol. vii, no. 1 1989.

Figure 6.1 Large scale manufacturing production and capacity utilisation 1977-1988

181

The above figure indicates that five years into the adjustment programme, average manufacturing capacity utilisation was still less than that of 1977, a year in which although the economy was already crippled, average capacity utilisation stood at 43%, compared to the 40% of 1988.

Manufacturing output, having stagnated in the 1970s, declined sharply in the early 1980s. Accordingly, the manufacturing sector's contribution to gross domestic product fell from 22% in 1973 to under 5% by 1983 at the beginning of the reform programme. The figure has since then clawed to 10% by 1990 (Synge 1995, p.438). The decline and gradual recovery has been more pronounced in the medium to large scale manufacturing sub sector. This sector has traditionally been prominent in food processing, vehicle assembly, cement production, paper, chemicals and export based processing such as cocoa and timber (ibid.). Manufacturing suffered during the period of decline from transport congestion, particularly at the Takoradi and Tema ports as well as the persistent over valuation of the cedi. Major rehabilitation works at the two ports is therefore expected to remove this particular bottleneck.

Small scale manufacturing

Small scale industries dominate the country's private sector manufacturing. The 1987 Industrial Census found a total of 8640 businesses, of which 97% were in manufacturing. A total of 7370 of these [88%] were classified small scale[24] with 85% of them employing less than ten workers. There were also twelve companies, including Unilever and Volta River Authority in the big business category (Ghana, 1987). The survey findings indicated a noticeable absence of a 'middle class' in the form of medium scale enterprises in manufacturing.[25]

Commentators such as Steel and Webster[26] posit that successful industrialisation must have an indigenous base, and the small to medium scale sector provides the base for expansion while helping to develop the experienced entrepreneurial and managerial class that is necessary to spur indigenous and efficient investment and management of large scale industries. The Ghanaian small scale enterprises, like their counterparts in other developing countries, have tended to be relatively labour intensive and to utilise low level of technology, an occurrence that has helped the sector expand while achieving employment and income distribution objectives. Increasingly however, improvements in technological up take has been noticeable especially in food processing and furniture.

Effects of adjustment on manufacturing

One of the strongest criticisms against Ghana's Bank and Fund supported adjustment programme has been the charge of de-industrialisation that critics say has resulted from the pursuance of the programme (see Zeebo 1991, Jon Kraus 1991)]. Indeed both the Ghana Chamber of Commerce and the Association of Ghanaian Industries have persistently complained about manufacturing industry losing out as a result of the over liberalised trade policy (Rothchild 1991, pp.134-135). The mass circulating Daily Graphic[27] in September 1988 reported that almost all Ghanaian owned garment factories had closed down because of unwinnable competition from cheap imports (West Africa 1988, p.1684).

General effect on industry

Adjustment policies affect industries differently and with varying incentives for investment in new capacity. Expenditure switching policies such as devaluation that raise the relative prices of tradables tend to favour industrial value added in exporting and import competing activities, but at the same time raising cost for industries that depend on tradable inputs. Liberalisation of the market place helps those companies which hitherto lacked access to allocated inputs such as foreign exchange, but also increases the competition for many import substituting industries. The net result of incentives therefore depend on the mix of policies, how well they are implemented and transmitted through price signals as well as the character of individual industries (Steel & Webster 1991, p.3).

Beyond the abstract, after declining from 19% to less than 12%, the share of value added of the industrial sector in GDP rose to over 14% by 1990 (Kapur 1991, p.11). The about 2% aggregate growth in share of value added by the industrial sector between 1983-1990 highlights the relative mediocre performance of value adding industry under adjustment in Ghana. Total manufacturing only accounted for 9% of GDP in 1990 (ibid.).

Manufacturing production in 1989 stood at 63% of its 1977 level. Although this is an advance on the 39% equivalent figure for 1984 (Parfitt 1995, p.57), considering the amounts of foreign capital pumped into the economy during the period of adjustment, and considering that the Ghanaian economy was already in free fall decline by 1977, it begs one to wonder whether the adjustment years were not wasted from the single perspective of industrialisation.

However, capacity utilisation has improved since the beginning of the programme as figure 6.1 shows. Non-metallic mineral production, including cement, [whose production has since doubled and capacity utilisation quadrupled between 1984 - 1989], rubber, wood processing and beverages in which capacity utilisation has tripled, have been prominent in the upsurge of industrial production. Others such as textiles and clothing, leather goods, paper products and printing, iron and steel products as well as electrical products and appliances have had a very turbulent period because of harsh competition from cheap imports. These firms also happen to be more dependent on imported inputs and have had to contend with the falling value of the cedi as well (ibid.)

Table 6.7
GDP of manufacturing at constant 1980 factor cost
(ten million cedi)

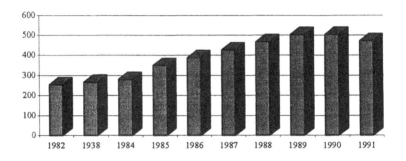

Source: UN African Statistical Yearbook, 1990/91 vol.1 p.2.12-4.

The gradual improvement to both industrial production and manufacturing output occasioned by new investment in machinery and parts, improved infrastructural provision, liberalised financial climate has dragged capacity utilisation from the paltry 20% for industry as a whole in 1985 to 62% by 1988 (Synge 1995, p.438) while as table 6.8 below shows, manufacturing capacity utilisation doubled from 18% in 1984 to 37% in 1990.

184

Table 6.8
Manufacturing capacity utilisation

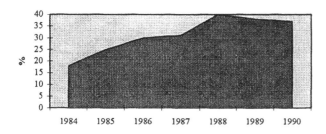

Source: UNDP/WB 1992, African Development Indicators p 254.

The nature of the effect of ERP cannot, therefore, at the level of the macro economy, be said to be spectacular or even positive. A United Nations Industrial Development Organisation and the International Labour Organisation joint Industrial Sector Review and Programming mission to Ghana noted that while "...It is generally agreed that the thrust of macro economic policy is correct... For many enterprises in private sector, the transitional costs now appear to be greater than the benefits they have so far undoubtedly gained" (UNIDO/ILO 1992, p.2).

The UNIDO/ILO report raised two specific issues:

• The impact of trade liberalisation which raised some demands for protection;
• The effects of tight monetary policy and the associated interest rates. The scarcity and high cost of credit being of great concern to Ghanaian industrialist. The constant fall in value of the cedi erodes the value of the equity investment of business people as well as raising the cost of inputs.

A number of useful developments have however, been recorded particularly at the level of the large scale manufacturing. The reopening of the Aboso Glass factory after more than a decade of idleness with a capacity of 25,000 tons per annum in 1987 was a most welcome development, particularly for the beverage brewing, beverage and pharmaceutical industries. The liberalised and investor friendly climate created particularly for international capital has also attracted significant new investment to the palm oil industry. A $15m palm oil mill was opened in 1987 to give impetus to agro processing. while existing cement factories more than doubled production within the adjustment period. A new factory producing cement from local raw materials instead of imported clinker also came on line at Tema (Synge 1995, p.438).

The large scale manufacturing sector definitely fared better under adjustment, particularly, subsidiaries of foreign multinational corporations such as Guinness, Nestle, Unilever etc. They had the capacity and access to credit limits beyond their indigenous competitors who have had to grapple with the high interest rates imposed under IMF influence. Compared to 1984 therefore, capacity utilisation had improved but nowhere near substantial, as table 6.9 shows.

Table 6.9

Large scale manufacturing productive and capacity utilisation 1977-1988

	1977	1983	1984	1986	1988
Index of manufacturing production (1977=100)	100	35	39	57	62
Average capacity utilisation (%)	43	30	18	35	40

Source: Ghana Statistical Service, Quarterly Digest of Statistics vol. vii no. 1 March 1989.

The effect of the adjusting regime on small scale industry has left much to be desired. It is the sector that has been most affected by the direction and content of the adjustment package. The small scale or micro enterprises have absorbed an increasing share of labour during the adjustment period as formal employment opportunities diminished under public expenditure cuts (see WB 1990). The Adjustment Programme has either consciously or unconsciously included measures that banished the laid off into self run businesses. But demand for goods and services provided by small and micro enterprises hardly kept up with the growing supply of labour in these activities. Government policy has also contracted aggregated demand in the economy leading to fierce competition. As has been the case elsewhere, units within this sector have witnessed income and productivity falls in areas characterised by easy entry and elastic demand (ibid.).

An analysis of industrial and especially manufacturing productivity during adjustment would not be complete without examining the World Bank's reaction to widespread criticism by the industrial sector as has been the case in Ghana. The World Bank claims that evidence adduced from surveys of manufacturing firms in Ghana negates the contention that the heavy dosage of adjustment reform witnessed in Ghana leads to de-industrialisation. The Bank relies on its own commissioned survey conducted by the Center for African Economic Studies at Oxford between 1992 and 1993. The survey claims to have taken in randomly chosen formal and informal enterprises of all sizes, including "unregistered enterprises excluded from official figures" [WB 1994, p.149].

The Bank claims that the aforementioned survey found much activity taking place in the small to medium scale enterprises with both output and aggregate employment increasing at 2% a year in their sample. The bank again claims that two -thirds of the increase in manufacturing employment since 1983 is attributable to new firms particularly in woodworking and metalwork sectors, where domestic resource costs are relatively low (ibid. p.151).

On the observable reduction in the number of employees by firms belonging to the medium to large scale category surveyed in which 63% have fewer workers in 1991 compared to 1983, the Bank's explanation is that the phenomenon is explained by firms downsizing to become more efficient [ibid. p 149]. This is obviously very questionable. Firms have traditionally downsized when the aggregate output per additional employee becomes negative. In this instant, firms have not just been able to meet labour costs. This needs to be differentiated from conscious downsizing as a business strategy.

The World Bank is emphatic that adjustment did not inhibit enterprise growth and that it radically changed relative prices [and the incentive environment] with emphasis on cutting cost as well as encouraging more efficient use of resources. Enterprises, the Bank argues, have therefore moved from one class to a higher during the adjustment period. Sixty seven percent of medium scale enterprises existing in 1993 begun as small firms, compared to only 50% of the old medium sized firms. The upward mobility, from the Bank's perspective, is the proof that new firms are in a better position to take advantage of the new environment.

The future

The structural problems embedded in the Ghanaian economy have not been eliminated during the twelve years of intensive adjustment practise. At best, these have only been minimised. Regarding manufacturing, growth has been held up by "continuing structural problems, and the dramatic increase in costs of spare parts and raw materials" as the value of the cedi continues to fall (Synge 1995, p.438).

A study by the IMF in 1991 and quoted by Synge (ibid.) found private sector response to the improved macro - economy unsatisfactory and that the process of reform itself had also forced the closure of some industries whose markets had hitherto been protected from the predatory instincts of transnationals and the rent seeking and dumping practising traders from within and without.

Prospects for development in the manufacturing sector would have to be looked at again taking on board, the reservations of indigenous industry. Small scale industry can for example, operate more readily with low levels of infrastructural and other non traded inputs while serving as a training ground for the development of the indigenous entrepreneurial class. Such developments would not mean much without a conscious policy in place to encourage and create an indigenous entrepreneurial class. The present over reliance on international capital and markets is therefore short sighted.

Prospects for investment in large scale industries may not be very favourable in the medium term as well. Adjustments have usually taken place only after serious deterioration in infrastructural services, financial systems and institutions. Yet some large scale industries may raise their capacity utilisation as adjustment borrowing makes resources available, most are reluctant to invest in new capacity until underlying infrastructural, financial and institutional conditions are improved (Meier & Steel 1989). It is, therefore, not surprising that manufacturing growth has stagnated, growing at an average of only 2.8% annually between 1988 and 1991 (Leechor 1994, p.170).

Policy makers would have to address the issue of affordable credit to the indigenous manufacturing sector. As the ILO/UNIDO team discovered, the non discriminatory monetary policy pursued as part of the adjustment process has squeezed profit margins to the level where profit alone has become inadequate for expanded production by the indigenous manufacturing sector (UNIDO/ILO 1992, p.8). The issue of credit for Ghanaian industry must be addressed urgently together with the adoption of policies that would strengthen the linkages between industry, agriculture, fisheries as well as mining.

Table 6.10
Selected economic indicators 1985 - 1994
(annual % change unless otherwise indicated)

	1985	1986	1987	1988	1989	1990	1991	1992	1993	1994
Output & Prices:										
Real GDP rate	5.1	5.2	4.8	5.6	5.1	3.3	5.3	3.9	5	3.8
Agriculture	0.6	3.3	0	3.6	4.2	-2	4.7	-0.6	2.5	1
Industry	17.6	7.6	11.5	7.3	4.1	5.4	3.7	5.8	4.3	2.8
Services	7.5	6.5	9.4	7.8	5.8	8.8	6.3	7.7	7	6.6
Per capita income	2.1	2.2	1.8	2.6	2.1	0.3	2.3	0.9	2	-
GDP deflator	20.6	41.7	39.2	34.2	27.5	38.7	20.3	12.5	24.5	27
Inflation (cpi annual av.)	10.4	24.6	39.8	31.4	25.2	37.2	18	10	25	24.9
Inflation (cpi end of year)	19.5	33.3	34.2	26.6	30.5	35.9	10.3	13.3	27.7	34.2

Source: Government of Ghana: 1995 Budget Statement.

While this chapter and the preceding one have examined the both the broad and the sectoral thrust of the Ghanaian adjustment experience, the next chapter would specifically look at weaknesses of the adjustment programme.

Notes

1 See World Bank, Ghana: Progress on Adjustment. 9475 - GH p 75.
2 By Ghanaian standards but nowhere near the experiences of other African countries.
3 WB, 1985 Report No GH 5366 - GH & WB 1985, Report No GH 5366.
4 The term used for Ghanaians who were expelled from Nigeria in 1982.
5 maize, cassava, cocoyam, and rice.
6 See Jon Kraus "The Political Economy of Food in Ghana" in Naomi Chazan & Tim Shaw (eds.) Coping with Africa's Food Crisis. p.109 table 4.3.
7 12,900 km being described either as poor or very bad.
8 Particularly for food crops.
9 Particularly for food crops.
10 The author, Zurich Leslie, was a member of both the original 1981 team as well as the 1984 team from KPMG Peat Marwick Management Consultancy. [1994 "Commercialisation of the Cocoa Board", Paper delivered at Southampton University on Oct. 14, 1994 p2. mimeo].
11 The World Bank's target being 55%.
12 The National Mobilisation Programme being one of the new 'revolutionary' organs established by the PNDC.
13 That is, workers who existed only on payrolls.
14 The fallacy of composition is a situation where a simultaneous expansion of exports in the face of inelastic world demand depresses rather than enhance export revenues.
15 See the Special Newsweek Supplement on Ghana, October 3, 1994.
16 Name changed to Ashanti Goldfields Company in line with its stock market floatation in 1994.
17 The precious Diamond Marketing Corporation was revamped and renamed to perform this function in the mid 1980s.
18 see Richard Synge, 1995 'Ghana: Economy' in Africa South of the Sahara 1995 p 439.
19 African Business March 1995 p 28 & May 1995 p 13.
20 Once the trade sanctions on the country had been lifted.
21 Now renamed Birim River Diamonds Ltd.
22 The country's gold is currently refined in Switzerland, the country's own refinery having been abandoned at about ninety percent completion after the 1966 coup d' estat.
23 See World Bank, 1994, Africa: Reforms, Results and the Road Ahead p.76.
24 Employing between one and nineteen workers.
25 This indicates an inherent inability of small scale industries to grow.
26 Small Enterprises under Adjustment in Ghana, 1991 WB Technical Paper No. 138 p.3.
27 State owned and generally very supportive of the government.

7 A general critique of adjustment in Ghana, 1983 - 1995

There is very little doubt that Ghana's Adjustment Programme has chalked a number of successes as the preceding chapters have related. Some of these indicators have been both significant and incontestable - growth rates, the resuscitation of the cocoa , timber and mining sectors and the re-establishment of confidence in the Ghanaian economy by international financial institutions and markets. The Programme has, however, attracted a number of criticisms spanning across all schools of development thought. Whereas writers such as Yeebo (1991), Ninson (1990), Onimode (1991), Mengisteab (1995), Stewart (1992), Bangura (1992) etc. have lambasted the Programme on ideological and political economy grounds, others such as Frimpong Ansah, Toye, Chazam etc. have taken umbrage on design grounds.

It is my intention therefore, to give prominence to the fault lines of the Programme not just from any particular school's proposition, but from an independent, even if structuralist position. I am however, ignoring all criticisms related to mass poverty for the next chapter. My explication is therefore, going to be conducted under specific themes and areas.

General political economy

a) Political

In examining the fault lines of Ghana's Adjustment Programme, it is almost imperative to begin with the specific ideological/political underpinning of the Programme. Liberalisation of the economy and particularly of international trade, has since the 1980s become the dominant ideology on the basis of which much of North - South economic interactions take place. The collapse of the communist governments of Eastern Europe has further fuelled this development.

While the Ghanaian and indeed the African experience provides evidence that state intervention has, by and large been inefficient, the diagnosis and prescriptions of the liberalisation school in replacing the state with the market is not without serious flaws. Firstly, neither recent empirical evidence nor history provide a strong basis for the claim that intervention is the underlying cause of the prevailing economic crisis. Secondly, the liberalisation school refuses to distinguish between the differences in the nature of the state and thus types of interventions, as it lumps all the above together as harmful to economic development. Finally, even if prevailing economic conditions were attributable to past policy failures, the liberalisation ideology does not still provide new solutions. The liberalisation position is at best a re stating of the discredited trickle down theory. As the United Nations Economic Commission for Africa [UNECA] stated on the subject, 'Africa's economic and social crisis has not developed all out of a sudden in so far as it has existed since the mid 1970s as a result of the cumulative impact of a number of adverse factors both internal and external.'[1] And yet it is the external factors that liberalisation ideologues refuse to acknowledge in the African situation.

Ghana's Programme also ignores the objective reality that some late comers to industrialisation have succeeded, Japan, Taiwan and South Korea etc.] through interventionist strategies (Sen 1988 & James Dietz 1992). Notwithstanding the evidence of successful intervention elsewhere, the Programme makes no attempt at examining which sectors or which particular cases open themselves to successful and efficient state intervention.

b) Markets and the state

The adjustment Programme refuses to differentiate between the various forms of state intervention. For example, the state's positive role in the procurement and distribution of agricultural inputs as well as credit to small scale agriculture is being put on the same weighing scale as the disastrous state ownership and operation of plantations A Programme that seems ideology driven in its worship of the market has serious limitations for the Ghanaian sphinx. The insistence by the Bank on privatising the external marketing of cocoa on a world market where size and the economies of scale are universally recognised by most businesses smacks of ideologically induced impairment.

It is equally important, in understanding why Ghana's adjustment attracts very little praise from Ghanaians, to recognise that Adjustment is built on the false premise of markets always knowing best. Not withstanding what free marketers claim, there is no such thing as a free market with a price mechanism adjudicating prices and allocating resources within the economy without political [state] or class guidance either directly or indirectly. Not since the nineteenth century when, some buccaneering and plundering European nations briefly attempted unadulterated *laissez faire* policies.-the Corn Laws and the Enclosure Movements marked the end of that experiment. Even if 'free markets' were not such a fallacy, the inadequate flow of information between producers and consumers, sellers and buyers and the rural and urban dwellers that would have underpinned any such intermediation of the price mechanism fatally flaws any such contraption.

c) Development

A recent study by the World Bank on Sub-Sahara Africa observed "... in the most fundamental sense, development depends on the capacity to initiate, sustain and accommodate change" (1989 p.38). The study found out that "weak capacity in both public and private sectors is at the very core of Africa's development crisis" (ibid.). And yet, Ghana's Programme marginalises spending on human capital development.[2] More importantly, the Programme is geared towards growth rather than development. Whereas development "... implies changes in technology and an increase in useful material resources" and "... improvement in the quality of life" (Hadjor 1993, p.100), growth pertains to the quantitative improvement of economic aggregates. Development encompasses the qualitative advancement of an economy [including its people] which may take the form of an enhanced capacity within the economy to sustain the achievement of greater welfare and economic independence for the mass majority of the population. Development must therefore encompass an indigenous ability to sustain technological progress while creating qualitative employment and social provision for citizens.

Contrary to the above, Ghana's Programme has concentrated on growth that is generated by increasing exploitation and export of primary products with very little value added. This form of production hardly has any linkages to the rest of the economy, especially the rural economy. The current gold boom is a good example of this tendency of growth without development. Without a conscious state led attempt at translating growth into development, private capital and the market for that matter, has been unable to turn the average 5% growth rate chalked over the past decade into meaningful development.

d) Vulnerability to international commodity markets

A major shortcoming of Ghana's SAP is the inadequate notice taken of the vulnerability of the country's primary products to world market upheavals. For example, when Ghana's cocoa production rose from 153,000 metric tonnes in 1984 to 300,000 metric tonnes in 1989, the net benefit to the economy of the increased production was whittled away by the decline of world market price for the commodity on the back of Ghana's increased production.[3] At the other extreme, while the value of cocoa exports [and thus Ghana's exports] declined per tonne in 1989, import prices, particularly oil, rose by 20% during the same period (Legum 1990, p.2).

World cocoa output rose by a third between 1983 and 1987 - the precise period of output growth by Ghana - and as was to be expected, cocoa prices fell through the floor established by the International Cocoa Agreement.[4] The fall in cocoa price had by 1989, amounted to 21% of the 1983 price level and yet Ghana's programmers, under the tutelage of the Bank and the Fund, had only provided for a 4% fall in price (Loxley 1990, p.16). Why the designers, banking on an increased cocoa output as the basis of the initial recovery could have got it so wrong is puzzling, recognising that the cocoa market is one of the most volatile in its downward fluctuations on the least pretext.

Gold, the current lead foreign exchange earner, is not exempt from the same price upheavals or vulnerability. The metal is currently enjoying a respectable rise in price levels, but the cyclical fall in metal prices is a well known phenomenon on the world market.

e) Foreign finance

A very strong weakness of the ERP is its extreme dependence on foreign financial flows, whether official or private. During the last Donors Meeting on Ghana held in Paris,[5] $1.6bn in Programme and project aid was pledged for 1996 and 1997 by both multilateral and bilateral donors.[6] This amount is equivalent to about 60% of the projected exports earnings for the period.[7] The very 'generous' levels of official funding lends itself to being used as powerful leverage by the 'donors'. The threat of withdrawing such would be enough to bring the government into line irrespective of the national interest. During the last donors conference, the external funders - both multilateral and bilateral - 'urged' the government to intensify its privatisation efforts, despite clear evidence that the privatisation agenda, especially of utilities and public services, needed to be re-examined in the light of experiences from elsewhere and the efficiency gains made by some of these bodies within the last five years under public ownership.

The over-reliance on foreign finance for the pursuit of adjustment has in the past adversely affected the country's balance of payment position. Arising from the non-disbursement of programmed loans and grants, largely from the International Development Association of the World Bank Group, the country experienced a large shortfall in its borrowings in 1994. Repayments however, continued apace, creating a net outflow of resources amounting to ¢84.96bn in 1994. And 1994 was the third straight year in which non-disbursement of foreign inflows as a result of perceived non-compliance with mechanistic conditionalities caused macro economic distress and deprived the state of the opportunity to use divestiture proceeds[8] to retire domestic debt or increase revenues (Budget Statement 1995, p.9).

The unhealthy reliance on foreign finance enumerated above goes beyond official sources. Foreign private capital and investors are vigorously been pursued, even if with relatively very little success other than in mining, to the neglect of the domestic capital. It is therefore not surprising that after more than a decade of adjustment, private saving as a percentage of GNP has not exceeded the pre - adjustment rates (Alderman 1994, p.50).

The foregoing can only bode danger for the country, particularly when local industries are not seen to be given equal attention and treatment. There is no empirical evidence available that any country within the last half century has made susbtantive progress without an indigenous industrial base. The collapse of the foreign owned and operated Meridien BIAO bank in June 1995 is a pointer to this danger. For while the domestic operations of the multi national banking institution was vibrant and profitable, the collapse of the parent holding company in Belgium led to a run on the Ghanaian operation, leading to the eventual take-over of the local operation by the Social Security and National Insurance Trust [SSNIT], a state owned institution that is in the process of divesting itself of its ownership of the Social Security Bank as part of the country's privatisation drive.

So strong is the desire to attract foreign investment that the inducement package available to foreign investors under the new Ghana Investment Promotion Centre Act, 1994[9] is probably the most liberal in the developing world. Seventy five percent of capital investment is allowed to be written off against tax in the very first year of operation. The remaining twenty five percent can also be written off in the same way within the susbequent four years.[10] The corporate tax in the non traditional export sector is fixed at 8% by the Act, while hotels pay a corporate tax of only 25%. For all other sectors, the corporate tax is now 35% (GIPC, p.12).[11]

The virtual 'sell-out' of Ghana's natural resources to transnationals without commensurate returns to the Ghanaian economy leaves the country a loser. The reduction of gold export duty from 20% to 6%, a reduction of company corporate tax from 50% to 45% for mining companies [and 35% for others], exemption from payment of import duties on plant and machinery as well as exemption from the Selective Alien Employment Tax[12] have radically reduced the revenue accruing to the state from the operations of these transnational mining and other concerns. And all these inducements when the cost of production is one of the cheapest anywhere in the world. Ashanti Goldfields Ltd.'s cost of production [with the deepest mines in the country and therefore the most expensive] is only $199 per ounce, well below the world industrial average of $230 per ounce (ibid.).

f) Trade and the colonial legacy

The Adjustment Programme stands the danger of reinforcing the dangerous structural imbalances moulded into the Ghanaian economic fabric by colonialism. By 1994, nearly 84% of all export earnings (see BUDGET STATEMENT 1995, p.9) was accounted for by gold, cocoa and timber, just as these three commodities had done from 1921 [see chapter 1]. The structural imbalance here lies in the absence of any noticeable forward or backward linkages to the rest of the economy. As long as gold, cocoa and timber were exported to meet the raw material needs of British and subsequently European needs, all was good. By the absence of linkages -and thus alternative domestic uses - the country becomes totally dependent on the external market, hence a price taker. Yet, this is the route favoured by adjustment under the mistaken guise of comparative advantage! Ghana's comparative advantage in the production of cocoa for example, was consciously and carefully nurtured by the British colonial administration,[13] to meet the raw material requirements of factories based in England, hence whatever advantage that allegedly exist for the production of cocoa beans in not natural but designed for a purpose in a grand scheme of British colonial and post colonial domination.

The overall dependence on primary commodities has not changed, and yet, industrialisation has been the tested root to development of all developed countries. Why then, should Ghana's economy, after more than a decade of adjustment, have nothing to show for diversifying exports and production? Primary commodities constituted 98% of all exports in 1965 and by 1987, primary commodities still constituted 97% of all exports. (Stewart 1992, p.30 Table 1.5). The adjustment Programme ignores the reality that:

> there are systematic forces at work in world markets which tend to reduce the gains of the poor countries in international trade; consequently, trade may actually widen the gap between the rich and the poor countries. Furthermore, adverse movements in terms of trade of poor countries transfers the benefits of technological innovations from poor to the rich (Singer & Ansari 1977, p.65).

Agriculture

The agricultural sector as a whole[14] has been one of the spectacular failures of Ghana's adjustment Programme. The food, animal husbandry and fisheries sub-sectors have hardly been touched by the economic and social changes being pursued under adjustment. Food production, as noted earlier in this chapter, has indeed declined on a per capita basis.

The agricultural sector generally suffered from 'under government' rather than 'over government' as the designers of the adjustment Programme would want us to believe. Once government revenues evaporated in the late and early 1980s, the country lost its ability to service the sector. And although some advocates of SAPs contend that getting government off the back of farmers, fishermen and herdsmen would raise productivity, this position is not borne out by empirical evidence in Ghanaian agriculture.[15]

The real issue of agricultural productivity in Ghana lies in the poor internal terms of trade, the subsidisation of urban agricultural consumption by rural agriculture, the poor access to credit for small holders [who produce the bulk of the country's agricultural output], the absence of alternative production infrastructure such as irrigation facilities, problems of communications etc. Even for export crop production, it is convincingly argued that the major sources of disincentives in developing countries are to be found in the effect of exchange rate distortions and high levels of taxation rather than direct government intervention. (Krueger, Schift & Valdes 1988. & Stryker, 1988).

The Fund and the Bank are relying on 'market forces' to reverse the fall in per capita agricultural production (Loxley 1988, p.28) but evidence from more than a decade of adjustment in Ghana points to the inability of markets to perform this function. Agricultural responses are determined not just by price, but by a myriad of factors including weather, credit, inputs, communications. With the removal of subsidies on inputs, the position of food croppers in Ghana has worsened (Smith 1987). The sharp drop in fertiliser[16] intake resulting from the privatisation of fertiliser procurement and marketing [referred to earlier in this chapter] is indicative of how unsuitable the market is for this purpose. In any case, it is quite revealing to note that not a single industrialised country goes without subsidising agriculture, especially food production. More than 50% of the total budget of the European Union is still spent on the Common Agricultural Policy.

It is pertinent to note that food imports as a percentage of export earnings rose from 10.5% in 1980 to 34.7% in 1989 (Mengisteab 1995, p.176 Table 8.3). This leaves us in very little doubt that the country's ability to feed itself - critical for an agricultural economy - has been compromised by the Adjustment Programme. In absolute terms, the level of inability is even more frightening since the increased percentage of 24.2% is on an export base that doubled within the 1980 - 1987 period. Loxley captures the tragedy of food production under agriculture when he writes:

> It is a sad commentary on Fund/Bank Programmes that the food production sector is treated as a virtual 'residue' in programmes of most countries producing crops for exports. The focus is on export promotion, and once consumer subsidies have been removed, the market prices of food are supposed to adjust in a 'trickle-down' manner (Loxley 1990, p.15).

But of course, the bankruptcy of the trickle down theory is widely recognised.

Cocoa has been portrayed as one of the unparalleled successes of adjustment in Ghana (WB 1994a). It is however, questionable whether the increased output recorded from 1986 was accounted for by increased productivity or simply a cessation of smuggling activities across the western and eastern borders of the country. And to what degree is any such productivity gain, if any, attributable to the revolutionary mobilisation of 1983/84 as opposed to IMF/Bank policy? In any case, the 50% increase in volume purchases by the Cocoa Board between 1983 - 1989 only led to a fall in total receipts.[17]

Industrialisation/industry

The relative backwardness of the Ghanaian and African economic structures, the unreliability of primary exports and the relative lag in their skill and institutional development are greater than those suffered by countries in Asia or America at the same stage of development and thus the need for industrialisation becomes even more pertinent (Lall 1992.). With the foregoing odds stacked against Ghana, there is in both the medium and long term, no alternative path to development but by industrialisation.[18]

Industrialisation is thus of major import to Ghana's developmental aspirations. Every country that has achieved sustained development has witnessed structural transformation from primary production towards industry. Industrial production is critical to raise growth of incomes and employment; diversifying exports, protecting the economy from worsening terms of trade for primary products, establishing linkages etc. (see Stewart 1994). Even the World Bank, in its watershed Berg Report claimed "Industrialisation has a crucial role in long term development; it is an important source of structural change and diversification; and it can increase the flexibility of the economy and reduce dependence on external forces" (WB 1981, p.91).

Industrial growth has since 1987, slowed down to the level where real per capita value becomes negative if annual population growth is brought into the equation. Even assuming the 2.8% growth for 1994 reported in the 1995 [see table 6.10] is allowed to stand,[19] the single largest contribution to industrial growth is still gold mining, which is basically extractive primary activity.

In the light of the above, the Adjustment Programme's drive to privatising existing state owned industry [as opposed to disposing off or liquidating those that are irredeemably insolvent] while pursuing an exercise of trade liberalisation is surely a guaranteed suicide attempt. Undifferentiated import liberalisation has thrown Ghanaian industry into unmoderated competition with multi billion dollar MNCs for the local market. Without the state's intervention to create a level playing field, local industry with any sizeable value added component has been unable to grow. So negative has the effect of this unfair competition been that by 1990, P V Obeng,[20] had to admit that "... the over-liberalisation of certain economic activities" was a mistake of policy (West Africa March 1990, p.359) even though nothing has subsequently been done.

The privatisation component of SAP has further damaged the country's potential for indigenous industrialisation. The capacity of any nation to develop and enhance its technological expertise ought to demand a very high priority from managers of the national economy. But the disposal of viable going concerns, such as the Cocoa Factories at Tema and Takoradi to foreign [German] interest at a time when productivity and profitability had increased appreciably, is cynical.[21] The country, as already stated in this and previous chapters, has no control over the sale of cocoa beans and in the rare instant of adding value to exports through processing, the facilities for such are being sold to foreign interest! If for any reason, and here only ideological grounds can justify this divestiture, the state needed to off-load such strategic and profitable production facilities, local industry should have been given the first bite of the cherry and in the absence of willing local consortia, the companies should have been floated on the Ghana Stock Exchange to achieve the same purpose.

Just as the import substitution advocates of the 1960s and 1970s saw unbridled protectionism as the panacea for industrial growth, the present free market ethos of Ghana's Adjustment Programme is mistaken in believing that there is a 'free market option' to industrialisation in the 1990s. There is a serious need to examine the basic structural problems of both the Ghanaian economy and Ghanaian industry which were not created by the 'market' but by the conscious disarticulation of colonialism. It would equally need a conscious state led response, utilising all forces in tandem, to give Ghanaian industry the take off it urgently needs. The present direction of adjustment is however, unable to provide this leadership.

Structural Adjustment ignores the reality of the shift in context of international trade. International trade, measured in terms of exchange values has shifted away from primary commodities to high-technology products and yet adjustment in its present formulation, is only shaping Ghana into an efficient primary producer!

I must emphasise, that successful industrialisation does not, however, mean building factories, adding to infrastructure or just adding to physical industrial capacity. It takes planning, appropriate human and material resource base, incentives and above all, forward and backward linkages to the other sectors of the economy to utilise factories and machinery efficiently and profitably for national development. The quality and determinants of the industrial process must therefore, be seen to be extremely important.

Employment

The Adjustment Programme has impacted negatively on both formal employment sustenance and the creation as well as the viability of job creation in a number of informal areas of production. At the formal level, the mass retrenchment associated with the Programme was not accompanied by any substantial increase in avenues for job creation. By 1993, some 86 enterprises had been privatised or liquidated with about 20,000 employees redeployed ostensibly to the private [informal] sector (ILO 1995, p.59). The redundancies at Cocoa Board and the Civil Service are additional to the 20,000 retrenched from privatised or liquidated enterprises.

The above retrenchments take on a serious magnitude when juxtaposed against the fact that while population grew by 3.4% between 1981-1990, labour force growth was only 2.8% (ibid.). Between 1985-1993, population growth slowed down to 3.2% while labour force growth only marginally increased to 2.9%[22] indicating in each case, a net loss of job creation. Abbey, credited with much of the design work of ERP 1, recognised the adverse effect of Ghana's chosen adjustment path on employment when he argued that for adjustment to be sustainable, the Programme:

> must seek to increase the rate of participation of the labour force in the economy. Significant segments of society may be precluded from effective participation in the absence of specific programmes designed with that objective in view and included as integral components of the adjustment Programme itself. (Abbey 1990, p.39).

The absence of appropriately designed programmes aimed at employment creation as an integral part of Adjustment is well illustrated by the desire of the funders of infrastructural projects to see home companies, using machinery-intensive methods, win contracts associated with their funding. Foreign funded projects, particularly road construction, have consistently been awarded under a World Bank formula. Invariably, such contracts have tended to go to foreign contractors and in the token instances where such have been awarded to Ghanaian contractors, such have been awarded on machine intensive construction basis rather than labour intensive.

There is enough evidence in feeder road construction that labour intensive methods are superior in that such methods generate more jobs and are 15% cheaper, 50% less foreign exchange is used and such feeder roads tend to be technically superior. A joint study by the European Commission and ILO on the use of labour intensive methods of road construction on a project in Ashanti Region found the utilisation of 1500-2000 workdays per kilometre, which was three times the employment creation rate of machine intensive construction. They also found 30% of the workers employed on this particular method to be female (EC/ILO 1994, p.48).

Monetary / fiscal policy

The area of monetary and fiscal policy has attracted a lot more attention than almost any other area of Ghana's Adjustment Programme. This attention is not just because of the specific policy measures and instruments deployed in this arena, but also because of the effect of such measures on other sectors. A good example is the effect of cost recovery, a policy instrument within the fiscal realm on the take up of educational and health facilities by the poorer sections of the population.

A lot of criticisms against the country's monetary and fiscal policies have been raised elsewhere in the last chapter and therefore my attention here is basically focused on three issues: devaluation; control of currency in circulation and retrenchment.

While the Fund and the Bank have a love affair with devaluation, devaluation *per se* is not curative in either the specific Ghanaian context or indeed in the broader African context (see Loxley 1990, p.11). The peculiar characteristics of the dominant export crop, cocoa in the 1980s is more important than traditional demand and supply analysis. The supply of cocoa is inelastic in the short term while demand is also fairly inelastic. Indeed, demand for cocoa on a per capita basis has been falling since the 1980s when additives/supplements started making serious inroads into cocoa usage. In the case of Ghana shipment figures between 1983 - 1986, the short run formal response to producer prices increases was accounted for by the existence of an underground market for cocoa in the system from smuggling to the formal sector. Real increased production has only led to falls in producer prices on the world market.

There was an inability of the managers of the economy to control the significant levels of currency in circulation. Currency in circulation increased by ₵152.7bn between January and December 1994, a rise of 63.7%.[23] What is not certain is whether the increase in money supply without a commensurate increase in economic productivity is occasioned by the free fall of the value of cedi or whether the astronomical growth in currency in circulation is causal to the free fall. There is however, no doubt that the two reinforce each other. Additionally, the state's inability to put its house in order, as exemplified by the profligate activities of the Ghana National Petroleum Corporation, is a major contributory factor to the rise of money supply (Budget Statement 1995, p.4). Equally critical is the percentage of total currency in circulation outside the banking system. Out of ₵392.2bn of currency in circulation as at the end of December 1994, only ₵23.6bn is lodged with the banking sector, including clearing houses.

As for fiscal policy, two types of reforms have almost cancelled out each other with respect to the government's ability to reduce its wage bill. The large numbers of laid off workers, including Cocoa Board's retrenchment, did not come cheap. The government was obliged to grant those laid off four months' gross salary plus two additional months' salary for every year of service. This imposed considerable burdens on the wage bill (Alderman 1994, p.41). In other areas, such as the Ghana Education Service, retrenchment did not mean a reduction of payroll numbers. Trained teachers simply replaced non-teachers and other permanent personnel in the Ghana Education Service with no net savings in payroll costs. Equally those who remained in the public service had their salaries raised in line with the new ethos of a slim and well paid workforce. It is therefore not surprising that despite retrenchment etc., government wage bill increased from under 25% of all government expenditure in 1982 and 1983 to over 35% in 1987 (ibid.).

External/internal trade

The unwillingness or inability of Structural Adjustment Programmes in general and Ghana in particular to address pertinent issues of international trade disequilibrium is one of the major problems confronting the adjustment process. The impact of international trade and its terms of exchange on the Ghanaian economy is most pronounced. Adopting an export-led growth strategy, therefore, seems pregnant with danger in the context of a refusal to address issues of international trade. By refusing to address and incorporate this reality into adjustment programming, the success or otherwise of Ghana's programmes has been reduced to a lottery. A major deterioration in gold prices would endanger whatever "success" has been chalked.

World cocoa prices continue to be volatile and depressed. Between December 1993 and January 1995, cocoa traded at the London terminal market between £926 and £990 per tonne,- depressed prices at that. This level is not only depressed at historical market level, but even more depressed in real terms, particularly with reference to the depreciation of sterling after the so-called *Black Wednesday* (Budget Statement 1995, p.2). Other than just the terms of trade and prices of primary export commodities, the role of exogenous variables in Ghana's [Africa's] underdevelopment is highlighted by the neo-marxist school of structuralists. Structural links with a powerful Europe in the form of trade, investment and financial ties represent the interference of colonialism carried into the present. Indeed, as Dos Santos postulates, economies such as Ghana's become "conditioned" by economic expansion and contraction that occurs in Europe and North America (Theolonio Dos Santos 1973, p.109). A depression in overseas markets therefore leads to a reduced demand for Ghana's raw materials as happened in the recession of the late 1980s.

The Adjustment Programme's heavy dependence on external loans, even if concessionary, has left the country with a heavy debt burden whose servicing might become an albatross if either gold prices fall significantly on the global market or if concessionary loans and grants dry up in the near future. the pledge of $1.6bn over 1996 and 1997 fiscal years exemplifies this dependence.

The disbursement and non - disbursement of this large portfolio of official finance has thus made the economy a pawn of foreign imposed and administered conditionality. The withholding of International Development Association's facilities in 1994, as an instant of this tendency, created a large negative flow in the country's net borrowing/payment position. This amounted to ¢84.9bn, 48.7% of the total capital expenditure for 1994. (Budget Statement 1995, p.8).[24]

The national debt, at $1398m in 1980 had skyrocketed to $4590m by 1993, with long term debt also increasing from $1162m to $3378m (table 6.9). The magnitude of the debt overhang becomes more striking when examined as a percentage of exports at 1994 levels, which comes to 377.7% (ibid.). National Debt as a percentage of Gross Domestic Product came to 72.6% by 1993.[25] This high level of debt [even by the late 1980s] prompted Ewusi to observe:

> The ERP [still the favoured term by Ghanaians] has not only increased the levels of indebtedness, but debt servicing to unrealistically high levels. One major problem resulting from the ERP is the increasing

dependency and vulnerability of the economy to external factors (Ewusi 1988, p.60).

The large amounts of official inflows also blur the balance of payment position of the country. The 1995 budget statement for example points to a surplus of $180m (p 2) for the 1994 financial year against a balance of trade deficit of $409.6bn - 7.6% of GDP (ibid. p.9). But the difference in the balances of trade and payment is not accounted for by trade in invincibles or earned income from abroad, but by grants and other official loans. The long term problem of the balance of payment disequilibruim at the start of the Adjustment Programme is therefore still prevalent, if even masked by official assistance.

Human capital development

Of all the criticisms against Ghana's Adjustment Programme, the most far reaching is its impact on human capital development. Cuts in public expenditure have almost inevitably, affected items which are essential for long term development, especially expenditure on human capital - health, education and training, as well as research and development in priority areas.[26]

The paradox of the Ghanaian situation is that both the Ghanaian government and the World Bank acknowledge the need for human capital development and yet their actions have been contrary to this acknowledgement. The Bank on the human capital had this to say: "... To survive and compete in a competitive world in the twenty first century, Africa would require not only literate and numerate citizens, but also highly qualified and trained people to perform top quality research, formulate policies and implement programmes essential to economic growth and development" (WB 1989, p.81).

The President of Ghana on the other hand, acknowledged the severity of adjustment on people on low incomes' ability to meet the increasing cost of educating their children and wondered how they 'managed' that.[27] One is forced to wonder whether the perpetual struggle within the Bank by factions wanting to determine the Bank's agenda is responsible for the gulf between its pronouncement above and the reality of its actions.

Environment

The extractive industry orientation of the adjustment Programme has serious environmental consequences both for the present and future generations of

Ghanaians. The overriding desire for growth rates, as opposed to development or quality of life improvements finds expression in environmental degradation.

Serious environmental consequences occur during surface mining operations as the various chemicals used and the by-products of such chemical reactions are released into the atmosphere. With the adoption of the surface option under the recovery Programme instead of the traditional deep mining operations, environmental consequences can no longer be ignored. Surface mining requires relatively lower investment and is thus the preferred option of international capital. Even Ashanti Goldfields Company, considered indigenous by Ghanaians, has found it necessary to follow the lead of new entrants to the Ghanaian mining scene such as Teberebie Goldfields, Canadian Bogosu engaged predominantly in surface mining operations. Ashanti Goldfields' substantial surface operations now yields about 100,000 ounces of gold a year (Yeebo 1991, p.199). The World Bank, in its Trends in Developing Economies 1994 publication, commented on Ghana thus: "Mineral production has polluted the air with corrosive and poisonous gases; discharges of heavy metals and cyanide are polluting water with potentially serious impact on human health" (p.193).

The negative environmental consequences of SAP extends to forestry. The desire for increased export earnings is typified by the jump in timber exports from \$34m in 1980 to \$165.4m in 1994.[28] This 'achievement' was at the cost of deforesting a large stretch of the country. Sawn timber exports had increased by 77% between 1979-1981 and 1989-1991. The average annual net trade in roundwood had also increased from 119,000 cubic meters in 1979-1981 to 205,000 cubic meters in 1989-1991 (World Resources Institute, 1994). The consequence of this was that 700,000 hectacres of forest and woodland was cleared within the same period with the major cause attributable to the timber trade (FAO 1992, Table 1). The above translated into a loss of about 1.3% of the country's forests and woodland each during the 1980 - 1990 period, with the total national stock of forest decreasing from 10.93m ha. in 1980 to 9.55m ha. in 1990.

Of equal importance to the country's environmental heritage and sustainability is the increasingly high cost of electricity and natural gas occasioned by cost recovery. Urban dwellers on low incomes are therefore, being driven to switch to cheaper but less ecologically friendly forms of energy such as fuelwood and charcoal especially for cooking.

Notes

1   See UNECA Document No. E/ECA/CM/10/37/Rev 2 p.8.

2   At least in the short to medium term.

3   Interview with P V Obeng, Chairman of Committee of Secretaries in West Africa March 5 - 11 1990 p 359.

4   The Organisation has never fully recovered since it lost its ability to stabilise prices through its buffer stocks in 1989.

5   The gathering is often referred to as the Paris Club.

6   Daily Graphic Thursday 15 June 1995.

7   Export earnings for 1994 amounting to \$1,206.6 billion.

8   The opposition to the sale of part of the State's share in Ashanti Goldfields Ltd. in 1994 was largely based on this. Opponents argued that the proceeds from the sale was not going to be put into any investment use but for balance of payment purposes.

9   Act 478 of the Parliament of Ghana.

10   see the Times newspaper of London 13 July 1995 p.40.

11   The same Act provides for a tax holiday of five years for investors in real estate, between three to ten years for agriculture and ten years for rural banking. Other tax concessions include accelerated depreciation allowances at the rate of 50% per annum for 2 years for plant expenditure and 20% per annum for building expenditure. A loss-carry-over of 5 years in all sectors is also allowed.

12   Bank of Ghana, 'The Economy of Ghana', Times 13 July 1995 p.40.

13   This indigenous textile industry in industry in Indian was equally subverted by the British colonial administration so as to create a source of raw material, in this case cotton lint, for the newly established textile mills of Manchester and Liverpool, assigning the Indian sub continent to just the production of raw cotton.

14   The exception being export crop production such as cocoa and palm oil.

15   For a good review of the literature on this, see Lipton M, 1989 "State Compression: Friend or Foe of agricultural liberalisation?" Indian Society of Agricultural Economics, Golden Jubilee Volume, Streeten, Paul, 1987: What Price Food? Agricultural Price Policy in Developing Countries, Shapiro, K & Elliot Berg, 1988 "The competitiveness of Sahelian Agriculture" Elliot Berg Associates, Mimeo.

16   This is not a situation where the use of fertiliser has been replaced by manure or some other such method.

17   Financial Times 26 Jan 1990.

18   For a vigorous defence of this route, see Chenery, HB et al., 1986 Industrialisation and Growth: A comparative Study. New York. Oxford Univ. Press for World Bank.

19   That is ignoring the difficulty of collection in an economy where data collection is still problematic while government sourced information is likely to exaggerate the positive and down play the negative.

20   Chairman of the Committee of Secretaries and effective Prime Minister during the PNDC period and presently the Advisor to the President on Presidential Affairs.

21   See Bank of Ghana Advert: Economy of Ghana. Times July 13 1995 p.40.

22   World Bank: 1994. Trends in Developing Economies p.195.

23   See Daily Graphic 4 May 1995

24   The capital budget for 1994 was ¢174.153bn

25   Standard Chartered Bank, Ghana: Country Report 1995.

26   See Frances Stewart 1994 for an exposition on this.

27   JJ Rawlings: Third Sessional Address to Parliament, 6 Jan 1995 p7 ISD.

28   See UNECA Document No. E/ECA/CM/10/37/Rev 2 p.8.

8 Poverty in Ghana

The elimination or minimisation of poverty is and must be the aim of any genuine interpretation of development, at least in the developing world. It is also a worthy national goal for countries of the industrialised North, even if the degree of urgency may not necessarily be the same, although that is getting less true of some countries. This objective in the Third World is probably one of the few areas of where students of development, development activists and allied professionals are in full agreement. Beyond this, there is hardly any consensus on other aspects of the problem 'child' called 'poverty'. This inability stems largely, but not exclusively from the failure to formulate and agree on a single concept of poverty.

There are presently three major concepts or approaches to poverty in mainstream thought. It has been argued that these three definitions or concepts are not sensitive to the experiences of the developing world. Vic George argues that "definitions of poverty used in advanced industrial societies are not sensitive enough to cope with the breath and depth of deprivation in the third world countries." (1988 p.27). While this assertion holds true, this chapter proceeds on more traditional lines because of the absence of starvation and famine in the specific Ghanaian condition.

Subsistence

The subsistence approach to poverty is the oldest and has its origins in the Poor Laws regime of nineteenth century Britain. The reference point under the Poor Laws was crude and largely limited itself to bread and bread-flour measurements, although some Parishes[1] routinely made insignificant allowances for other necessities.[2] The work of nutritionists in later years inevitably led to a re-evaluation of the mechanics of the subsistence concept, with emphasis no longer placed on bread or bread-flour but on calories and related quantities of nutrients. A family was thus deemed to be in poverty if the family income was "not sufficient to obtain the minimum necessaries for the maintenance of merely physical efficiency" (Rowntree 1901, p.86). A family under Rowntree's formula, was treated "as being in poverty if its income minus rent fell short of the poverty line. Although allowance was made in the income for clothing, fuel and some other items, this allowance was very small and food accounted for much of the greatest share of subsistence" (Townsend 1993, p.30).

The subsistence approach became the standard approach both to measurement and conceptualising poverty not just in the first three decades of this century in Britain but by extension in all former colonies including Ghana, where the Guggisberg Ten Year Development Plan (1920-30) saw 'development' as a pre - requisite for moving subjects of the colony from poverty. In Britain, even the 'radical' Beveridge Report on social security that set the tone for post war welfarism operationalised its poverty threshold and thus the level of state assistance on the subsistence concept (Beveridge Report, 1942).

Although the history of subsistence among former British Colonies is best known for India and perhaps South Africa, it was also very important in Ghana. But it was more than just a historical import from Britain. The subsistence approach is still fundamental to the positioning of such international organisations as the World Bank and the International Monetary Fund among others, on poverty in the developing world. They rely on a 'poverty line' developed "by estimating the minimum income required to provide for adequate nutrition while allowing for a proportion of total expenditure for non food items" (Hasan 1978, p.31). To some extent, this is sanctioned in the USA too, subsistence still remains the centre-piece of measuring poverty today (Townsend 1993, p.30).

The shortcomings of the subsistence concept are not difficult to find. The most critical for the purposes of this work is the implicit assumption that human needs are primarily physical needs, that is, for food, shelter and clothing. Townsend (1970 & 1993), Lister (1990), argue that human needs also include social needs. People are not just biological cells requiring replacement of energy lost or used. They are social beings expected to perform socially demanding roles as workers, citizens, parents, wives, fathers etc. Human beings are equally not just consumers but producers of goods and services as well as being active participants in complex social, economic and political relationships (Townsend 1993, p.31).

Basic needs

Arising out of the structural and other weaknesses of the subsistence approach, especially as pertains to the developing world, the desire for a re - conceptualisation of poverty resulted in the formulation, or more accurately, the adoption of the 'Basic Needs' approach by the international community led by the International Labour Organisation. The ILO's perception of Basic Needs included two elements:

> Firstly, they include certain minimum requirements of a family for private consumption: adequate food, shelter and clothing, as well as certain household furniture and equipment. Secondly, they include essential services provided by and for the community at large, such as safe drinking water, sanitation, public transport and health, education and cultural facilities... The concept of Basic Needs should be placed within the context of a nation's overall economic and social development. In no circumstances should it be taken to mean merely the minimum necessary for subsistence, it should be placed within a context of national independence, the dignity of individuals and peoples and their freedom to chart their destiny without hindrance (ILO 1976, p.24-25).

The influence of the Third World and the politics of the 1970s - such as the New International Economic Order, Détente, North/South dialogue, etc. - is clearly visible on the imprimatur of the basic needs approach. The Basic Needs approach has influenced a number of radical attempts at both fighting against poverty [particularly in developing nations] and setting the international co-operative development agenda. The Brandt Commission Report (1980) incorporates the spirit of this new internationalist approach,[3] in the same way as the various Development Plans in Ghana and elsewhere attempted to achieve in the 1970s. The introduction of the Human Development Index by the United Nations Development Programme in the 1980s is a logical follow up on the basic need conceptualisation.

However, the Basic Needs approach's greatest deficiency is its muddled inter-connection between the community and the individual. How was the individual going to fairly and equitably access the communal resources both in the context of the existing market ethos and that of existing social stratification? Townsend, in his critique of the Basic Needs approach, introduces the linkage between individual poverty, national wealth, organisation of trading and other institutional relations as well as re-distribution. He wrote:

> The more the concept of poverty is restricted to an insufficiency of income to cover basic individual physical goods and facilities, and even

collective goods and facilities, the easier it is to argue that the national growth of material wealth is all that is required to overcome the phenomenon. By constrast, the more the concept is widened to an insufficiency of income to cover in addition basic social needs like health, welfare, the fulfilment of obligations of family, citizenship and relations at work, and community participation, the more it becomes necessary to admit that a complex combination of growth, redistribution and re-organisation of trading and other institutional relationships and the reconstitution of traditional with new social associations has to be evolved (1993 p.33).

This wider definition runs counter to conventional interpretations of North - South relations because it invokes existing methods of satisfying social needs - some of which are more successful in poor countries than in rich industrial countries. The wider definition is more in accordance with the idea that development is everyone's problem and not just that of the Third World.

Relative deprivation

A third pathway or formulation is the relative deprivation concept pioneered by Townsend in "Poverty in UK" in 1970. In this formulation, Townsend argues that poverty has to be 'situated' through time in relation to social and institutional structures and not simply denoted by low disposable income (Townsend 1993, p.35). From this perspective:

> People are relatively deprived if they cannot obtain, all or sufficiently, the conditions of life - that is, the diets, amenities, standards and services - which allow them to play the roles, participate in the relationships and follow the customary behaviour which is expected of them by virtue of their membership of society, they may be said to be in poverty (ibid. p. 36).

Thus the concept of poverty is located within a particular socio-cultural milieu, as opposed to an abstract synchronisation. It needs to be pointed out that poverty here is not the same as inequality, although the two are connected and have some bearings on each other. The concept of relative deprivation, like all concepts in the behavioural sciences, is not without critics, with Amartya Sen as probably the most vocal of its critics. Sen,[4] in his critique argues *inter alia* that:

Relative Deprivation is essentially incomplete as an approach to poverty, and supplements [but cannot] the earlier approach of absolute dispossession. The maligned biological approach, which deserves substantial reformulations but not rejection, relates to this irreducible core of absolute deprivation, keeping issues of starvation and hunger at the centre of the concept (Sen 1981, p.22).

Whatever the approach [but more so with subsistence] to classify a person or even a group as poor by virtue of their inability to meet a norm, or a set of norms has its own conceptual and empirical problems. How do you define the set of norms? How do you for instance quantify an agreed minimum of clothes, food and shelter needed to sustain life in universalist terms when the body functions of individuals are influenced by age, sex, height, weight etc., indices that are not constant even for the individual? And what of an individual who has the resources to meet the set of norms but does not do so either because of ignorance or wilfulness? Is such a person to be considered poor? And how do you quantity values that a community holds dear?[5] It is worth noting that poverty is more than insufficient resources to surmount physical deprivation. There are social and psychological effects of a ramifying character which prevent people from realising their potential. Additional resources are required to meet these equally 'basic' needs.

Mass poverty

While the foregoing refers essentially to individual or case poverty, the incidence of mass poverty is of particular importance in Ghana and other developing countries. Mass poverty differs from case or individual poverty where a relative few are poor in a general affluent society. The term helps to direct attention to 'structural causes'. With mass or general poverty, poverty is the norm and not to be poor is the exception. In the former, poverty is often attributed [if even wrongly] to various characteristics - moral, genetic, familial, environmental, educational, racial, social etc., while in case of the latter, explanations have to be sought elsewhere (see Galbraith, 1980).

> Mass poverty is largely the function of acute, often contrived socio-economic inequality, which in turn is engendered and reinforced by acuminate, often deliberately organised, social stratification. It is not static, fortuitous, ahistorical and purely economic phenomenon, but a dynamic, structured, historically conditioned, and multi dimensional experience of the peoples of the South (Bandyopadhyaya 1988, p.263).

In Ghana, where 36% of the population was said to be below the poverty line in 1987-88, a conclusion of mass poverty becomes indisputable (Boateng 1990, p.13).[6] The mass nature of national poverty is also signified by the low level of per capita national income, $450 in 1992 (WB 1995, p.304). Even at the relatively more accurate purchasing power per capita calculation, per capita income is still less than $1000.

Causes of poverty

The causes of poverty, and thus under-development - if we view development to include the equalisation and creation of communal wealth to permit social, work and citizenship roles to be performed - are many. The perception of the causes have throughout modern history, travelled the whole distance from the absurd to the scientific.

The traditional 'old' establishment saw poverty as resulting largely from the inherent weaknesses of the poor - and they feared the spread of a kind of social infection. People were poor because they were either lazy or did not have it in them to do otherwise. To this class the causes of poverty "rest overwhelmingly in individual and sub - cultural defects and disposition" (Townsend 1993, p.6). Structural factors and the like are totally absolved from blame. This position is of course, false or at best inadequate in explaining individual or mass poverty. Explanations need, therefore, to be found elsewhere, and it is in furtherance of this search that the roles of both the global political economy and national government come in for examination.

Global politico - economic structures

So significant is the role of global economic and political arrangements in the impoverishment of individuals, communities and nations of the Third World that, some writers have tended to see such arrangements as the fundamental cause of world poverty (see Bandyopodhyaya, 1988). Notwithstanding this, the poverty of the Third World is treated as if it has no bearings on the accumulated wealth of the developed world.

Social stratification, and by extrapolation poverty, is in the twentieth century, global in character. It is the by-product of colonialism and neo-colonialism of economic, political and social arrangements which in turn originated from capitalism and imperialism. It is therefore, impractical, if not unethical, to attempt to separate national and individual poverty from world poverty since the two are intrinsically linked. Within the theatre of global economic relations, a country and its people, manoeuvred into economic disenfranchisement by powerful global forces would relatively be poor on the global scale, no matter how egalitarian its internal distribution of resources would be. A good internal distribution would at best, only lessen the extent of individual poverty but would do nothing for national poverty.

The post colonial period still witnesses unequal terms of trade, the use of official trade and aid policies of northern governments and international financial institutions to entrench northern interests, the perversion of the developing world by multinational corporations of the north as well as the dominance of international political and economic space by the industrialised north. This, side by side with the freedom and status of the Ghanaian bourgeoisie and civil-bureaucracy, allowed economic, political and social doctrine to be formulated in a way that siphons off a disproportionate percentage of the fruits of a slow growing GNP for themselves. By so doing, they sentenced the mass of citizens to poverty.

Unlike the umbilical cord between a mother and a baby, the link between the developed metropolis and the peripheral developing country paradoxically transfers nourishment from the weaker to the stronger. While Ghana and other developing countries are 'encouraged' to be primary commodity producers, - comparative advantage promoted to support this - developed countries are continually moving up to even higher technology led production sophistication. Tragically, the prices of primary commodities have consistently fallen in real terms since the mid 1970s while manufactured products have done the very opposite. The effects of the two markets [in their contrasts] has been to reduce earnings from developing countries while increasing developed world earnings. If the price of cocoa, for example, had stayed at even its 1975 levels, instead of its historical slump, at least a multiplier effect of five to ten percent of GDP could have been achieved, expanding GDP to levels far higher than the 1980 - 1990 period witnessed .

In the specific case of Ghana, the foreign domination of the economy allow the transfer abroad of potential surplus of the economy in the form of visible export profit or concealed profits inherent in unequal exchange. Amin, looking at this occurrence in the early 1970s, argued that while private transfers, income from investment and a large part of current services [which conceal transfer of profits] total about ₵100m or 6% of GDP in 1968. On the hypothesis that labour in Ghana's export sector should be rewarded half the wage rate of labour in developed country, the real drain from the country to the international system is ₵350m or 17% of GDP (Amin 1973, p.250).

National policies/structures

The causes for both individual and mass poverty can also be located within individual countries and their structures or pursuit of policies. While the global environment marginalises a country - thus denying such a country the resources to fight poverty - the ability of the privileged in society to protect and extend their privileges equally creates havoc on poverty levels (see Elliot 1975, p.2).

The introduction of a small dependent capitalist sector in the traditional agricultural communalistic economy in Ghana, largely in the form of cocoa, timber, mining, import and export and general recorded trade, aggravated the traditional stratification of society, leading to class domination and exploitation of the mass of the people by the few that had been co-opted into the 'modern' sector. The co-opted, in the post colonial state is isomorphic to the ruling capitalist class in the various metropolises of [Paris, London, Bonn, New York etc.] global economic and political power. Symbiotic linkages between the ruling political and commercial classes in both the global metropolises and the Ghanaian periphery has relegated the mass of the people, who are outside these structures of linkage, to irrelevance in the distribution and ownership of resources.

On this link between the global and national players vis a vis poverty, Bandyopdyaya commented:

> while impoverishing the South and enriching the North through the colonial drain, imperialism also created structural and socio - cultural distortions in the colonies which further retarded their economic development and made them heavily dependent ... It created in the colonies, a dualistic socio -economic structure, consisting of a small capitalist sector superimposed on, and draining the wealth of a vast pre - capitalist agricultural sector (op. cit. p.266).

The end result of the above distortions is the rise of poverty. Poverty arises because the poor do not have assets - skills, land, capital or labour power - which are needed to generate an adequate level of income. Secondly, they are prevented from using these assets by unemployment or lack of demand for what they produce; or the economic conditions are such that the rate of return on their productive assets does not generate enough income.[7]

Specific to mass poverty, the following explanations have been advanced at one time or the other as responsible for mass poverty:

1. 'Naturally Poor'. Here, countries are said to be naturally poor in terms of physical or natural resource endowment. However, the experiences of Japan, Taiwan, Hong Kong, Singapore and Israel do not support this contention. Either they have insufficient land or they lack the natural resources in the traditional sense and yet they are all very rich countries.
2. The political system of administration has often been advanced as an explanation for the poverty of nations. The political 'right' stresses the absence of free 'enterprise' as being the cause of mass poverty while the

'left' argue that the appropriation of the gains of production by the land and capital owners leaves no incentive for peasants to increase productivity. Empirical evidence does not however, seem to support to any credible extent, either of these absolutes. China and India, endowed almost equally, have attained different levels of mass prosperity with China obviously the better off.[8]

3. Prebisch addresses the issue from another angle. He argues that poor countries, producers in the main of raw materials and other agricultural products, suffer persistently in terms of trade with industrial countries (Prebisch, 1963).

Features of poverty in Ghana

Ghanaian poverty in consonance with most developing countries of Africa and South Asia, is quite widespread and on the mass scale. An analysis of the national household surveys of 1974 by Ewusi (Ewusi, 1976) indicated that about 75% of the Ghanaian population at that time had incomes which placed them below the poverty line of $100. UNICEF (1986) estimated that 30 - 35% of urban households and 60 - 65% of rural household were below their respective poverty line of $307 and $130 [1978 prices]. Ghana also generally exhibits a relative inequality between the various decile groups with the poorest 10% of the population only earning 6.45% of the ₵280,764 attributed to the wealthiest 10% of the population as the 1987 - 1988 survey showed (see table 8.1).

Table 8.1
Characteristics of the distribution of individuals by per capita household expenditure (CHHE)

Decile	Expenditure cut-off (constant ₵)
1	18,119.0
2	23,897.0
3	29,300.0
4	35,272.0
5	40,897.0
6	47,583.0
7	56,239.0
8	68,684.0
9	91,420.0
10	280,764.0
Mean PCHHE	49,471.0

Source: Boateng et al. 1990: A Poverty Profile of Ghana p 13.

214

It is worth mentioning that the average Ghanaian household devoted 50.6% of its expenditure on food in 1991 - 1992 (see Table 8.2) with the rural household spending a higher 52.2% (ibid.).

Urban/rural

Poverty is predominantly concentrated in rural Ghana, irrespective of how it is defined; whether in monetary terms or in terms of basic needs provision [amenities as well as food and other items like fuel and clothing for household consumption].This is also true of both case/individual poverty or mass poverty (see Ewusi, 1976, Boateng et al. 1990, Alan Roe & Hartmut Schneider 1992). In analysing a survey undertaken in 1974/75, Ewusi found that while 75.4% of the population fell below the poverty line,[9] the rural component was 85.08% while the urban sector accounted for 53.48% (ibid.).[10]

Expenditure

Another exercise conducted in 1987 - 88 concluded that 83.3% of the poorest 20% of the population were to be found in the rural part of the country while 54.5% of the wealthiest 20% are found in urban areas. While the average resident of Accra had an average expenditure of ₵149,542 in 1987/88, the average non Accra resident had an adjusted expenditure of ₵63,940 (Glewwe & Twum-Baah 1991, pp. 25-26).

The dichotomy between urban and rural dwellers becomes even more striking in relation to expenditure on food. The poor, as stated earlier, are predominantly engaged in agriculture and are thus rural based. Yet rural dwellers spend 52.2% of all expenditure on food, while the urban average is 48.65% (see Table 8.2).

Table 8.2
Mean annual household cash expenditure by locality
and expenditure group (cedi)

| | LOCALITY | | | | LOCALITY | | | |
	Accra	Other Urban	Rural	Country	Accra	Other urban	Rural	Country
					%	%	%	%
EXPENDITURE GROUP								
Food & Beverages	367,575	348,198	234,925	276,511	48.5	48.8	52.2	50.6
Food & Tobacco	102.89	15,313	21,688	18,948	1.4	2.1	4.8	3.5
Clothing & Footwear	82,921	56,948	43,903	51,107	10.9	8	9.7	9.3
Housing & Utilities	82,189	70,161	35,201	48,652	10.8	9.8	7.8	8.9
Household goods, operation and services	57,815	43,900	34,071	38,924	7.6	6.2	7.6	7.1
Medical care & expenses	18,664	26,032	22,046	22,691	2.5	3.7	4.9	4.2
Transport & Communications	58,472	43,288	27,399	34,501	7.7	6.1	6.1	6.3
Recreation & education	37,657	42,392	18,012	26,057	5	5.9	4	4.8
Miscellaneous goods & services	42,356	66,818	13,097	29,397	5.6	9.4	2.9	5.4
All groups	757,938	713,050	450,342	546,788	100	100	100	100

Source: GLSS 1995 p.147.

The poverty gulf between urban and rural extends more significantly to the provision and uptake of basic economic and social rights such as the right to education. While 65% of all Ghanaian adults surveyed in 1991 - 1992 were literate, the equivalent for rural Ghana was 48.8% (see Table 8.3). The effect of this is seen more in agriculture where farmers, predominantly rural, find themselves unable to adopt agricultural practices being encouraged by the Ministry of Agriculture because they are unable to read accompanying instructions.

Table 8.3
Adult literacy rates by sex and locality [Percentage]

| | URBAN | | | RURAL | ALL |
	Accra	*Other Urban*	*All*		
Male	84.7	71.2	74.8	53.5	60.8
Female	73.1	51.1	57.0	28.3	38.5
All	78.3	60.3	65.0	40.0	48.8

Note: Adult refers to anyone aged 15 years and over. Any one who could write a letter in English or any Ghanaian language was counted as being literate.
Source: Ghana Living Standards Survey 1995, p.16.

Treated pipe-borne water was only available to 13.8% of rural dwellers, compared to 100% in Accra and 67.5% for all other urban areas (see table 8.14). The prevalence of water borne diseases in Ghana is, therefore, not surprising considering the inadequate provision of safe drinking water for the majority of the population living in rural Ghana. Again, the gross impoverishment of both the country and rural dwellers in particular, is exemplified by the fact that only 30.8% of the residents of Accra, the most affluent part of the country, have flush toilets with only 1.4% of rural dwellers enjoying the facility. Sixty one percent of our rural folk have to make do with pit latrines, as against less than thirty percent of all urban dwellers (table 8.12). In housing, 98.3% of Accra residents and 96.2% of all urban residents live in houses with cement constructed floors, as against 69% of all rural dwellers (table 8.15). Even in illness, rural dwellers are worst off, with rural women at the bottom of the pile (table 8.7B).

Geographical

The northern regions [Northern, Upper East and Upper West] constitute 40% of the land mass of Ghana but are less densely populated. The three together account for 14% of agricultural output (Roe & Schneider 1992, p.35), have one main crop cycle, and the least rainfall in the country. Ewusi in 1976 found that the then Northern and Upper Regions scored 13 and 13.9 for Physical Quality of Life Index ([PQLI][11] compared to between 36 and 52 in all other Regions (ibid.).

In terms of farming, the northern Regions are sparsely populated with 20% of the country's population but 40% of its land mass. It is worth noting however, that the Upper East Region has a population density of 87 persons per km., which is five times the average density of the North as a whole (ibid. pp.35-36). Poverty is more prevalent in Northern, Upper East and Upper West Regions than the rest of Ghana (Ewusi 1976). The World Bank in its 1990 World Report wrote about the three northernmost Regions thus: " ... In Ghana's Savannah Regions a typical family of seven lives in three one-room huts made from mud-bricks, with earthen floors They have little furniture and no toilet, electricity or running water. The family has a few possessions, apart from three acres of unirrigated land and one cow, and virtually no savings" (p. 24)

The 1987 - 1988 Living Standards Measurements Survey also found that the savannah areas of Ghana, particularly the rural savannah, were over-represented among the poor. The urban and rural savannah combined constituted 25.4% of the population but 54.2% of the poorest 10% and 41.5% of the poorest 30% (Glewwe & Twum-Baah 1991, p.47). The three Northern Regions are the most under resourced, just as the incidence of malnutrition is highest in the Northern, Upper East and Upper West Regions (Sarris & Shams 1991, p.80).

Occupational

Surveys have reported a correlation between employment status and poverty in Ghana. The First Ghana Living Standards Survey (1987-1988) found that 85% and 87% of the 'very poor' and 'poor' respectively were self-employed but only 4% and 6% respectively were in government employment. This finding confirmed the view that a government job was a relative way out of poverty. Poverty was also greatest among non-cocoa farmers[12] with only 6% and 18% respectively in the 'very poor' and 'poor' engaged in cocoa farming (Roe & Schneider 1992, p.34)

The link between poverty and agriculture is shown in various studies. In 1970, 43.3% of the farming population or 80.3% of all small holders or 1.95 million rural people were below the poverty line. This shot up to 67.3% of the total farming population in 1984 [1984 has to be interpreted in the context of the 1983 famine] and settled at 54% of the total farming population being below the poverty line in 1986 (Sarris & Shaw 1991, p.66)

The GLSS survey of 1987-1988 concluded as per the table 7.4, that 65.10% of the income of the poor came directly from agriculture. Thus the link between agriculture and poverty is further confirmed. The agricultural poor were also the least likely to receive educational scholarships in a country where education still provides a workable route out of poverty (see Table .4)

Table 8.4
Source of income by poverty groups

	All	Non-poor	Poor
Employment income	7.30 (100)	8.10 (86.6)	4.40 (13.4)
Agricultural income	55.60 (100)	52.90 (74.0)	65.10 (26.0)
Non-farming self employment	28.20 (100)	29.70 (82.0)	22.80 (18.0)
Actual and implied rent	1.70 (100)	1.60 (72.9)	2.10 (27.1)
Educational Scholarship	0.08 (100)	0.10 (89.4)	0.04 (10.6)
Remittances received	4.10 (100)	4.10 (77.4)	4.20 (22.6)
Other Income	3.0 (100)	3.50 (89.7)	1.40 (10.3)
All	100 (100)	100 (77.8)	100 (22.2)

Source: Oti Boateng et. al. 1990 p.21.

The nature of occupation is a more important correlation with poverty [if the 1987- 1988 survey is correct] than whether the head of the household is employed or not. Indeed the household with an unemployed head was better off than where the head was either a cocoa farmer or a non-cocoa farmer. The unemployed was only slightly worse off than the average Ghanaian (Glewwe & Twum-Baah GLSMS 1991, p.33). Glewwe and Twum-Baah argued that individual unemployment is neither concentrated among the poor nor is it a major cause of poverty. Twum-Baah (1983) explained this as resulting from extended family mode of living, with its network of social relationships and economic security. As long as such unemployment [largely urban] remains minuscule, transfers would make up for any loss of income, but where unemployment becomes *en masse*, this traditional insurance would be unable to provide for the victims.

Basic needs

The most useful avenue for analysing poverty in low and middle income developing countries is the use of Basic Needs Indicators or Provision. This is particularly helpful in the case of Ghana where as a result of the preponderance of the informal sector, the compilation of national accounts is at best a thankless exercise and at worst, a piece of enlightened guesswork. The traditional social cohesion, as indicated by the extended family system, also softens the unequal distribution of individual wealth and accumulations as an adequate means of assessing or analysing poverty.

The adoption of basic needs does not however, infer that such a route is smooth. The difficulty of reducing publicly supplied services like subsidised public transport and others such as clean drinking water, an alternative sewerage system or public provision of education [quality as well as quantity] ad infinitum to a single numeraire is often side-stepped by separating private consumption from basic indicators (Oti-Boateng 1990, p.4). However, any meaningful poverty analysis in Ghana must take on board, both private consumption and public consumption of not just goods and services provided by the 'market', but also of basic needs provision and facilities. This section will, therefore, concentrate on analysing the provision and utilisation of Basic Needs provisions from the standpoints of urban-rural, gender and locality where applicable.

Health provision

The uniqueness of poverty and its perception *vis a vis* health provision in developing countries is reflected in the 1988 Ghana Living Standards Survey. The survey based on self-reporting found that the incidence of illness increases as people move from very poor categorisation to poor and average Ghanaian.

This trend was also present in a similar Living Standards Survey in Ghana's Western neighbour, The Cote d'Ivoire (Oti- Boateng 1990, p.24). The credible explanation for this occurrence is the greater propensity for the rich or well off to classify themselves as ill. What constitutes illness in the mind s of the rich and poor are different. In my own Ghanaian experience while the middle and well off classes will often report to clinics and hospitals when they contract malaria, or a common cold - thus staying away from work - the poor will normally treat such as an irritant, self medicate and report to work. The poor cannot in this scenario afford to be ill and would not self-report such as illness. This is therefore reflected in the answers of the various categorisations in tables 8.5 and 8.6

Table 8.5
Percentage of individuals ill during the past 28 days by locality and poverty group

	Very Poor	Poor	All
Rural	24.3	29.6	35.2
Urban (excluding Accra)	24.3	33.9	38.4
Accra	*	33.3	38.9

Notes:
1. * There are no individuals classified as 'very poor' in Accra
2. 'Very Poor' relates to the lower poverty line of one-third of mean per capita consumption.

Source: Oti Boateng et. al. 1990, p.24.

Table 8.6
Percentage of sick individuals who consulted health personnel by locality and poverty group

	Very Poor	Poor	All
Rural	29.5	37.5	44.4
Urban (excluding Accra)	41.5	41.9	50.8
Accra	*	57.1	59.1

Source: Oti Boateng et. al. 1990 p.24.

The variance in table 8.5 even within the categorisation reflects the depth or otherwise of health provision in rural, general urban and the capital. Also significant is the difference between the poor rural population (37.5%) who consulted health workers and the same for the Accra 57.1%, a 50+ percent of the rural consultation rate [table 8.6].

A significant element of health provision and uptake is the type of consultation experienced. Among 460 people in Accra who reported ill during the survey sample period of GLSS(1) (1990), 188 (40.9%) did not see a health worker (see tables 8.7A & 8.7B). But of those who did, 91.9% (272) consulted a doctor. The corresponding figures for rural Ghana is 55.6% not consulting a health worker. But of the 1454 who did (44.4% of the rural sample), 38.9% (566) consulted a doctor, with 31.3% consulting a Medical Assistant.

Table 8.7a
Type of consultation by ill people in sample by locality and poverty group

	RURAL	URBAN (excluding accra)	ACCRA
Doctor	566	518	250
Nurse	182	52	9
Medical Assistant	455	117	2
Other	251	60	11
None	1819	724	188
All	3273	1471	460

Source: Oti Boateng et. al. 1990, p.25.

8.7b
Type of health practitioner consulted by locality and sex (%)
Locality   Country

	Accra		other Urban		Rural		Country		
	male	female	male	female	male	female	male	female	all
Physician	86.8	87.5	57.3	67	39.4	41.8	48.3	53.7	51.2
Nurse/midwife	1.3	5.8	7	6.4	18.9	20.8	14	15.1	14.6
Med. Assistant	2.6	0.8	13.9	10.5	19.5	19.1	16.6	14.8	15.6
Pharmacist	6.6	1.7	6.6	5.9	6	7.7	6.3	6.6	6.4
Traditional	2.6	4.2	12.7	7	13.8	8	12.6	7.3	9.7
Other	-	-	2.5	3.2	2.3	2.6	2.2	2.5	2.4
Total	100	100	100	100	100	100	100	100	100
Sample size	76	120	316	373	645	765	1057	1258	2295

Note: Others include spiritualists and traditional birth attendants.
Source: Ghana Living Standards Survey, 1995 p.20.

The above comparison reflects the predominance of doctors in Accra. There are very few doctors in rural Ghana. Equally important is the use of Medical Assistants in rural areas. Thus from a policy perspective, table 8.6 reflects the success of the medical assistantship project as making the case for more Medical Assistants to be trained. Of concern however, must remain the disparity of medical provision between rural Ghana[13] where the bulk of the country's wealth is produced and Accra, the parasitic seat of government and influence.[14]

Table 8.8
Where consultation took place for those who were ill and consulted someone by poverty group

	VERY POOR	*POOR*	*ALL*
Hospital	23	192	1020
Dispensary	0	10	46
Clinic	38	281	1046
Other	18	117	361
All	79	600	2473

Source: Oti-Boateng et al. 1990 p.25.

Table 8.8 presents an interesting picture of the health provision and intake landscape. For the very poor,[15] clinics are the most important sources of treatment. The preponderance of hospital visits by the rich is also established by the fact that although the very poor and poor record 29.1% and 32% intake respectively, the national average is pushed up to 41.2% because of the relatively high intake by the rich.

It is estimated that 61% of all Ghanaians have access to health services, although hundreds of thousands in the rural areas depend on herbalists and other forms of unorthodox health care (Assenso-Okyere 1993, p.3). So important is the role of herbal medicine in particular that a number of well managed herbal clinics and hospitals are being set up by both the government and the private sector to improve health care delivery. The government owned Centre for Research into Plant Medicine Mampong-Akuapem has attracted a lot of interest both from within and outside of the country from practitioners of orthodox medicine. Indeed some aspects of herbal medicine such as herbal first aid and traditional birth delivery methods have been incorporated into the country's Primary Health Scheme.

While health delivery, especially immunisation has improved considerably over the years, such as the proportion of one year olds immunised increasing from 34% in 1981 to 67% in 1989, and with 40% of all births now attended by trained professional health personnel (ibid.), the same cannot be said for general public health. Diseases such as yaws and yellow fever, which had virtually been eliminated by campaigns of early 1960 and early 1970s, have re-appeared in the 1980s and 1990s as health provision degenerated (see Sarris& Shams 1991, p.79 & Loewenson 1993). It is estimated that the under-5 mortality rate, which had come down from 215 per 1000 in 1960 to 157 in 1980 had risen to 170 by 1991 (World Resources Institute, 1994, p.272 table 16.3).

Expenditure on health care in 1982/83 was only 23% of its 1974 value on a per capita basis, (ibid.). For the rural population, the consequences of decreased provision is even more acute, recognising the traditional urban bias of medical allocation and delivery. In a typical year, 79% of the total health budget goes to medical care, of which Korle-Bu Teaching Hospital, the biggest in the country, alone appropriates 22%, with Public Health Delivery only 12% and training 6%. Eighty percent of total health expenditure is typically recurrent (ibid.). In the 1995 Budget provision for example, 88.58% (₵65,448,995.00) of the total provision was earmarked for recurrent expenditure with only 11.42% being 'development' expenditure on health (Budget Statement 1995). The total health budget itself was only 8.11% of the total expenditure, compared to the allocation of 10.47% to Roads and Highways.

Education

Education is another recognised category of Basic Needs that calls for examination in the context of poverty analysis in Ghana. Education does not only enhance empowerment and therefore expanding opportunity to move out of poverty, but its provision also increases productivity and employability. The GLSS(1) published in 1990 saw lack of education as a causal contributory factor to poverty. As a result of poverty (in lack of education), individuals only have the opportunity to work in lowly paid jobs. I have shown (above) that people in government jobs are the least likely to fall below the poverty line and since education is often a pre-condition of obtaining a government job, it is by implication recognised by many people to be a major route out of poverty (Boateng et al. 1990 p 27).

Significantly, educational provision also mirrors the various strata of inequality by location, gender, income group etc. established by the preceding pages. Table 8.9, for example, captures the inequality of literacy achievement between the sexes, both for adults and children. While the gap has somewhat closed between male and female literacy rates between 1970 and 1990, there are still unacceptable differences among both adults and infants by gender.

Table 8.9
General literacy levels - percentage

	1970	*1990*
Adult - Female	18	51
Adult Male	43	70
Gross Primary School Enrolment		
(%age of age group)		
Female	31	65
Male	58	81

Source: Compiled from World Resources, 1994 -19 95 p.276 table 16.5.

Table 8.10
School attendance rate by region, age and sex (%)

REGION	AGE GROUP 6 - 11 Male	Female	12 - 15 Male	Female	16 - 18 Male	Female	19 - 25 Male	Female	6 - 25 Male	Female	All
Western	83.6	75.7	83.2	75.5	60.3	47.3	8.8	6	64.5	54.3	59.5
Central	77.6	72.4	83.3	71.4	61	51.7	26.8	6.1	68	53.7	60.8
Gt. Accra	87.8	85.4	93.2	77.7	65.9	52.5	33.3	15.4	72.8	61	66.6
Eastern	87.5	83.5	90.4	81.1	57.1	36.5	19.6	5.6	73.5	57.5	65.6
Volta	80	81.4	82.7	81.5	63.5	31.8	40.9	15.4	69.5	61.1	65.6
Ashanti	89.1	81.8	94	76	55	36.3	21.6	6.1	70.1	53.4	61.7
Brong Ahafo	86.1	83.5	83.3	82.5	65.9	53.6	19	6.4	69.6	62.1	66
Northern	57.2	31.3	63.3	31.5	40.9	22.6	30.6	12.8	51.1	25.8	39.7
Upper West	34.3	33.8	30.8	35.5	42.1	33.3	13	6.7	31.1	28.4	29.8
Upper East	30.2	31.9	44.8	34.1	14.3	15	22.2 -		31.1	28.4	29.8
All	77	71.9	81.5	70.8	56.9	41.1	24.6	8.5	64.9	52.4	58.8

Source: GLSS 1995 p.14.

Table 8.10 is significant. The three northern most Regions in Northern, Upper West and Upper East are again the worst resourced in terms of education. While the national average for the 6-11 year group attending school is 74.45%, the three regions average a poor 36.45% attendance. Also worth mentioning from table 6.10 is the gender gap between boys and girls regarding attendance. Even though it is comforting to see the gap narrow from the high differential between 19-25 age group of 24.6% to 8.5% in favour of males to 77%-71% for age group 6 - 11, the existence of the gap still has implications for both future and present policy options. Table 7.10 reveals a very worrying scenario. The national uptake of education for the 12-15 year group (76.6%) entering formal schooling between 1983-1986 (data referring to Sept. 1991-Sept. 1992) was higher than the uptake of 6-11 year group (74.6% and beginning from 1987-1992). The later period coincides with increasing percentages of educational costs on parents.

Table 8.11
Education and the poor (percentage)

	Poorest 10%	Poorest 30%	All Ghana
Education of household head			
None	80.3	71.7	53.9
Primary	3.5	6.9	8.1
Middle	15.7	20.6	31.3
Secondary: 'O' Levels	0.0	0.0	3.0
Secondary: 'A' Levels	0.0	0.0	0.3
Teacher Training	0.0	0.5	1.8
Other post secondary	0.0	0.3	0.4
University	0.0	0.0	1.2
School attendance by household members:			
Age 6 - 10	43.2	57.2	66.8
Age 11 - 15	46.0	60.5	70.8

Source: Donald Rothchild 1991, Ghana: The Political Economy of Recovery, p.103.

Table 8.11 establishes the link between education and poverty. The educational attainment of the head of household plays a major role in determining the household's access to resources through the employment market. While 80.3% of the poorest ten percent of the population had no formal education, one can not find heads of households with secondary school education or better in the poorest 10% of the population. The lack of access to formal education is thus established as a concomitant to poverty in the Ghanaian situation.

Water sanitation and housing

The degree and severity of mass poverty in Ghana can also be gauged by examining the provision of safe drinking water, sanitation and housing for the population as a whole.

Table 8.12
Distribution of household by locality and type of toilet used (%)

	Urban Areas			Rural	Country
	Accra	Other Urban	All		
Type of toilet:					
Flush	30.8	12.1	17.6	1.4	7.1
KVIP	13.2	12.3	12.6	3.7	6.8
Pit latrines	13.7	36.5	29.9	61.3	50.3
Pan/bucket	29.3	23.0	24.8	4.0	11.3
None	11.3	12.9	12.4	28.6	22.9
Other	1.7	3.2	2.8	1.1	1.7
All	100.0	100.0	100.0	100.0	100.0
Sample	461	1123	1584	2938	4522

Source: GLSS 1995 p.53.

Rural households are once again, worse off than their urban counterparts in the provision of toilets facilities with 28.6% having no access to any kind of toilet infrastructure and having to use the bush (free range) for such purposes. For the country as a whole, 3/4 of a million households have no toilet facilities, with 40,000 of these in Accra, 110,000 in other urban areas and a colossal 620,000 in rural areas (see Table 8.12).

For sanitation services in general, only 63% and 60% respectively of urban and rural dwellers had access to safe sanitation infrastructure in 1990 (Table 8.13). The urgency of improving sanitation services in Ghana is self apparent if public health, particularly cholera and other wind and water borne communicable diseases are to be brought under control. Good sanitation goes a long way in fighting diseases and enhancing good health of the population. Of concern is the deterioration of access to safe drinking water by the urban population from 72% coverage in 1980 to 63% in 1990.

Table 8.13
Access to safe drinking water and sanitation
(% of population)

	Safe drinking water*		Sanitation services	
Year:	Urban	Rural	Urban	Rural
1980	72	33	47	17
1990	63	39	63	60

Table 8.14 paints an even worse picture of safe drinking water provision. Only 36% of the population have access to treated pipe borne water, with only 13.8% of all rural dwellers enjoying the facilities of treated pipe borne water. This highlights the widespread nature of mass poverty in Ghana. The country definitely qualifies for membership of the poor category of nations since 34.2% of the population (table 8.12) still depend on untreated spring or river water to meet their daily requirements.

Table 8.14
Distribution of household by locality and source of drinking water (%)

SOURCE OF WATER	URBAN AREAS			RURAL	COUNTRY
	Accra	Other	All urban		
Pipe borne	100	67.5	76.9	13.8	36.0
Indoor plumbing	19.3	3.7	8.3	0.3	3.1
Inside stand-pipe	40.4	25.8	30.0	2.2	12.0
Water Vendor	0.7	2.1	1.7	0.3	0.8
Tanker	-	2.7	1.9	0.1	0.8
Neighbour	16.3	8.3	10.6	1.6	4.7
Private outside standpipe	22.0	6.7	11.1	0.8	4.4
Public tap	1.3	18.2	13.3	8.5	10.2
Well	-	18.3	13.0	37.1	28.7
Well with pump	-	3.5	2.5	21.1	14.6
Well without pump	-	14.8	10.5	16.0	14.1
Natural sources	-	14.2	10.1	49.1	35.4
River/Spring	-	14.0	10.0	47.3	35.4
Rain	-	0.2	0.1	0.9	0.6
Other	-	-	-	0.9	0.6
All	100.0	100.0	100.0	100.0	100.0
Sample size	460	1125	1585	2935	4520

Source: Ghana Statistical Service, GLSS 1995 p.51.

The prevalence of poverty is also reflected in the poor construction quality of the country's housing stock. The Third Ghana Living Standards Survey[16]found that nearly sixty three percent of all houses in Ghana had their outside walls constructed with mud as against less than thirty four percent constructed with cement. However, 82.9% of all houses in Accra (and 62.3% in all urban areas) had their walls constructed with cement, as against 14.9% in rural Ghana. Even in housing provision, the urban rural divide is manifested as table 8.15 shows.

Table 8.15

Percentage distribution of household by locality and main construction material of walls, floor and roof

| | URBAN AREAS | | | RURAL | COUNTRY |
	ACCRA	*OTHER*	*ALL*		
OUTSIDE WALL MATERIAL					
Mud	9.8	32.1	25.6	82.5	62.6
Wood	3.3	2.6	2.8	0.6	1.3
Corrugated iron	3.7	0.8	1.6	0.6	1.0
Stone	0.2	2.2	1.6	0.8	1.1
Cement	82.9	62.3	68.3	14.9	33.6
Other	0.2	-	0.1	0.6	0.4
MAIN FLOORING MATERIAL					
Earth	0.7	3.1	2.4	29.4	20.0
Wood	0.4	1.1	0.9	0.3	0.5
Stone	0.2	0.2	0.2	0.2	0.2
Fibre glass	-	0.3	0.2	0.1	0.2
Cement	98.3	95.4	96.2	69.9	79.1
Other	0.4	-	0.1	-	0.1
All	100.0	100.0	100.0	100.0	100.0
Sample size	461	1124	1585	2939	4524

Source: Ghana Living Standards Survey 1995, p.54.

Adjustment effects on poverty

Investigating the effects of the adjustment process on poverty is an extremely complex task in the Ghanaian situation. The examination has to be carried out in the context of trends in the poverty of the nation state, mass poverty and case (individual and household) poverty, even though our concern here is centred on the last two. In each of these definitions, the effect of poverty might not be such as to bring out a clear cut message or picture. While a particular policy might pull poverty along a progressive direction, a second policy within the same package might just do the opposite, thus blurring the overall effect.

228

A number of policy instuments are used in adjustment programmes the world over, with the Ghanaian programme being no exception. The instruments encompass the whole gamut of money and credit policy, fiscal policy, pricing, labour markets, trade and trade liberalisation etc. The instruments have impacted and indeed will continue to impact on various poverty groups in Ghana by influencing aggregate demand, supply, overall price levels, including the composition of demand and supply and therefore relative prices.

There is also to consider, the struggle between the short term and the long term developments in assessing the effects of structural adjustment on poverty. Although labour restraint, for example, might negatively affect poverty in the short term, should such restraint enable the economy to turn around and start increasing output, more jobs would be created in the long term. This potentially can then lead to improved wage rates in the long term if distribution of the gains of increased production is equitable. But the long term includes so many variables that one cannot take the outlook for granted.

Another complication to the assessment of the impact of adjustment on poverty is the tendency to see the growth rate of GNP as the ultimate test of success in developing world. However, more important than mere growth rates, is the removal of illiteracy, ill health, malnutrition and social and cultural deprivation. These should be seen as valuable goals in their own right and not just as enhancing the 'economic growth' process. The development and expansion of the above and other Basic Needs must not be seen *only* or even *primarily* as expansions of 'human resources'[17] -but as a valuable end in itself. (Sen 1994, p.4).

Incomes

While it is difficult to generalise the effects of adjustment on the various income segments in the economy, it is still a worthwhile exercise as income levels have bearings on the sate of poverty in any given country. In examining the impact of adjustment on income levels (as these contribute to poverty or otherwise) one is conscious of the time frame of more than a decade of adjustment within which wages and incomes may swing from the positive axis of the pendulum to the negative (illustrated by table 8.16).

Table 8.16
Population, informal and formal sector wages (deflated by ncpi)
and aggregate labour shares

	Population (million)	informal sector (unskilled construction)	Indices of real wages in public sector	formal sector
1977	9.85	100.00	100.00	100.00
1978	9.99	81.46	77.17	62.60
1979	10.12	62.21	72.58	50.63
1980	10.24	60.92	66.60	52.85
1981	10.37	46.90	37.60	31.47
1982	10.50	38.62	32.05	26.86
1983	11.99	23.58	22.12	21.67
1984	12.39	31.45	22.05	31.90
1985	12.72	61.13	53.27	45.99
1986	13.05	67.74	76.57	75.38
1987	13.39	56.68	71.85	76.33
1988	13.74	55.73	65.09	76.23
1989	14.10	55.29	68.39	77.03
1990	14.47	52.58	62.21	78.32

Source: Alexander S Harris, 'Household Welfare During Crisis and Adjustment in Ghana' Journal of African Economies, vol. 2 no. 2 p.215.

While real wages in the informal sector doubled from 23.58 in 1983 to 67.74 in 1986 largely as a result of improved monetary policy, by 1990, the levels had fallen again to 52.58 (see table 8.16). For the public sector from an all time low of 22.05 in 1984 when the reform package took effect, real wages reached 76.57 of the 1977 figure before decline set in reaching 62.21 in 1990. The non-public formal sector has relatively held firm, with the indice improving from 21.67 consistently and reaching 78.32 of its 1977 value in 1990.

On income of the poor, Harris argues that:

> it is not likely that incomes of the poor in Ghana have deteriorated after the outset of ERP...... comparing the real incomes in 1989/90 to those of the pre-adjustment peak of 1977/78, it appears that the urban non-poor group seem better off, and those in rural savannah and south marginally better, while real income of other groups (including the poor) although it surpassed this peak in 1987/88, was slightly below this level in 1989/90 (ibid. p 229-30).

This analysis is, however, against the grain of evidence, as shown by table 7.16. Real wages had risen appreciably from the low 1981-1983 figures but were still short of the 1977/78 period. Sarris' analysis is again at best income centred, ignoring the very serious decline in public (free or near free) provision of education, health, transport and publicly consumed services. While incomes were increasing, the cost of living would have increased even further than the increases in real income when previously socially provided services are brought into the equation.

The Trades Union Congress took up the position of Sarris and other World Bank/IMF apologists in 1988 that:

> although the various statistical indicators are moving in the programme, the going is still hard for the working people .....The effect of the World Bank and IMF sponsored economic policies are the cheapening of the local currency.....the high rate of unemployment and a rising cost of living brought about by the decontrolling of prices, removal of subsidies on essential goods and services, and the partial freeze on wages and salaries of the working people (TUC 1988, p.32).

The boast of adjustment raising real income is inconclusive. For example, cocoa farmers, traditionally amongst the well off in Ghanaian agriculture, and hailed by World Bank as beneficiaries of adjustment, were found by Glewwe and Twum-Baah,[18] not to be better off than the average Ghanaian but even worst off than the average Ghanaian in terms of income (Glewwe & Twum-Baah 1991, p.33).

The lower employment in the formal sector (see table 8.16) generally raises the supply of labour to the informal sector, thereby reducing the real earnings of the poor engaged in the informal sector. Unemployment reduces not only the incomes of the poor in the short term, but also lowers their longer term potential for employment (see Blanchard & Summers 1986). Heller and others however, postulate that the particular economic circumstances of Ghana, as in the case of Thailand at adjustment, warranted the reverse, that is a rise in real wages.

This rise in real wages was necessitated by the need to improve "supply performance of the economy" hence the raising of the real minimum wage from 13% of its 1975 level at the onset of the ERP to about 30% of the same by 1985 (Heller 1988, p.19). While Heller and others. go on to claim that the rise in real wages benefited the poor, this "benefit" needs to be put in perspective. Only a small percentage of the country's labour force is employed in the formal sector and thus could have benefited from the said raise. And even within the formal sector, employers were not obliged to give their workers the government announced raises of the minimum wage as implementation of announced increases was to be on the basis of "ability to pay".

It is also pertinent to keep in focus, the philosophy of adjustment programmes not only in Ghana, but all over the world (including conservative pro-market Britain) to make countries pursuing such programmes (and in this case Ghana), attractive to foreign investors as a low wage economy. In pursuance of this, the Ghanaian state de-controlled prices during the period but retained the Prices and Incomes Board with the sole function of regulating wages! The government's determination to keep wages low is exemplified by the fact that in 1988, while a number of companies agreed to a 30-50% wage increases through the negotiation process, the Prices and Incomes Board decreed that such increases must not exceed 25% [Mbia 1989, p.3]. The additional caveat of "ability to pay" has been consistently used to keep wages low.

Distributional effects

Extensive price control under the previous regime of controls had shifted the supply of goods and services to the parallel market where the poor were victimised by their inability to access these goods and services from official sources. De-controlling prices did not necessarily make the poor worse off, as argued in the preceding chapter, (the only exemption being public provision of basic needs) *vis-a-vis* the powerful in society and their social and political acolytes at the point of purchase (see Heller 1988, p.17). It only confirmed price levels existent in their 'real world'.

The problem of the poor at this stage was, and still is, income. Agriculture, the predominant occupation still suffers an internal terms of trade disadvantage and therefore, the incomes of agricultural workers have not kept pace with other sectors of the economy. The critical mass of inequality for the poor can and should, therefore, be located here.

It is also useful to bring to bear, the peculiar nature of Ghanaian inequality. Ghana had traditionally had one of the lowest inequality thresholds in the developing world with a Gini co-efficient of only 0.3471 in 1988 as table 8.17 below indicates.

Table 8.17
Inequality in consumption expenditure in five countries

	Gini co-efficient	Thiel T	Thiel L	Log variance
AFRICAN				
Ghana	0.3471	0.2141	0.2046	0.3998
Cote d'Ivoire	0.4350	0.3530	0.3254	0.6079
Mauritania	0.4144	0.3074	0.3062	0.6297
NON AFRICAN				
Jamaica	-	0.3487	0.3203	0.6044
Peru	0.4299	0.3534	0.3194	0.5967

Source: Glewwe & Twum-Baah p.57.

The above does not mean, however, that the contribution of distribution to poverty reduction can be very significant, at least from the absolutist and basic needs traditions. The prevalence of poverty on the large scale as enumerated in this chapter and the existing low threshold of inequality limits the effectiveness of distribution *per se*, but does not totally negate its contribution, not least from the relativist school. The widening differentials arising from adjustment cannot be ignored (not at the expense of social disarticulation), particularly in the public services and between export crop farmers and food crop farmers. The relatively fairly good distribution of resources prior to adjustment served to ameliorate social polarisation.

Labour market

The upheavals that characterised both industrial relations, remuneration relationships and labour market employment generation etc. affected the poverty profile of the country. The huge number of workers retrenched was bound to have serious effects on the numbers in poverty. As indicated in chapter 5, by the end of 1991, 15% of the core civil service for example had been laid off, excluding the thousands who suffered the same fate at Ghana Education Service. At the Ghana Cocoa Board, about 57,000 names were removed from the payroll between 1983 and mid 1989 (see chapter 5). Indeed Yeebo (1991, p.205) estimates that over 100,000 jobs were lost in the public sector (excluding the civil service) between 1982-1989.

The implications of the above job losses are obvious. With the public sector providing the surest employment route out of poverty, the loss of such large job numbers reduced from the Ghanaian economy, in the short to medium term at least, the opportunity of a commensurate number either staying out of poverty or climbing out of the poverty trap. It must not be forgotten that these were not just any jobs but public sector jobs, the plum jobs in the body politic.

The closing down of a number of productive state enterprises, such as the African Timber and the Plywood Factory at Samreboi in Western Region further reduced paid industrial employment availability in one of the most depressed rural districts in the country where the only alternative employment available was small holder farming.

The correlation between decreasing public sector and other formal sector job losses and the shifting of labour to agriculture and the non-formal sector is established by Table 8.18 below:

Table 8.18
Percentage of labour employment

	Agriculture & Informal sectors	Government	Parastatal & other formal sector
1977	81.9	6.6	11.6
1978	80.7	7.8	11.5
1979	82.2	6.4	11.4
1980	85.8	6.5	7.7
1981	88.5	6.8	4.7
1982	87.2	6.5	7.7
1983	87.9	6.0	6.1
1984	85.5	5.9	8.6
1985	85.3	6.1	8.6
1986	86.3	6.2	7.5
1987	86.7	6.3	6.9
1988	88.1	6.7	5.3
1989	87.7	6.8	5.5
1990	87.8	7.0	5.2

Source: Compiled from Quarterly Digest of Statistics figures.

Notwithstanding the government machinery shedding jobs from 6.5% in 1982 to 5.9% in 1984, the government's share of direct labour had again reached 7% by 1990. This was because a number of new institutions of governance[19] such as the Board of Public Tribunals, the National Investigations Committee, the Confiscated Assets Committee, the Office of the Special Public Prosecutor, the

Office of Revenue Commissioners (to name a few), as well as new mass movements[20] of the PNDC had become more integrated into official government accounting. But the critical sectors, for employment purposes, were still the parastatal/formal and the agricultural/informal sectors. While the former's share of labour decreased from 8.6% in 1984 to 5.2% in 1990, the latter's increased from 85.5% to 87.8% during the same period. Agriculture, from the previous analysis was the least viable route out of poverty (as it contributed the greatest employees to poverty) with the parastatals at the other end of the scale as regards poverty. The implication here is that labour was being moved from well paid (and thus more poverty averting employment) to the agricultural/informal sectors, where the probability of moving out of poverty was the least favourable.

From an equity perspective, the increased differential of 5.7:1 prior to 1983 to 10.5:1 by 1991 (see chapter 5) in the civil service changed the nature of equity in that requirement of the labour market. And since the public sector has historically been the lead sector on employment income in Ghana, the precedent was there for the private sector to follow.

The above creates the picture that no jobs were created during the adjustment period with the potential of making a mark on poverty. This impression would be misleading as the increasing growth of the service sector (hotels, insurance, financial services, private medicine etc.) testifies (see 1995 budget statement). However, the nature of services job creation is such that apart from those at the apex of the sector, the majority of the jobs created are low paying hotel and other clerical jobs compared to the manufacturing and industrial jobs that had been lost.

Public provision

If one is to put a finger on a rough factor that has had the most adverse effect on poverty (whether case or mass) in Ghana, the person would have difficulty naming another factor that comes anywhere near the curtailment of public provision of service (such as health, education , water, sewerage agricultural extension, electricity etc.) functions which the state has viewed as critical up to national development until the introduction of the Economic Recovery Programme in Ghana.

Public provision of these services had given Ghana a human development capacity consistently above the sub Saharan African average. For example, Kenya has a gross educational enrolment ratio of 13% fifteen to twenty years ago while Ghana was already enjoying a 37% enrolment ratio (WB 1993, pp 127 & 175). While Ghana had a population per physician ratio of 12,900 during this same time frame, oil rich Nigeria had a ratio of 20,200 (ibid. p 127 & 249).

The lower level of public provision, a component of the cost recovery regime, led to hospital fees being introduced in 1983. The fees were increased in 1985 and have consistently been adjusted higher every year since then. We have established in chapter five that the poor were least likely to report sick, (that is to utilise medical services). The increasing cost of hospital attendance (hospital fees) is, therefore, felt most by the poorest of the society who are the least capable of paying. While the legal minimum wage is ₵1200 per day, a day's admission at any state hospital, let alone private ones, currently costs the individual not less than ₵2000 per day.[21]

The introduction of "cost recovery" in health went hand in hand with a decrease in public investment in health provision. Per capita health expenditure decreased from $4.93 constant dollars in 1972 to $1.63 in 1987 (Carrin 1992, p.31 Table 3.4).

Decreased public provision was not limited to health or indeed to education, (the consequence of which as discussed earlier, is the fall in employment rate), but to other utilities. Between 1983 and January 1986 for example, water rates rose by 150%, postal tariffs by 365% and electricity by 1000%.[22] Public welfare was thus compromised by these measures leading invariably, to a deepening of poverty.

Increasing rural inequality

One of the far reaching consequences of the broader Structural Adjustment Programme on equity, and thus poverty in rural Ghana has been the increasing social and economic inequality and diversity in recent years. While aspects of this occurrence have a positive potential - included in this category is redeployment of civil and public servants to the hinterland under the local the local government decentralisation programme adopted by the PNDC in the mid 1980s, the economic causes of the increasing inequality have essentially rested on the enhanced price differential between export crops such as cocoa, coffee, cotton etc. and non-export food crops. Producer price reform under adjustment altered the internal rural terms of trade, making exports the most lucrative.

National food security/agriculture

The effects of SAP on poverty can also be examined from the angle of agriculture and food security. The credit policy pursued as part of banking and monetary reform impacts negatively on agriculture. Agricultural workers, as already established, form the biggest poverty group in the economy. Largely because of this and also conceding to the fact that agriculture credit has not been the most profitable form of banking in Ghana, previous regimes had moved to ring fence a proportion of available credit to agriculture. Interest on such credit was also mandated to be lower than for other sectors and small scale farmers equally became a priority for agricultural credit. The Financial Sector Adjustment Programme (FINSAP) deregulated credit. Sectoral fencing, was deemed incompatible with the new market ethos of credit supply and management in the economy, hence losing its place in the scheme of things. The lower interest rate extended to agriculture was also abolished by FINSAP.

With Banks no longer required by regulation to advance credit to agriculture and small holders on favourable terms, rural farmers, amongst the least able to provide the type of collateral security ordinarily demanded by banks, have become increasingly unable to access credit from regular sources, thus suffering productivity and income losses. And with the deterioration of the terms of trade between export crops and food crops, the little available credit is channelled to export crops. This not only leaves most farmers (majority of Ghanaian farmers cultivate food crops) poorer, but critically compromising national food security. The relative decline in the production of food crops coinciding with FINSAP is not unconnected and since agriculture provides the highest percentage of income for the poor, their fate is thus worsened.

The welfare position of food farmers has been more problematic since 1986 as a continued decline in food terms of trade, a faster feed-through of the effects of devaluation and other policies into consumer prices, the slowing down of the growth of food production as well as the elimination of the fertiliser subsidy, combine to reduce the real income of farmers (Roe & Schneider 1992, p.91).

The above further pushes farmers and thus most rural dwellers into increased poverty (see Heller 1988, p.3).The liberalisation of food imports, above and beyond making up for local shortfalls, adds to the downward spiral of agricultural prices in real terms and lower incomes for the already poor Ghanaian farmers. These imports are generally cheaper than locally produced food but often of a worse quality as a result of the large scale chemical rich method of producing rice and beef, for examples in Europe and America.

The inability of the country to establish a creditable national food security has other disastrous outcomes for poverty. Lower incomes have resulted in Ghanaians spending nearly two-thirds of their income on food in 1987-1988 (applies to both 'poor' and 'non-poor'), a proportion higher than the country did in 1950 (Rimmer 1992, p.5).

Poverty alleviation under adjustment

The instrument of poverty alleviation under adjustment has been the Programme of Action to Mitigate the Social Cost of Adjustment (PAMSCAD). Proposals for the establishment of PAMSCAD were presented to the Paris

Donors Conference on Ghana in 1987 and accepted by implementation beginning in 1988. The drawing up of PAMSCAD saw UNICEF playing a leading role.

PAMSCAD was a series of projects undertaken largely by community groups and part or wholly funded by foreign pledges administered by the government. The aim was to generate works (and incomes) through the construction of basic needs facilities and provide both work and training for retrenched workers in rural and urban deprived areas. The programme was transitional in nature, at least in terms of design and was to have a quick-time implementing regime (WB 1992a, p.15).

Why PAMSCAD?

PAMSCAD was the admission by both the government of Ghana and the multilateral and bilateral donors (who had supported and promoted the adjustment over the previous four years)[23] that the social consequences of reform were massive and needed corrective action. The social disenchantment and the increasing impoverisation of the people could no longer be overlooked if the programme was to stay on course; neither could the increasingly militant stance of the Trades Union Congress nor the barrage of criticism emanating from the universities and other progressive[24] circles be ignored.

PAMSCAD was, therefore, both a recognition and an attempt to lessen the worse effects of a market led adjustment in the Ghanaian situation. The social consequences of adjustment had been ignored in both the drawing up and pursuance of adjustment because of the fixation of lead players[25] with aggressive economic growth theories and rates. Social consequences only came in for belated attention in the form of PAMSCAD only when the consequences threatened to derail the pursuit of the 'golden fleece'. No wonder PAMSCAD was designed as an interim scheme to effectively buy time for economic growth.

Character of PAMSCAD

The designers of PAMSCAD saw the programme seeking "... to address the needs of vulnerable groups who are in a precarious condition due to the adjustment or due to earlier period of economic decline" (PAMSCAD 1987, p.1). The designers, from the above quote, had no intention of revising or incorporating poverty alleviation into the main thrust of the programme. They only grudgingly accepted that adjustment was largely responsible for the increased vulnerability of the poor in society to the forces of deprivation and poverty. Forever free marketers, they could not, accept total responsibility and needed to drag in "earlier period of economic" decline as also responsible for the social and commercial impoverisation of the mid 1980s!

PAMSCAD had the overall aim, according to Yeebo, of mobilising the population into undertaking viable community economic projects, through which it was hoped the thousands of retrenched workers would be re-employed outside the public sector. The government estimated that a thousand rural and small scale enterprises were going to be established through the instrumentality of PAMSCAD (ibid. p.216). The scheme was also to generate community initiatives, re-train retrenched workers, encourage small scale industries and provide basic needs such as water and improved sanitation facilities to rural communities [ibid.].

The Programme was in its initial and 'exciting' phase funded to the tune of $84m with a foreign exchange component of $37.6m over a three year period by external donors. It was also expected to create 40,000 mostly unskilled jobs during its 'initial' phase. Feeder road construction using labour intensive methods, non-formal education, basic level health projects were some of the other activities targeted for PAMSCAD assistance [PAMSCAD 1987, p.1].

With the prevailing levels of social deprivation, the selection of projects had to be critical in the success or otherwise of PAMSCAD. The government in recognising this, established that:

> the criteria for the selection of projects under the programme was that they should have a strong poverty focus, high economic and social rates of return, modest institutional requirements permitting speedy implementation; and in sensitive areas, a *high profile to enhance the sustainability of adjustment* [ibid. p.21].

Assessment

Assessing the effectiveness and contribution of PAMSCAD to poverty alleviation leads one through the uncharted territories that all hyped up programmes must need conjure. The dilemma here, as is often the case, is where to draw the line as regards the objectives of the programme. If one were to go by the volume of literature and official publications and mutual back slapping of such bodies and agencies such as UNICEF's description of PAMSCAD as " a good example of what is meant, in practice, *'adjustment with a human face"* [UNICEF 1990, p.10], then one is tempted to positively assess the Programme. On the other hand, sticking to the text of the programme and practical achievements on the ground can only lead one to conclude that

PAMSCAD was and is, a gargantuan political fraud perpetuated on the poor of Ghana by the government and its international backers.

But on the positive side, (even if insignificant), a number of small scale targeted projects, were completed in 1989. The World Bank asserts that by the end of 1989, twenty community initiated projects under PAMSCAD had been completed and another one hundred and ninety-eight started during the initial phase of PAMSCAD [Rothchild 1991, p.12]. This is obviously only a ripple of the sort of programme needed to protect the poor and vulnerable from the ever worsening impoverishing effects of the Economic Recovery Programme.

Notwithstanding the above 'success' of which both the government and international donors such as the World Bank and UNICEF never stop publicising, PAMSCAD has had very little positive impact on the lives of the millions of Ghanaians it was set up to help. A number of factors explain the programme's lack of success in living up to its publicity claims:

Funding

PAMSCAD was mainly funded by the international community as already discussed. An amount of about $84m was pledged at the 1987 Donors Conference in Paris over a three year period. While this level of funding was seriously inadequate, the slow realisation of pledges made disbursement even more difficult. Even the World Bank, had to concede that the gap between headline pledges, disbursement and identification of suitable projects had led to 'bottlenecks' in programme implementation. If PAMSCAD could be that underfunded in its high profile years, it should not come as a surprise that only ¢288,000,000 (about $288,000) was allocated to PAMSCAD in the 1995 budget year.

Basic needs approach

Another reason for PAMSCAD's failure to make any meaningful headway in poverty alleviation was (and still is) its over reliance on the 'basic needs' approach. Projects favoured invariably included toilets, boreholes, schools and health posts.[26] While there is no dispute over the need for these projects, they are still in the main, not income generating. Surely, the generation of income by the retrenched and the disadvantaged of society ought to be the priority in poverty alleviation. The maintenance of these 'basic needs' projects was not provided for by PAMSCAD, leaving communities to shoulder the burden. People using KVIP[27] toilets, for example, had to pay for the privilege anytime they responded to nature's call. The proceeds were then used either by the local community or a local government agency to maintain the facility.

PAMSCAD's approach on one hand assisted particularly rural communities to build these facilities but on the other hand, imposed extra financial burdens on the community by encumbering the communities with increased financial outlays on both construction[28] and maintenance. By not raising rural standards and incomes through employment generation and lowering the cost of health care, education, mass transport etc., whatever else is done only amounts to surface dressing.

Non-integration

The Programme of Actions to Mitigate the Social Costs of Adjustment suffered from its non integration into mainstream adjustment policy. Arising out of its isolation, PAMSCAD did not have any effect on the reform process itself. The same market policies, which created the increased impoverishment in the first place, were pursued with increasing intensity after 1987, creating more casualties along the way.

If poverty alleviation via PAMSCAD was going to be effective, the instrument of alleviation ought to occupy centre stage or at least be prominent in a multi purpose integrated reform package. In the pursuit of PAMSCAD, promoters found it useful to ignore the empirical conclusion that poverty was causal to economic decline, and that economic regeneration could not be devoid of poverty reduction. Outside the main thrust therefore, PAMSCAD becomes at best, a belated mop up exercise. Jolly captured this succinctly when he saw PAMSCAD as a belated appendage to the Economic Recovery Programme rather than a part of it [Jolly 1988, p.171].

From the foregoing, it is difficult not to see PAMSCAD as an exercise in political gimmickry with the sole aim of preventing societal rebellion against the harsh reality of the free market solutions being imposed on Ghana under Structural Adjustment.

Notes

1 The smallest unit of local government administration in England and Wales.

2 See Report ... on the Poor Laws, 1834 p 22.

3 The Brandt Report can be said to be an attempt by the ruling establishment to 'contain' the negativity of the existing global political relations, rather than re-structure the politico-economic foundations of the system.

4 See Sen A., 1981, Poverty and Famines: An essay on Entitlement and Deprivation, "Poor, Relatively Speaking" in Oxford Economic Papers 35 (1983) 153 - 169 and Townsend's reply to Sen, "A Sociological Approach to the Measurement of Poverty - A Rejoinder to Professor Amartya Sen" Oxford Economic Papers, 37 (1985) 659 - 668.

5 See MG Quibria & TN Srinivasan (eds.), 1993: Rural Poverty in Asia: Priority Issues and Policy Options. Oxford Univ. for Asian Development Bank p7.

6 The poverty line was draw at two-thirds of the mean per capita household expenditure. This amounted to ₡32,981, or $96 per annum at nominal 1990 exchange rate.

7 David Woodward [Debt, Adjustment and Poverty in Developing Countries 1992] views the lack of access and or resources as the most critical causes of poverty in the developing world.

8 See World Resources 1994 - 95.

9 Defined in the survey as $100 per capita household income.

10 It is useful to note here that the poverty line at historical 1975 $100 was higher than the line drawn by the GLSS of the late 1980s and early 1990s, reflecting the relative decline of Ghanaian living standards.

11 A composite measure which combines infant mortality, life expectancy and literacy.

12 Explaining in part, the poverty of the Savannah North.

13 According to the World Bank's 1995 World Development Report, 65% of all Ghanaians are rural based.

14 Ghana presently has one of the worst population/physician ratios in the developing world. The World Bank's Social Development Indicators (1993) put the ratio as one physician to 22,970 as against 1:12,900 15-20 years ago. Togo, has a ratio of 1:11,954, Kenya 1:10,133, Malaysia 1:2,701, South Korea 1:1,366, etc.

15 Recognising that poverty is largely rural.

16 Conducted between Sept. 1991 and Sept. 1992.

17 That is the accumulation of human capital.

18 Analysing the 1987 - 1988 Ghana Living Standards Survey.

19 These new bodies, seen as revolutionary organs of the 'revolutionary' PNDC government paralleled some existing institutions. For example, the Board of Public Tribunals shadowed the existing judicial system, the Office of Revenue Commissioners duplicated the work of the Internal Revenue Service, The National Investigations Committee that of the Police and other existing investigative bodies in the public domain.

20 The Committees for the Defence of the Revolution (CDRs) and the 31st December Women's Movement being the most prominent.

21 This excludes the government approved charges for every medical attention from consultation to major operations.

22 see West Africa (magazine), January 13, 1986 p 78.

23 These bodies included 14 donor governments and 12 multilateral organisations some of which were the Fund, Bank, UNICEF, UNDP, WFP, IFAD, ILP, CIDA, USAID and ODA (UK): source Zaya Yeebo 1991, p.215.

24 The National Union of Ghana Students (NUGS) and some of the other left leaning pressure groups which initially supported the PNDC in 1982 are worthy of mention.

25 Government, Fund and World Bank.

26 This preference invariably originating from the need to easily quantifiable projects for propaganda purposes.

27 Kumasi Ventilated Internal Pit latrines were designed by the Engineering Faculty of the University of Science and Technology, Kumasi for use in rural and surb urban Ghana. The design was such that such toilets did not need piped water as the traditional ones do.

28 PAMSCAD did not completely meet the cost of any selected project but only assisted with part of the cost, leaving the local community to provide the additional funding.

9 Conclusion

In the preceding chapters, I have sought to explain and analyse what informs the Ghanaian political economy, how structural and managerial lapses reduced the capacity of the country and economy to grow out of poverty, how and why the Structural Adjustment Programme was adopted, the nature and degree of poverty in Ghana and how adjustment has affected poverty.

My principal conclusion is that economic development has been partially but perhaps only temporarily restored, and that social development has in some senses worsened. The two[1] are poorly integrated. As a consequence, economic growth may be smaller, and more uncertain, than might otherwise be the case. Important social objectives - such as the massive reduction of poverty, have demonstrably not been fulfilled. Structural adjustment programmes are largely responsible for the unsatisfactory outcomes and prospects. Far from being one of the rare successes of international Structural Adjustment Programmes in Africa, Ghana represents another example of national accommodation to dependency in an emerging global economic system.

This is of course a very general thesis, which has to be subjected to close examination and clarification. I cannot claim to have provided necessary substantiation of its comparative and global institutional aspects. But in modern conditions, nations states are increasingly involved in international systems and networks, and analyses of national events have to be placed in context.

So, while acknowledging the many limitations of this book, I have risked reference to the wider setting to show the lines on which economic theory is inadequate to explain events and needs to go beyond national frontiers. But I have tried to substantiate the historical process within Ghana itself and to use cross-national examples to reach conclusions applicable to the country.

A theoretical analysis of Ghanaian development and the shortcomings of international [and national] policies inevitably leads to conclusions which have to be drawn about alternative policies which need to be put in place. The steep economic decline that confronted the country in the late 1970s and early 1980s has been arrested in at least, the short to medium term. This was however, achieved at a high cost, especially social and long term economic sacrifices. If policies are not put in place as a matter of urgency to offset the social and economic distortions, these will come back to haunt the economy in the next decade or two. The increased poverty and socio-economic polarisation that accompanied adjustment - which represented those sacrifices - have the potential of being the seeds of tomorrow's macro economic stagnation or even collapse.

Let me begin with education. The policy of shifting ever - increasing proportions of the burden of educating tomorrow's workforce on individuals, as against the society represented by the state, is already resulting in a decline in the uptake of educational places in schools. Education, be it general or specialised, pays for itself in the long run by enhancing the absorption of knowledge and the aptitude to learning, thereby improving the cost-effectiveness of later training. Specialised education, for example, increases the skill levels available for employment and higher productivity, apart from simultaneously contributing to the reduction of household poverty in Ghana and enhancing the varying capacities and confidence of the population as a whole. Again, the history of development this past half century clearly establishes an indisputable link between levels of education and economic take-off.[2]

'Cost Recovery' under adjustment is equally compromising the health of the nation. The people of any nation are the greatest assets that any nation can have and public investment in the health of its most important asset can only be beneficial to increased wealth creation and well being. Under the present direction of adjustment, the population as a whole is becoming vulnerable to the encroachment of increased ill health through poverty.

The cumulative impoverishment of the mass of the population is stretching the traditional safety net of kinship to a breaking point as increasing levels of social costs are pushed on to individuals. The family system has historically redistributed the surplus of the extended family to cater for all the needs of the kith and kin. However, with the state reneging on social obligations previously accepted, the individual cells in the great web of the extended family are increasingly becoming unable to take on additional obligations and at the same time, unable to accumulate the needed surplus for redistribution. The last bastion of security for the Ghanaian poor, whose numbers are swelling as the casualties of the Economic Recovery Programme mount, has been weakened.[3]

The evidence from the study indicates that adjustment has in the short term at least, increased mass poverty both by the distributive policies pursued and by the mortgaging of the Ghanaian economy to the 'market' and international capital. However, the establishment of relative macro economic stability as a result of the adjustment measures[4] paradoxically provides the country with a rare window of opportunity to move both the country and the majority of its citizens from the depths of poverty.

To do this, those in charge of administration would have to thread a delicate path between restructuring the economy in a way that meets both the development aspirations of the country and retains the confidence of international money markets. In restructuring the economy, poverty alleviation should be seen as a major pillar of the process alongside other priorities and not as an ineffective after-thought *a la* PAMSCAD. The problem is to persuade internal and external opinion of the advantages of this change.

How is that change to be achieved? The recommendations underlined below are not exhaustive but serve as a useful starting point. I have tried to set out a number of areas of policy requiring international and national collaboration: a big reform in agriculture; a social basis for economic growth; more equitable distribution of internal resources ; greater priority for health; the consolidation of education; the restructuring of the labour market and a programme for the environment.

1. Agriculture/rural development

Attempts at poverty reduction must start with an integrated agricultural and rural development programme. As the preceding chapters have pointed out, poverty in Ghana is essentially a rural phenomenon. The bulk of both the poor and the population at large live in rural areas where agriculture is the premier occupation. Food expenditure also constitutes more than half the household expenditure of the Ghanaian family. Thus whether in fighting poverty, inflation or economic stagnation, agricultural productivity is at the heart of effective action. To achieve this, the following is suggested.

1.1 Food and agriculture should be the central plank of a reform programme along the lines suggested by the Lagos Plan of Action.[5] Emphasis here must be on increasing the yield per acre (as against just increasing acreage) through better husbandry, the control of post-harvest losses, supply of improved and more drought-resistant crop varieties, promotion of water and soil conservation, improvement in hand tools design and usage, promotion of irrigation and revamping the extension services department of the agricultural ministry.

1.2 Increasing real incomes of the rural poor through increased land yields and food availability. It must be remembered that the ERP in its infancy emphasised the rehabilitation of export agriculture, ignoring food production for home consumption. Equal emphasis, if not a higher priority, must now be given to food agriculture[6] as a matter of policy imperative.

1.3 Ringed agricultural credits for farmers with particular attention going to small-holder producers must be introduced. Financial and allied institutions would have to be re oriented to see credits to agriculture as a potentially viable business as opposed the previous conception of agriculture as a non profitable area of investment. To this end, the Bank of Ghana must re-assess the role and functions of its Rural Banks with the aim of tailoring their operations to suit the rural economy. This will not be easy, but must be urged and directed consistently. Under this re-orientation, the form of credit should be essentially input led, rather than cash led. Rural farmers and cottage industrialists must be organised into associations and similar groups possibly along lines not unsimilar to the Grameen approach.

1.4 Critical linkages between rural agricultural producers and the market economy must be established. This can be done by opening up rural areas via improved road networks, financial infrastructure, re-introduction of a slimmer but more business oriented marketing boards or companies to operate on quasi-commercial lines buying up agricultural surplus from producers, selling inputs available at cost prices[7] to farmers, providing credits against purchases of agricultural inputs and encouraging the introduction of high yield seeds to rural agriculture. This would accommodate the legitimate demands and needs of Ghanaian agriculture while avoiding the excesses, inefficiency, corruption, bureaucratic bungling and the general waste that characterised the operations of previous marketing boards in particular and the agricultural bureaucracy in general.

1.5 To improve the quality of life in rural Ghana and help rural dwellers to move out of poverty, simplified techniques and technologies must be developed for and encouraged in rural Ghana as a matter of urgency. Existing technologies are either too sophisticated and therefore, unsuitable,[8] or have not changed for more than a century. These technologies and techniques should be developed from local knowledge and materials on a 'next stop' basis.[9] There are local models developed by local research institutions such as and the Technology Transfer Centre of the University of Science and Technology for this very purpose and which have been allowed to remain largely unknown. The state would have to come in and move these beyond their successful pilot stages to mass commercial usage.[10] On the basis of available reports, these measures could involve:

- Improving traditional methods of crop storage to reduce post harvest losses, which can account for as much as 30% - 50% of the harvest;
- Designing and improving manually operated cereal and legume grinders as well as millet threshers as a matter of urgency. A Technical Task Force could be set up for this purpose;

- Improving cooking arrangements to reduce fuel wood consumption and release labour for other uses in the household, particularly for female members of the household;[11]
- Design and encourage the use of manually operated extraction presses to enable rural dwellers, and especially women ,to extract oil from locally produced seeds. This would add value to the product and thus increase agricultural incomes;
- One new strategy is to use wind-power and simple solar energy for pumping water, grinding, cereals and legumes and for small-scale production of electricity. So that they catch on speedily, these units must be subsidised by the state in the short to medium term.. 'Pump-priming' is a long-established state practice which deserves wider application in Ghana.

1.6 To stimulate local development in rural areas, functional local institutions would have to be involved in a new partnership. The partnership should draw strength from across political, economic, social and cultural divides. This way, development can be self sustaining in each given area. Previous attempts at rural development had failed precisely because the top down approach was adopted. A new partnership in which the government is only one of several parties, even if it is the facilitator, would help build up the needed domestic support for progress.

1.7 Above all else, the distinctive urban bias associated with the Ghanaian state would have to be abandoned. This is the counterpart of giving priority to agricultural development as suggested above. It is ironic that the well-equipped Cocoa Clinic operated by the Cocoa Board is located in Accra where no cocoa is grown![12] Accra, already boasting the biggest teaching hospital in the country as well as a number of government hospitals and the bulk of private hospitals, was again chosen in the early 1990s for construction of the one and only Social Security and National Insurance Trust Hospital.[13]Resources now would have to be shifted to rural Ghana if poverty alleviation is to be successful. Although such a strategy has proved to be difficult in many parts of the world - there are examples of substantial success - as in Malaysia.

2. A social basis for Economic growth

To secure economic and social growth while reducing the level of poverty in Ghanaian society, a different type of macro economic restructuring would have to be effected, building on both the success and the lessons of the ERP. This new process would have a longer time frame than is implicit in the present adjustment programme, recognising that there is no quick fix for Ghana's development problems. The following would be some of the options available in achieving the foregoing:

247

2.1 The role of government has to be larger, and not smaller, in the optimal long term strategy for rural development. Leaving market forces to dictate the rate and level of rural development would be short sighted since the market is not equipped to perform that function. Indeed, supply-side rural development is an investment in both people and the economy that recognises poverty elimination as both a social and economic imperative.

2.2 The Ghanaian government must wrestle the lead of policy initiative from external actors while keeping them on board. Development is achieved by people and institutions with a direct stake in the outcome of development. For too long during the adjustment period, as my analysis on shows, Ghana had virtually handed over the policy and reform initiative to the World Bank and the International Monetary Fund. The global agenda of these institutions blinds them to the Ghanaian reality. Inappropriate policies are designed from afar and pressure is applied on the government to pursue policies not suited for the Ghanaian situation, as the VAT debacle proved.

2.3 The needed resources for economic empowerment [and poverty reduction], can be released through sustained campaigns to get her international creditors, both institutional and bilateral, to convert their debt holdings into equity investment. This necessarily invites international campaigning organisations to do what they can to embolden government to pursue this objective in various fora. This would have the benefit of reducing the debt repayment burden while boosting investment equity in the economy.

2.4 Value adding strategies must be emphasised as the favoured course of action for both industry and agro processing. This was a prominent feature of chapter six. This would involve rejecting the free market non-interference regime pursued by the ERP. Value added production would for example, enable the necessary linkages to be built between rural agricultural and the rest of industry. Such industries or operating units can be and must be encouraged through an incentive package to locate in rural Ghana closer to the source of raw materials. This would also create non farm wage income and help reduce poverty while extending the rural economy. Agro processing must also aim at improving national food security by creating the wherewithal for storage and the banishment of post harvest losses among rural agricultural producers.

2.5 Increased productivity per acre for cocoa production without increasing acreage will raise incomes of cocoa farmers without compromising the availability of rich and fertile land in southern Ghana for food crop production. Using cocoa and cocoa by-products to create upstream manufacturing units in soap and fertiliser manufacturing as well as processing cocoa beans to butter must be pursued as a component of increased productivity and value in the cocoa industry. Soap making can be done on a cottage industry basis with the technology developed and passed on by central government bodies. These are all examples of the strategy discussed above of regenerating agricultural self - sufficiency alongside wider, and cross-national, objectives.

2.6 In formulating growth strategies, care must be taken to understand the consequences of various policy options on different socio-economic groups, including a better appreciation of the transitional costs of such policies. The extended emphasis on the stability instruments that bring down demand, particularly for rural production without counter balancing measures must be abandoned in favour of more holistic approaches to restructuring and economic growth. Global inequality must not be deepened at the expense of local capacity for subsistence. That is what the above analysis teaches. The great problem has been the failure to counter - balance Structural Adjustment Programmes with strong domestic strategies.

2.7 Privatisation of state owned and profitable enterprises cannot be pursued unless the indigenous private sector has the expertise and resources to successfully manage such enterprises. If not, the state must consider giving such enterprises commercial autonomy to pursue their commercial interests while remaining in state ownership. Off loading such to multinational corporations only reduces the indigenous capacity to develop, and creates unbalanced, and in the longer run, unsuccessful economic relationships as well as unbalanced social relationships.

2.8 It is desirable that government work within the ambit of the international community to influence policies pursued by OECD countries. To ignore the fact that a large part of the external imbalance of the Ghanaian and indeed African economy,[14] was caused by policies pursued by this group of countries is to side-step a major component of the problem. If a reversal of OECD policies were to occur, it would reduce the magnitude of required adjustment in Ghana and elsewhere. This would make adjustment more successful and may possibly give Ghana the conditions and opportunity to specifically tackle increasing poverty in a major way.

3. More equitable distribution of resources

In this conclusion, I have so far, concentrated on the promotion of economic and social development among other things to *prevent* the growth of poverty. To effect poverty alleviation, the distribution of resources between urban and rural as well as between income groups would have to be made more equitable. Towards this end, the following measures are recommended:

3.1 The design of both broad adjustment as well as its component units must now incorporate equity and distributional justice into its growth focus. It is myopic, if not misleading, for Ghanaian policy makers and their legion of foreign 'advisors' to assume that accelerated economic growth would automatically have positive distributional impacts. It is equally false to operate on the basis that a PAMSCAD style 'mop up' anti-poverty scheme would have any impact on the incidence of mass poverty.

3.2 Intervention must be both strategic and specific. For policy purposes, intervention in the budget share of a particular commodity is less important than the fraction of the particular commodity accounted for by the poor. In food expenditure for example, Oti Boateng established that although the poor made up 35.9% of the population, they accounted for only 14.1% of market purchases of food [1990 p18]. Intervention here must be directed towards the staple food eaten by the poor.[15]

4. Greater priority for health

The health of the nation is too important to be left to market forces. This is even more so for rural dwellers. To tackle poverty, the following measures would be worth examining:

4.1 Expenditure on health as a percentage of GDP, must be raised to at least 1970s levels. The bulk of the increased expenditure should go into primary health care and immunisation through out the country but more especially the rural areas, where most of the disadvantaged live. It has been proven in other countries, such as Zimbabwe that comprehensive immunisation can and does lead to increased life expectancy while appreciably reducing infant mortality.[16]

4.2 Increased emphasis on primary health care must go hand in hand with the production within the country of common drugs. This would not only eventually reduce the cost of such drugs, but also increase total health delivery capacity in the economy. Increased outlays on health must be on *per capita* terms and not just in absolute figures. The health delivery ideology that places curative medicine at the apex of the system would also have to be jettisoned and be replaced with one that makes primary health care the main principal weapon for the future. Primary Health Care, being more rural friendly, would best serve the hinterland where both the majority of the population and the productive wealth of the country can be located.

4.3 Special nutritional support for children. There is an urgent need for intervention in supplementing the feeding programmes of children in rural poor communities. The increasing cost of living has to be countered by assisted feeding programmes for children in the short term while attention is focused on increased food productivity in the medium term. The UNICEF estimate of one and a half million undernourished children in Ghana in the mid 1980s has to be revised to about two million in the mid 1990s for the purposes of estimating the scale of the required action.[17]

4.4 A national health insurance scheme should be set up as a matter of priority to provide universal coverage as against the present 'cash and carry' favoured by structural adjustment but which further impoverishes the vulnerable.

5. The consolidation of education

The relevance of formal as well as skills education have already been argued in this thesis. In the same vein, I have established that the uptake of education since the introduction of 'cost recovery' under adjustment has been declining. This was one unexpected, and deeply problematic, finding from this research. To counter this destructive trend and help people move from poverty, the following are recommended for consideration which arise from the above structural analysis.

5.1 The immediate abandonment of the cost recovery concept in education as well as health;

5.2 Increase state expenditure on education, with the bulk of the increased funding going to basic education and skills development. Increased revenues can be generated from efficiency gains. The Auditor General's Report for the 1994 fiscal year pointed out billions of the cedis being wasted because of inefficiency and inadequate controls in financial administration.[18]

5.3 Equality of treatment in the provision of educational infrastructure between urban and rural areas. The practice where rural communities have historically been made to carry the burden of building school structures while urban areas are largely provided for by the state must cease and in its place, the state should make rural provision, its priority for the next ten years at least.

6. The restructuring of the labour market

The low income/low wage strategy involved in formal sector adjustment involves low skill production methods, use of the informal sector, part time work and casual labour. The schema also involves weak environmental and health standards, poor social investment and limited infrastructure. The strategy is to maintain low wages by high unemployment and poor social development of labour, thus contributing to the erosion of workers bargaining power. Low wages also lead to widening inequality in the distribution of incomes and wealth. From this, the Structural Adjustment Programme is evidently a reformulation of the discredited old low wage/cheap labour thinking that was the hallmark of the country's periphery status during the colonial and neo-colonial phases of national life.

6.1 To therefore usher in development and reduce poverty, the strategy in the medium term must of necessity be to turn the economy into a fair wage economy through training, enhanced skill development, social regulation and increased labour productivity. Collaboration with neighbouring governments, particularly under the auspices of the Economic Community of West African States (ECOWAS) to establish minimum conditions of employment and expansion of the public sector in critical areas such as education and health, will help establish a more stable labour market as well as reduce poverty.

7. A programme for the environment

The state, to sustain growth in all its dimensions, must invest in measures and technologies that would reduce the country's reliance on natural occurrences such as rainfall for agriculture. Investment must be directed at increasing the quantity of land under irrigation, checking soil erosion, soil enriching measures such as organic fertiliser application, conservation of forest and foliage etc.

At the industrial level and especially in mining, the regulatory climate needs tightening to protect the citizenry from disease and other environmental hazards. What is needed here are regulations that are transparent, fair, and which strike an equitable balance between exploitation, protection and conservation.

New directions in policy

I have attempted to relate the specifics of the Ghanaian analysis to the overall responsibilities of not only the Ghanaian government, but also to those of international agencies like the World Bank and the International Monetary Fund. International as well as national policy strategies must, on this analysis, be changed. In the Ghanaian case, theories of development as expressed in SAPs have not worked, as has the national administration of those programmes. The state has seemingly withdrawn from efforts to take a different direction; almost gliding along with the momentum of the Bretton Woods duopoly. At both national and international levels, key policies must take a different direction. While the author would be the first to apologise if the conclusion seems over-ambitious, the logic of the need to adopt a new social development plan for Ghana seems unavoidable.

I have sketched seven areas of policy initiatives to be adopted internationally and nationally, which flow from the analysis in this work of the history of Ghana, its current social and economic situation, and the influence of Structural Adjustment Programmes applied to Africa in general and Ghana in particular. I recognise that changes in IMF and World Bank policies may require the restructuring of these (and other) international agencies, so that there might be representation of more countries in the management of these bodies. Closer consultation and agreement between professional advisors from outside and from inside, as well as a new Ghanaian government department of planning to restore, or achieve local democratic control of policy development and administration is also called for. However, it would be wrong to give any impression that policies can be changed without acknowledging that adjustments have to be made in the balance of institutionalised power both internationally and within the Ghanaian polity to make these policies viable.

Notes

1 That is economic and social development.
2 See World Bank, 1992, Ghana 200 and Beyond chapter. 3 for comparative statistics between Ghana and NICs on literacy levels at take off.
3 ERP and Structural Adjustment are used interchangeably in the Ghanaian context.
4 The most significant factor here is the increased confidence in the Ghanaian economy by the international community and markets.
5 The O.A.U's Lagos Plan of Action exhorts African governments to improve the use of input packages, modify techno-economic structures of production with aim of providing incentives to farmers to increase production [AU, 1982, Lagos Plan of Action, Geneva. International Institute for Labour Studies, p 10].
6 Including animal husbandry and fishing.
7 The state would have to meet the difference between the cost price and the market price in the form of subsidies. The subsidies need not be cash subsidies but can be offset against tax liability of the boards or companies. If the developed world still finds it necessary to subsidise agriculture, then Ghana should not shy away from doing likewise.
8 These are often unaffordable as well.
9 That is, moving a lever above what is already present and appreciated.
10 Ghana Research institutions, particularly the University of Science and Technology have produced or developed a large range of useful implements, machines and technologies which only need state support to popularise.
11 The Ghana Living Standards Survey (3) found females bearing the blunt of fetching fuel wood as well as other domestic unpaid duties [p 6 Table 4.6].
12 This is rather like the Fishery inspection units in Spain which are located in the heart of the country and not at any of the Ports.
13 The Social Security and National Insurance Trust [SSNT] is the state 'quango' responsible for contributory pension administration in the country.
14 For which the Bretton Woods institutions have and continue to have substantial responsibility.
15 Which happen to be locally produced staples as opposed to imported food.
16 See World Bank, 1994a.
17 See Giovanni Andrea Cornia et al., 1988 Adjustment with a Human Face: Ten Country Case Studies vol. 2 p 116.
18 Report submitted to Parliament as required by the Constitution and reported in the Ghanaian Times of Sept. 4, 1995.

Bibliography

Abbey, JL. (1987), *Ghana's Experience with Structural Adjustment.* mimeo. Accra.

Abbey, JL. (1990) "Ghana's Experience with Structural: Some Lessons" In (ed.) Pickett, James & Hans Singer. *Towards Economic Recovery in Sub- Saharan Africa,* Routledge: London.

Acquah, Ione. (1958) *Accra Survey,* University of London: London

Adda, William. (1989). "Ghana." In (ed.) Ramandham V, *Privatisation in Developing Countries,* Routledge: London.

Adu-Boahen. (1975). *Ghana: Evolution and Change in the Nineteenth and Twentieth Centuries.* Longman: London.

Ahmad, Nasseem. (1970) *Deficit Financing, Inflation and Capital Formation: The Ghanaian Experience 1960 - 1965.* Munchen. Weltforum Verlag.

Alderman, Harold. (1994). "Ghana: Adjustment's Star Pupil." In (ed.) Sahn, David E *Adjustment and Policy Failure in African Economies.* Penguin. London.

Amin, S, (1973) *Neo-Colonialism in West Africa* Monthly Review Press. New York.

Assenso-Okyere W.K., (1993) *Policies and Strategies for Rural Poverty Alleviation in Ghana* ISSER Technical Publication No. 57, Legon.

Bachar, Edmar L. (1987). "IMF Conditionality: Conceptual Problems and Policy Initiatives." *World Development* vol. 15:12.

Bandyopadhaya, J,. (1988) *The Poverty of Nations* Allied Publishers New Delhi.

Barbara, WJ. (1964). "The Movement in World Economy." In: (eds.) Harwitz MJ & Harwitz M, *Economic Transition in Africa*. Northwestern Univ. Evanston III.

Bate, Robert. (1981)*Markets and States in Tropical Africa: The Political bias of Agricultural Policies*. Univ. of Calif. Berkeley.

Berechot, Moret, Bosboom. 1985. *Study of Public Enterprise Sector in Ghana*. Final Report vol. 1 A.Management Consultancy Report. Nov. Accra.

Berg, Robert J & Jennifer Seymour Whitaker (eds.)](1986). *Strategies for African Development*. Univ. of Calif. Berkeley.

Beveridge Report, (1942) *Social Insurance and Alllied Services* cmd 6404, HMSO. London.

Bhagwati, JN & TN Srinivasan, (1975). *India.*. National Bureau of Economic Research [Foreign trade regimes and economic development]. New York.

Birmingham, WB. (1966). "An Index of Real Wages of Unskilled Labourers in Accra." In (eds.) Birmingham et al. *A Study of Contemporary Ghana*. George Allen & Urwin. London.

Blanchard, Oliver J, and Summers, Lawrence H, *Hysteresis and the European Unemployment Problem*, Havard Institute of Economic Research Discussion Paper Series No. 1240, Cambridge.

Boateng, Oti et al (1990). *A Poverty Profile of Ghana* Ghana Living Standards Survey (1) Ghana Statistical Service/ World Bank. Accra.

Brown, Merritt. "Macroeconomic Data of Ghana" *Economic Bulletin*. No. 1 & 2.

Burns, Allan. (1946). "Political and Other Changes in the Gold Coast." (Speech to Parliamentary Association, 24 Oct.). London.

Busia, KA. (1950). *Social Survey of Sekondi - Takoradi*. Crown Agents for the Colonies. London.

Carrin, Guy (1992) *Strategies for Healthcare Finance in Developing Countries*, Macmillan. Basingstoke.

Chazam, Naomi. (1983) *An Anatomy of Ghanaian Politics: Managing Political Recession*, 1969 - 1982., Westview Boulder Colo.

Commander, Simon, John Howell & Wayone Seini. (1989). "Ghana: 1983 - 87." In (ed.) Commander, Simon. *Structural Adjustment and Agriculture*. ODI. London.

Cord, Jacobeit, (1991) "Reviving Cocoa: Policies & Perspectives on Structural Adjustment in Ghana's key sector" in Donald Rothchild (ed.) *Ghana: The Political Economy of Recovery*. Lynne Reinner. Boulder.

Cordova, J (1986). "El Programa Mexicano de Re ordenacion Economica, 1983 - 1984" in Sela, el FMI, el Banco Mundial y la *Crisis Latinoamericana* (mexico: siglo xxi editores).

Cornia, G. et al.[eds] (1987). *Adjustment with a Human Face* vol. 1.Oxford Univ. New York.

Crook, R. (1990). "State, Society and Political Institutions in Cote d' Ivoire and Ghana." *IDS Bulletin* vol. 2.

Dietz., James L, (1992) "Overcoming Development: What has been Learned from East Asian and Latin American Experiences" *Journal of Economic Issues* 26 No. 2 June.

Dixon, Chris & Michael Hefferman. (1991). *Colonialism and Development in Contemporary World*. Mansell. London.

Dos Santos, Theolonio. (1973). "The Structure of Dependence." In (ed). Wilber, Charles K. *The Political Economy of Development and Under-Development*. Random House. New York.

Dowse, RE. (1969). *Modernisation in Ghana and the USSR: A Comparative Study*. Routledge London.

Elliot Charles, (1975) *Patterns of Poverty in the Third World*. Praeger New York.

Emily, Card. (1975). "The Political Economy of Ghana." In (ed.) Rochard Harris. *The Political Economy of Africa*. Schenkan. Cambridge, MA.

Esseks, John D. (1971). "Government and Indigenous Enterprises in Ghana." *Journal of Modern African Studies* (May).

Ewusi K, (1976) "Disparitis in Levels of Regional Development in Ghana" *Social Indicators* Vol 3 No. 1.

Ewusi, Kodwo, 1976 "*Measures of Levels of Development Among Regions and Localities in Ghana*" Paper presented at the seminar on urbanisation and rural development, Legon.

Ewusi, Kodwo. (1974). *The Distribution of Monetary Incomes in Ghana*. University of Ghana (ISSER) Legon.

Ewusi, Kodwo. (1987). *Structural Adjustment and Stabilisation Policies in Developing Countries: A Case Study of Ghana's Experience in 1983 - 86*. Ghana Publishing Corp. Tema.

Ewusi, Kodwo. (1988). *Trends in the Economy of Ghana*. ISSER Legon.

Feinberg, Richard. (1986). *The Changing Relationships between World Bank and International Monetary Fund*. Unpublished. Overseas Development Council. Washington.

Fieldhouse, DK. (1971). "The Economic Exploitation of Africa: Some British and French Comparisons" In: (eds.) Gifford,P & WR Lewis, *France and Britain in Africa*. Yale Univ. New Haven.

Fitch, Bob& Mary Oppenheimer. (1966). "Ghana: End of an Ilusion." *Monthly Review* vol. 18 (3).

Freidland & Rosberg. (1964) *African Socialism*. Stanford Univ. Press. New York.

Frimpong-Ansah, JH. (1991). *The Vampire State in Africa: The Political Economy of Decline in Ghana.* James Currey. London.

Genould, Roger. (1969). *Nationalism and Economic Development in Ghana..* Praeger. New York.

George, V, (1988). *Wealth, Poverty and Starvation: An International Perspective.* Harvester Wheatsheaf. Hemel Hempstead.

George, V, 1991. *Poverty Amidst Affluence: Britain and the United States,* Edward Elgar. Vermont.

Ghatak, Subrata. (1995). *Monetary Economics in Developing Countries.* St Martins. New York.

Gilbraith, John Kenneth (1979) *The Nature of Mass Poverty* Harvard University Press. Cambridge, MA.

Gwendolyn, Mikell. (1989). *Cocoa and Chaos in Ghana.* Pergamon New York.

Hadjor, Kofi Buenor (1993), *Dictionary of Third World Terms* Penguin. London.

Hart, Keith. (1982). *The Political Economy of West African Agriculture.* Cambridge University. Cambridge.

Hasan, P. (1978) "Growth and Equity in East Asia" In *Finance and Developing.* July.

Hawkrow, Sir. William & Partners. (1956). *Report on Preparatory Commission on the Volta Dam.* vol. 1. HMSO London.

Healy, Derek (1972). "Development Policy: New Thinking about Interpretation". *Journal of Economic Literature* (September).

Heller & Allan A Tait. (1983). *Government Employment and Pay: Some Comparisons.* IMF Occassional Paper No. 24.. Washington.

Heller et al (1988) *The Implications of Fund Supported Adjustment Programmes for Poverty* IMF Occassional Paper No. 58.

Herbst, Jeffrey. (1993), *The Politics of Reform in Ghana, 1982-91.* Univ. of Calif. Press Berkely.

Hodder-Williams, Richard, (1984). *An Introduction to the Politics of Tropical Africa.* George Allen. London.

Howard, Rhoda. (1978). *Colonialism and Under development in Ghana.* Croom Helm. London.

Huq, MM, (1989), *The Economy of Ghana: The first 25 years since Independence..* Macmillan. Basingstoke.

Hutchful, Ebo. (1987) *IMF and Ghana: The Confidential Record.* Zed Books London.

Institute of Statistical and Social Research. (1993). *State of the Ghanaian Economy.* Legon.

Ishan Kapur et al. (1991), *Ghana: Adjustment and Growth, 1983-91.* IMF Washington.

Ishrat Husain. (1993). *Trade, Aid and Investment in Sub- Saharan Africa.* Paper delivered at the Royal African Society Conference. Oxford (21 - 23 March). mimeo.

Jolly, Richard, (1988) " Poverty and Adjustment in the 1990's" In *Strengthening the Poor: What have we Learned?* ed. John Lewis Overseas Dev. Council. Washington.

Kapur et.al. (1991) Ghana: Adjustment and Growth, 1993-1991. IMF Washington.

Kay, GB. (1972). *The Political Economy of Colonialism in Ghana: A Collection of Documents and Statistics, 1900 - 1960.* Cambridge Univ. Press Cambridge.

Killick Tony. (1966). "The Economics of Cocoa." In (eds.) Birmingham WB et. al. *A Study of Contemporary Ghana.* vol 1.. George Allen & Urwin London.

Killick Tony. (1978). *Development Economics in Action: A Study of Economic Policies in Ghana.* Heinemann. London.

Killick, Tony. (1966). "The Volta River Project." In (eds.) Birmingham et al. *A Study of Contemporary Ghana.* George Allen & Urwin Ltd. London.

Killick, Tony. (1972). "The State Promotion of Industry: The Case of Ghana Industrial Corporation." *Ghana Social Sciences Journal.* vol. 2 (1).

Krassowski, Andrzej. (1974). *Development and the Debt Trap.* ODI Institute. London.

Kraus, Jon (1988). " The Political Economy of Food in Ghana." (eds) In Naomi Chazan & Tim Shaw. *Coping with Africa's Food Crisis.*Lynne Reinner. Boulder, Colo.

Krueger, Anne, Maurice Schift & Alberto Valdes. (1988). "Agricultural Incentives in Developing Countries: Measuring the Effect of Sectoral & Economy-wide Policies" *World Bank Economic Review* 2 (3).

Kuznets, L (1966). *Modern Economic Growth: Ratio, Structure and Spread.* Yale Univ. New Haven.

Lall A, (1992). "Structural Problems of African Economy." In (eds) Frances Stewart et.al. *Alternate Development Strategies.*

Leechor, Chad. (1994). "Ghana: Front-runner in Adjustment." In Ishrat Husain & Rashid Faruqee. *Adjustment in Africa: Lessons from Country Case Studies.* World Bank. Washington.

Legum, Colin (1990) "Ghana : Where All is Gold that Glitters, but Oil Cost Retard Recovery" In *Third World Report,* NH/2 F ebuary.

Leith, Clark (1974) *Ghana: Foreign Trade Regimes and Economic Development.* Columbia University Press. New York.

Leith, Clark & Michael Lofchie (1993). "The Political Economy of Structural Adjusment in Ghana" in (eds) Robert Bate & Anne Krueger *Political* and *Economic Interaction in Economic Policy Reform*. Blackwell. Oxford.

Lewis, Arthur W. (1952). "World Production, Prices and Trade 1870 - 1960" *Manchester School of Economics and Social Studies*, 20 (1).

Lewis, Arthur W. (1954). "Economic Development with Unlimited Supply of Labour." *Manchester School of Economics and Social Studies*.

Lewis, Arthur. W. (1971). "Report on Industrialisation of the Gold Coast, 1953." In (ed.) Dalton George. *Economic Development and Social Change.*. The Natural History Press. New York.

Lister, R.,(1990) *The Exclusive Society*, CDAG London.

Loewenson, Rene (1993) "Structural Adjustment & Health Policy in Africa" *International Journal of Health Services* vol 23 (4).

Loxley, J. (1988): *Ghana: Economic Crisis and the Long Road to Recovery*. North - South Institute. Ottawa.

Loxley, John. (1990). "Structural Adjustment in Africa: Reflections on Ghana and Zambia." *Review of African Political Economy* 47.

May, Ernesto. (1985). *Exchange Controls and Parallel Market Economies in Sub -Saharan Africa: Focus on Ghana.*. World Bank Staff Working Paper no. 711 Washington.

Mbia. H.T., (1989) *"Towards a National Wages Policy in Ghana"* Oct 10 mimeo. Tema.

Mengisteab, Kidane (1995), "A Partnership of the State and the Market in African Development: What is an Appropriate Mix?" *In Beyond Economic Liberalisation in Africa.*

Mensah, JH. (1962). "Comprehensive Economic Planning in Ghana." Paper prepared for Economic Commission for Africa *Conference on Planning*. nd (circa Sept. 1962).

Michaeli, M. (1962). *Concentration in International Trade*, North - South Holland Amsterdam.

Missaglia, Marco. (1993). Theory and Policy of Structural Adjustment. A Note. In (eds) Gianna Vaggi. *From Debt Crisis to Sustainable Development*. St. Martins Press. New York.

Mosley, Paul, Jane Harrigan & John Toye . (1991) *Aid and Power: The world Bank and Policy - based Lending*. vol 1. Routledge. London.

Myint, H (1980) *Economies of Developing Countries*. Hutchison. London.

Myrdal, Gunna. (1968). *Asian Drama*. Twentieth Century Fund. New York.

Nashashibi, Karim et al. (1992). *The Fiscal Dimensions of Adjustment of Low Income Countries*. IMF Washington.

National Liberation Council. (1967). *New Deal for Ghana's Economy* Government Printer. Accra.

Nellis, John R. (1986). *Public Enterprises in Sub- Saharan Africa*. World Bank Discussion Paper No.1.

Niculescu, BM. (1954). "Fluctuations in Incomes of Primary Producers: Further Comment." *Economics Journal.* 64.

Nkrumah, Kwame. (1958). "African Prospects" *Foriegn Affairs.* Oct. 1958

Nkrumah, Kwame. (1961). *I Speak of Freedom.* Praeger. New York.

Nkrumah, Kwame. (1966). *Neo- Colonialism: The Last Stage of Imperialism.* International Publishers. New York.

Nurske, R. (1953). *Problems of Capital Formation in Underdeveloped Countries.* Blackwell. Oxford.

Nzongolia, Ntalaja. (1987). *Revolution and Counter Revolution in Africa: Essays in Contemporary Politics.* Institute of African Alternatives & Zed Press. London.

Ofori - Attah, J. (1975). "The Stagnation Crisis in Ghana: A Call for Pragmatism." *Universitas.* vol. 4 (May).

Omaboe, EN. (1966). "An Introductory Surey." In. (eds.) Birmingham et.al. *A Study of Contemporary Ghana.* George Allen & Urwin London.

Omaboe, EN. (1966). "The Process of Planning." In (eds.) Birmingham et al. *A Study of Contemporary Ghana.* George Allen & Urwin. London.

Omaboe, EN. (1969). *Developments in the Ghanaian Economy between 1960 - 1969.* Ghana Publishing Corp. Accra.

Owusu, KN.(1989). *"Ghana's Cocoa Industry: Overview of the Industry, Challenges, Prospects and Constraints"* Paper delivered at the National Seminar on the Cocoa Industry, 15 -17 Nov.

Poggi, Gianfranco. (1978). *The Development of the Morden State.*Hutchinson. London.

Poku, Adaa. (1985). "Solution for Ghana's Labour Crisis" *Talking Drums* (28 Jan).

Prebisch, Paul (1963) *Towards a dynamic Development Policy for Latin America.* New York.

Rado, ER. (1985). *Ghana Revisited.* Centre for Development Studies, University of Glasgow.

Ray, DI. (1986). *Ghana: Politics, Economics and Society.* Printer. London.

Richards, Jeffrey. (1989). "Ghana: The Political Economy of Self Rule." In (eds.) Donald O'Brien & Richard Rathbone. *Contemporary West African States.* Cambridge Univ.

Rimmer, Douglas, (1992). *Staying Poor: Ghana's Political Economy, 1950 - 1990.* Pergamon (for World Bank). Oxford.

Rooney, D. (1988). *Kwame Nkrumah: The Political Kingdom in the Third World* IB Taurus & Co. London.

Rostow, W. (1952). *The Process of Economic Growth.* Norton. New York.

Rothchild, Donald (1991) *Ghana : The Political Economy of Recovery* Lyne Reinner. London.

Rowntree, B . (1901) *A Study of Town Life,* Macmillan London.

Sarris, Alexander & Hadi Sham.(1991). *Ghana Under Structural Adjustment. The Impact on Agriculture and the Rural Poor.* IFAD New York Univ. New York .

Schift, Maurice & Alberto Voldes. (1992). *The Plundering of Agriculture in Developing Countries* World Bank. Washingon.

Schumpeter, J. (1939). *Business Cycles..* McGraw Hill. New York.

Seers, Dudley & CR Ross. (1952). *Report on Financial and Physical Problems of Development in the Gold Coast.* Government Printer. Accra.

Seidman, AW. (1978). *Ghana's Development Experience.* East Africa Publishing House. Nairobi.

Sen, A, (1994) *Beyond Liberalisation: Social Opportunity and Human Capability.* STICED. London.

Sen, Amartya [ed.] (1988) "Development, Which Way Now" In *The Political Economy of the Development and Underdevelopment,* Randon House. New York.

Shaw, Timothy M (1992). "Africa after the Crisis of the 1980s: The Dialectics of Adjustment." In (eds.) Hawkesworth Mary & Maurice Kogan. *Routledge Encyclopaedia of Government and Politics.* Routledge. London.

Shaw, Timothy M. (1993) *Reformism and Revisionism in African Political Economy in 1990s.* St Martins Press. New York.

Singer, Hans W & Ansari, Javed A. (1977). *Rich and Poor Countries.* London. George Allen & Urwin.

Smith, S. (1987). *Structural Adjustment in Ghana: Its Impact on Smallholders and the Rural Poor.* IFAD. mimeo. Rome.

Steel, WF. (1972). "Import Subsistitution and Excess Capacity in Ghana" *Oxford Economic Papers* 24 (2).

Steel, William & Liela Webster. (1991). *Small Enterprises under Adjustment in Ghana.* Washington. Technical Paper no. 138. World Bank.

Stewart, Frances. (1994) "Are Adjustment Policies in Africa consistent with long run development needs?" In Van Geest, William (ed). *Negotiating Structural Adjustment in Africa.* James Curry. London.

Stryker, D. (1988). *A Comparative Study of Agricultural Pricing Policy.* World Bank. Washington.

Synge, Richard. 1995."Ghana: Economy" *In Africa South of the Sahara.* Europa. London.

Szereszewski, R. (1965). *Structural Changes in the Economy of Ghana, 1891 - 1911.* London. Weindenfeld & Nicholas.

Szereszewski, R. (1966). "The Macro Economic Structure." In: (eds.) Birmingham et al. *A Study of Contemporary Ghana.* George Allen & Urwin. London.

Tait, Davis J. (1991). "Institutional Impediments to Workforce Retrenchment and Restructuring in Ghana's State Enterprises." *World Development* vol. 19 (8).

Tangri, Roger. (1991). "The Politics of State Diverstiture in Ghana." *African Affairs* 90.

Tanzi, Vito. (1987). "Quantitative Characteristics of the Tax Systems of Developing Countries." In (eds) David Newberry & Nicholas Stern. *The Theory of Taxation for Developing Countries*. Oxford Univ. New York.

Taylor, Lance. (1991). *Income Distribution, Inflation, and Growth: Lectures on Structuralist Macro economic Theory*. MIT. Cambridge.

Toye, John. (1990). "Ghana's Economic Reform 1983 - 1987: Origins, Achievements and Limitations" in (eds.) Pickett & Singer.Towards *Economic Recovery in Sub Saharan Africa* . Routledge. London.

Twum-Baah (1983) "Some Indicators of Labour Under utilisation in Ghana" ISSER *Discussion Paper* No.12 University OF Ghana.

Uphoff, NI. (1970). *Ghana's Experience in Using External Aid for Development, 1957 - 1966*. Univ. of Calif. Berkeley.

Walter, D (1963). *Report and Economic Survey, 1962*. Accra.

Wood, Adrian. (1988). *Global Trends in Real Exchange Rates, 1960 - 84*. World Bank Discussion Paper no. 35. Washington.

Wood, Adrian. (1988). *Global Trends in Real Exchange Rates, 1964 - 1984*. World Bank Discussion Paper No. 35. Washington.

Yankey, AK. (1985). "How Ghana's Labour Movement see the IMF". Lagos. *Guardian* (Nigeria). 10 Dec.

Zurick, Leslie, (1985). *Ghana Cocoa: A Role for or In Rehabilitation*. Peat, Marwick, Mitchel & Co. Mimeo.

Zurick, Leslie. (1994). *"Commercialisation of the Cocoa Board."* Paper delivered at Southampton Univ. (Oct. 14). memeo.

Official publications

Africa Business.

African Economic Digest.

CPP. (1962). *Programme for Work and Happiness*. Government Printer. Accra.

Economic Commission for Africa, (1989). *African Alternative Framework to Structural Adjustment Programmes for Socio-Economic Recovery and Transformation*. Addis Ababa.

EC/ILO. (1994). *Employment and Structural Adjustment in Ghana*. Brussels.

FAO, (1992). *Production Year Book 1991*. Rome.

GATT. (1992). *Ghana: Trade Policy Review.* vol 1. Geneva.

Ghana Commercial Bank. *Quarterly Economic Digest.*

Ghana Statistical Service (1989), *Quarterly Digest of Statistics* vol vii no.1.

Government of Ghana. (1957). *Ghana Economic Survey.* Government Printer Accra.

Government of Ghana. (1962). *Ghana Statistical Year Book.* Central Bureau of Statistics. Accra.

Government of Ghana. (1963). *Seven Year Development Plan.* Government Printer. Accra.

Government of Ghana. (1965). *Seven Year Development Plan: Annual Plan for the Second Year.* Ministry of Information. Accra.

Government of Ghana. (1966). *Proposed Letter of Intent, IMF Standby Agreement.* Ministry of Finance (April 1966). Accra.

Government of Ghana. (1966). *The Budget Statement, 1966/67* (July).Government Printer. Accra.

Government of Ghana. (1967). *Report on Structural and Recommendations of Public Services in Ghana (Mills-Odoi Commission)* Government Printer. Accra.

Government of Ghana. (1969). *Budget Statement, 1969/70.* (July) Government Printer. Accra.

Government of Ghana. (1981). *Reviewing Ghana's Economy: Report by Council of State on Economic and Fiscal Policies.* Government Printer. Accra.

Government of Ghana. (1983a). *Summary of PNDC's Budget Statement and Economic Policy for 1983.* Ministry of Finance. Accra.

Government of Ghana. (1983b): *JJ Rawlings: Ghana;s Moment of Truth.* Information Services Dept. Accra.

Government of Ghana. (1984). *Economic Recovery Programme, 1984 -86: Review of Progress in 1984 and Goals for 1985 & 86.* Second Meeting of Consultative Group for Ghana. (Paris) Ministry of Finance. Accra.

Government of Ghana. (1986). *Ghana: Agricultural Policy: Action Plans and Strategies, 1986 - 1988.* Ministry of Agriculture. mimeo. Accra.

Government of Ghana. (1987a). *National Industrial Census.* Statistical Service Board. Accra.

Government of Ghana. (1987b). *National Programme for Economic Development* (Revised). Govt Printer. Accra.

Government of Ghana. (1995). *Budget Statement.* Ministry of Finance. Accra.

Government of Ghana. (1995). *Ghana Vision 2020.* Paper presented at the CBI Ghana Investment Conference. Ghana Investment Promotion Centre. (July 14). mimeo. London.

Gt. Britain, (1944). *Report on Cocoa Control in West Africa,* 1939 - 43. HMSO cmd 6554 London.

Gt. Britain. (1946). *Statement on Future Marketing of West African Cocoa*. HMSO cmd 6950. London.

Gt. Britain. (1952). *White Paper on Volta River Project*. London. HMSO cmd 870.

IDS Bulletin, *Structural Adjustment and Macro Economic Policy: Ghana 1983 - 92*, 1994 vol 25 (3).

ILO, (1976) *Employment Growth and Basic Needs: A One- world Problem*, Report of the DG., ILO Geneva.

ILO. (1995) *World Labour Report*. Geneva.

JF Kennedy Library. (1961). *National Security Files*.

OECD. (1984). *Development Assistance: Efforts and Policies of Members of the Development Assistance Committee in 1983*. Paris.

OECD. (1995). *Geographical Distribution of Financial Flows to Aid Recipients*, Development Assistance Committee. Paris.

Standard Chartered Bank. (1995). *Ghana: Country Report*. London.

Trades Union Congress (1968) *The Condition of the Ghanaian Working Class: Letter to the Chairman of NLC* Accra. (May, 8 1968).

Trades Union Congress (1988) *"Economic Survey of Ghana 1980-1987"* mimeo. Accra.

UN ECA (1983). *Statistical Year Book*. Addis Ababa.

UNECA (1983) *The Lagos Plan of Action*. Addis Ababa.

UNECA (1989). *Africa's Alternative Framework to Structural Adjustment Programmes for Socio- Economic Recovery and Transformation*. Addis Ababa.

UNECA Document No. E/ECA/CM/10/37/REV 2.

UN (1990) *Africa Statistical Yearbook 1990/91* Vol 1.

UNDP/WB (1989) *African Economic and Financial Data 1989*. Washington.

UNDP. (1990). *Human Development Report, 1990*. Oxford Univ. New York.

UNICEF (1986) *Ghana: Adjustment Policies and Programmes to Protect Children and Other Vulnerable Groups*, UNICEF, Accra.

UNICEF (1989) *The state of the World's Children* New York.

UNIDO, (1991) *African Industry in Figure.s*

UNIDO/ILO (1992) *Industrial Sector Review and Programming Mission to Ghana*. Geneva.

United Nations. (1985). *Africa Year Book, 1984*. New York.

United Nations. (1985). *African Development Indicators*. New York.

World Bank. (1974). *Towards more effective Self - reliance: The Role of the Manufacturing Sector in Ghana*. Washington.

World Bank. (1981). *Accelerated Development in Sub-Saharan Africa. An agenda for action*. Washington.

World Bank. (1984). *Ghana: Policies and Programmes for Adjustment*. Washington.

World Bank. (1985). *Ghana: Agricultural Sector Review*. Report no. GH 5366 mimeo. Washington.

World Bank. (1987) *Ghana: Policies and Issues of Structural Adjustment*. Report no. 6635 -GH.. March 30. Washington.

World Bank. (1988a). *Annual Report*. Washington.

World Bank. (1988b). *Education in Sub- Saharan African*. Washington.

World Bank. (1989). *Africa: Adjustment and Growth in the 1980s*. Washington.

World Bank. (1989). *Sub- Saharan Africa: From Crisis to Sustainable Growth*. Washington.

World Bank/UNDP. (1989). *African Economic and Financial Data*. Washington.

World Bank. (1991). *The African Capacity Building Initiative*. Washington

World Bank. (1992a) *Ghana 2000*.

World Bank. (1992b). *Prospects for major Primary Commodities, 1990 - 2005*.

World Bank. (1992c). *Trends in Developing Economies*. Washington.

World Bank (1993) *Social Indicators of Development Papers*. Washington.

World Bank (1994), *World Debt Table* Washington.

World Bank. (1994a). *Adjustment in Africa: Lessons from Country Studies*. Washington.

World Bank. (1994b). *Adjustment in Africa: Reforms, Results and the Road Ahead* Washington

World Bank. (1994c). *Trends in Developing Economies*. Washington.

World Bank (1995) *World Debt Table* Washington.

World Resources Institute/ UNEP/UNDP. (1994). *World Resources 1994 - 1995*.. Oxford Univ. New York.

For Product Safety Concerns and Information please contact our EU
representative GPSR@taylorandfrancis.com Taylor & Francis Verlag GmbH,
Kaufingerstraße 24, 80331 München, Germany

Printed and bound by CPI Group (UK) Ltd, Croydon, CR0 4YY

08/05/2025

01864364-0001